Praise for Risk Thi

In Risk Thinking, Ron Dembo sets out a rigorous framework to assist corporate leaders to appropriately assess and mitigate risk in devising a strategy to prosper in today's world characterized by radical uncertainty. He provides an analytic toolkit based on maximal use of forward-looking data and expert opinion to make strategic assessments of inherently uncertain future developments. His approach forces decision makers to consider the complete spectrum of possible futures in establishing strategy. For this reason, I strongly recommend this book. Had we central bankers employed Dembo's risk thinking approach and analytical tools we could have avoided the Great Financial Crisis.

David Dodge,
former Governor of the Bank of Canada.

This is a thoughtful and lucid account of the problems that beset our approach to risk management systems - and a clarion call for a new, more systematic approach to cope with a world of "radical uncertainty." Dembo illustrates the arguments with powerful examples of what can go wrong with current risk management systems in areas ranging from autonomous cars to climate change - and Angela Merkel's political challenges around nuclear power. He then demonstrates how a different mentality could - and should - deliver better results, not just for humans but in AI processes too. A provocative and clear manual for anyone trying to assess risks today.

Gillian Tett,
Financial Times, Chair of Editorial Board and Editor-at-large, US.

Globalisation has made the difficulties facing us extremely complex and inextricably intertwined. It has accelerated the pace of change, making traditional problem-solving methods too limited, if not entirely inadequate. And the stakes have never been higher; from pandemics to climate impacts, our decision makers need to truly see the entire world and be enabled to act with their very best. I'm a risk thinker. To succeed as a test pilot, astronaut and spaceship commander, I had to learn how to be one. Enjoy this book; it's insightfully written, fun to read, and key to navigating our uncertain future.

Col. Chris Hadfield,
engineer, test pilot and astronaut,
formerly Commander of the International Space Station
and NASA's Director of Operations in Russia.

Ron Dembo has been at the forefront of risk management thinking for decades, and this book is the culmination of his deep engagement on this important topic. We can all think of major recent failures to manage risk: in the economy, financial services, health care, climate change, aviation, and so on. Looking forward, as the world becomes ever more complex, managing risk will be both more important and more difficult. In Risk Thinking, Ron provides an effective and refreshingly practical framework for addressing this challenge. This book will help people in all walks of life manage risks of all types and sizes.

Mike Pedersen
Chairman, Business Development Bank of Canada,
Former President and CEO, TD Bank,
America's Most Convenient Bank.

Thinking about risk has been a critical part of life for bankers, asset managers, investors, business leaders, and regulators for hundreds of years. How to manage risk has evolved and become radically more sophisticated. Ron Dembo shows very clearly that some of the risk tools, as well as 'forecasting' and the way we have had to 'think' about Risk now have to be looked at radically differently.

Dembo argues that the 'Risk Thinking' lens for this radically uncertain future is the way of the future. This includes separating the deterministic problems – those that can be managed by planning, practicing and efficiency – from the stochastic problems that need 'Risk Thinking' as opposed to more traditional thinking about risk. In 'Risk Thinking' a leader ultimately forms a risk strategy and makes an informed decision to 'bet' or 'hedge' on certain scenarios after using science, data, information, NLP, AI and most importantly crowd sourced expert opinions that identify a distribution of risk and identifies the 'black swans' that are sadly no longer once-in-a-lifetime events. A must read for those of us who manage, regulate, or oversee businesses.

***Anatol von Hahn**,*
formerly head of the Canadian banking business for Scotiabank.

Risk Thinking is a convincing, compelling, and accessible read. Dembo is a spell-binding narrator who retells world-changing events such as the Apollo 13 return to earth, Angela Merkel's shut down of the German nuclear industry, the financial melt-down of 2008, and the recent Texas snowstorm using scenarios to model alternatives. Eloquent graphics throughout help the reader grasp his method - linking uncertainty distributions with causal scenario trees that play out real world options. Dembo astutely argues that managing radical uncertainty calls for the right combination of diverse human expertise, the inclusion of outlier opinions, data, and machine learning. For organizational leaders at all scales, boards, policy makers, design thinkers and foresight practitioners this book is both a call to action and a practical guide.

***Dr. Sara Diamond**,*
currently President Emerita of OCAD University Canada's "university of the imagination." She was President and Vice-Chancellor for 15 years, stepping down on June 30, 2020.

Ron Dembo articulates the need for risk thinking, that is, a new way of perceiving, understanding, betting and hedging in our era of radical uncertainty: the era of converging crises. Harnessing risk thinking would transform how financial regulators, institutions, portfolio and risk managers respond to interconnected global risks driven by climate change using data, algorithms, and expert input. The telling result would be better operational and business decisions to protect our economies and societies. Realizing this differentiating capability requires not only the novel approaches to machine learning and artificial intelligence that Dembo elegantly describes, but also a new breed of decision makers and managers who do whatever it takes to build a culture of risk thinkers.

Sanjay Khanna,
Futurist, ESG & climate risk expert.

Risk is an innate part of the human condition. For every choice we make, there is an internal calculation on the risks and benefits – a series of steps in logical thinking that sometimes happen in the blink of an eye. In a world of constantly accelerating change, the ability to fully understand and minimize risk is becoming essential to our survival in the face of challenges like a global pandemic or irreversible climate change. In *Risk Thinking*, Ron Dembo gives the reader tools to unravel the mysteries of risk in an accessible and eloquent way. This is a must read for any strategic thinker and emerging leader looking to thrive in an uncertain world.

Dr. Phil De Luna,
Carbontech Innovator and selected as one of Forbes 30 Under 30.

Other books

Seeing Tomorrow: Rewriting The Rules Of Risk, Ron S. Dembo
And Andrew Freeman
By Ron S. Dembo; Andrew Freeman
John Wiley and Sons, 1998

Upside, Downside: Simple Rules of Risk for the Smart Investor.
By Ron S. Dembo; Daniel Stoffman
Doubleday Canada, 2006

RISK
THINKING

...in an Uncertain World

Ron S. Dembo

ARCHWAY
PUBLISHING

Copyright © 2021 Ron S. Dembo.

All rights reserved. No part of this book may be used or reproduced by any means, graphic, electronic, or mechanical, including photocopying, recording, taping or by any information storage retrieval system without the written permission of the author except in the case of brief quotations embodied in critical articles and reviews.

This book is a work of non-fiction. Unless otherwise noted, the author and the publisher make no explicit guarantees as to the accuracy of the information contained in this book and in some cases, names of people and places have been altered to protect their privacy.

Archway Publishing books may be ordered
through booksellers or by contacting:

Archway Publishing
1663 Liberty Drive
Bloomington, IN 47403
www.archwaypublishing.com
844-669-3957

Because of the dynamic nature of the Internet, any web addresses or links contained in this book may have changed since publication and may no longer be valid. The views expressed in this work are solely those of the author and do not necessarily reflect the views of the publisher, and the publisher hereby disclaims any responsibility for them.

Any people depicted in stock imagery provided by Getty Images are models, and such images are being used for illustrative purposes only. Certain stock imagery © Getty Images.

ISBN: 978-1-6657-0701-5 (sc)
ISBN: 978-1-6657-0700-8 (hc)
ISBN: 978-1-6657-0699-5 (e)

Library of Congress Control Number: 2021909848

Printed in the United States of America.

Archway Publishing rev. date: 09/09/2021

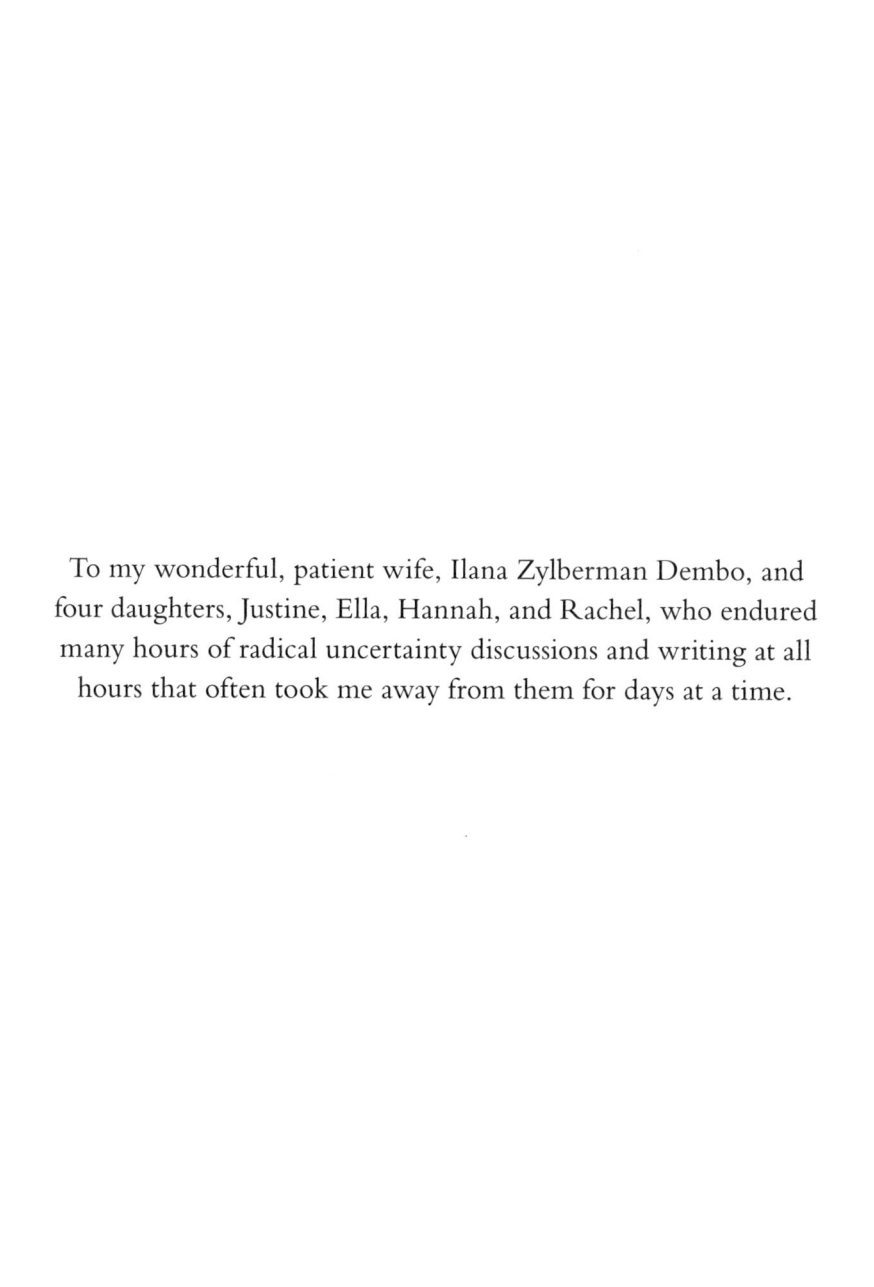

To my wonderful, patient wife, Ilana Zylberman Dembo, and four daughters, Justine, Ella, Hannah, and Rachel, who endured many hours of radical uncertainty discussions and writing at all hours that often took me away from them for days at a time.

CONTENTS

About the Author xiii
Preface xv
Foreword xvii

Chapter 1 Quantifying Uncertainty 1
Chapter 2 Addressing Radical Uncertainty 19
Chapter 3 Why Forecasting Is Overused 47
Chapter 4 Risk Thinking: A Different Way to
           Look at the Future 73
Chapter 5 Real Risk Thinkers (or Not) 81
Chapter 6 How Do We Create Scenarios? 101
Chapter 7 Can We Teach AI to Risk Think? 119
Chapter 8 Measuring the Financial Risk of
           Climate Change 133
Chapter 9 Analyzing Political Decisions around
           Energy and Climate 155
Chapter 10 Measuring Financial Risks During the
           Covid-19 Pandemic 169
Chapter 11 Strategy: Embedding Risk Thinking in
           Decision-Making 185

Conclusion: Risk Thinking at Its Best 209
Author's Note 223
Acknowledgments 231

Appendix 1 Algorithmic-Scenario Generation 233
Appendix 2 Strategy for an Electricity Distributor 253

Further Reading 265
About the Author 267

ABOUT THE AUTHOR

Dr. Ron S. Dembo, one of the world's leading authorities on risk management, is an academic, successful entrepreneur, and consultant to some of the world's largest corporations and banks. He has had a distinguished academic research career as a professor of Operations Research and Computer Science at Yale University and as a visiting professor at MIT.

He is the founder of Riskthinking.AI, a company dedicated to the science-based measurement of climate change financial risk. The goal of Riskthinking.AI is ultimately to facilitate the proper pricing of climate risk into the financial markets. Riskthinking.AI has created the world's first, most comprehensive data exchange for measuring climate change financial risk worldwide. His patented algorithm for the automatic generation of multifactor scenarios makes it possible to measure and price the impacts that result from multifactor climate change shocks operating simultaneously. He is also the cofounder of ClimateRiskLabs.org, an initiative to create a worldwide network of research institutions working on the intersection of finance and climate change.

He was the founder and CEO of Algorithmics Incorporated, growing the firm organically from a start-up to the world's largest enterprise risk-management software company, with offices in 15 countries, more than 70% of the world's top 100 banks as clients, and consistent recognition as one of Canada's 50 best-managed companies. Algorithmics was sold to Fitch in 2005 and later to IBM in 2012.

In 2005, he founded Zerofootprint, an innovative technology company focused on climate change. During his tenure, Zerofootprint facilitated carbon reduction programs in more than 250 companies worldwide and developed innovative solutions for changing behaviour. In 2018, Zerofootprint merged with CarbonX, a blockchain company developing innovative investment products for carbon reduction.

In May 2007, Dr. Dembo was made a lifetime fellow of the Fields Institute for Research in Mathematical Sciences for his contribution to Canadian Mathematics. In October 2007, he was awarded a Distinguished Alumni Medal from the University of Waterloo for his exemplary leadership in risk management and environmental protection.

In addition to three previous books, he has authored more than 60 refereed technical papers on finance and mathematical optimization and holds many patents in computational finance and software for climate change. He has also received numerous awards for his work in mathematical optimization, finance, and climate change.

PREFACE

Humans are remarkable toolmakers. Other species make them as well—apes use sticks to fish for termites and crack nuts with rocks, crows use twigs to retrieve grubs from tree bark, and octopuses use coconut shells for protection—but we, *Homo sapiens*, are by far the most creative. From controlling fire to making iPhones, from building the axled wheel to constructing the International Space Station, our toolmaking abilities and cleverness have allowed civilisation, culture, and our species itself to flourish.

We can also often predict the future and thus influence it. Our imaginations allow us to see the many ways that events might unfold and then take actions to get the results we want. As someone who has flown three rockets to space, travelling at tremendous speeds, I very much appreciate our ability to accurately predict and control how and where things are likely to be.

This book is the crossover between those two ideas: predicting the future and harnessing tools.

My first spaceflight was on Shuttle *Atlantis*, to build a section onto the Russian space station *Mir*. The challenge was immense: doing something no one had ever done before, in a highly complex technical environment where even small mistakes could kill everyone. Right up to the moment of launch, we were scrambling to improve our odds of success by predicting the future in a document NASA calls a Fight Plan. Yet we were unable to meet the deadline; *Atlantis* left Earth without a written plan, facing radical uncertainty.

When we landed back in Florida eight days later, I realised something: everything that had happened in space, despite the real-time, ad hoc planning and continuous surprises, ended up being somewhere within the scope of what we had prepared for. We'd had total success, and it was the direct result of how astronauts train; we visualise desired outcomes, analyze risks of all probable events, and then repeatedly simulate them, alone and in combination, until we've learned how to deal with the inevitability of things going wrong.

That is the very essence of *Risk Thinking*.

Ron Dembo and his team have developed a new tool that uses the latest technologies of machine learning accessing global data sets, employs high-speed computing with elegant algorithms, runs scenarios weighing the complex, interconnected risks of all possible events, and predicts actionable futures. Using this risk thinking tool allows us, the crew of spaceship Earth, from smaller businesses to investment banks and to global leaders, to make the right decisions for mission success.

It's a timely tool. Globalisation has made the difficulties facing us extremely complex and inextricably intertwined. It has accelerated the pace of change, making traditional problem-solving methods too limited, if not entirely inadequate. And the stakes have never been higher; from pandemics to climate impacts, our decision-makers need to truly see the entire world and be enabled to act with their very best.

I'm a risk thinker. To succeed as a test pilot, astronaut, and spaceship commander, I had to learn how to be one.

Enjoy this book; it's insightfully written, fun to read, and key to navigating our uncertain future.

Chris Hadfield
Colonel, Astronaut. Ret'd.

FOREWORD

A Better Way to Battle Uncertainty

Have you ever looked into a storm cloud just as lightning strikes? The white-hot flash sears sky and retina alike—a lethal and near-instant reminder of how temperamental nature and our planet can be. Greek myth depicts the lightning bolt as the weapon of Zeus, a terrible force to strike down his enemies. In the Vedic tradition, it is the god Indra who wields this world-breaking fire. Throughout history, lightning has captured both our imagination and our fear. Not only does it stun our senses, but it can wreak devastation around us, sparking wildfires, disrupting air traffic, triggering power outages or power surges, and reducing buildings to cinders in seconds. In rare cases, lightning also kills.

We often talk of lightning as random. "Lightning never strikes the same place twice" is how we reassure someone that a bad event will not repeat. But it can, and it does. That lightning defies our expectations is the prime source of its power, just as the unpredictable uncertainty in so many of nature's extreme events is the root of its destructive ability—the timing of freak flooding, the persistence of drought, or the precise location that a hurricane will hit.

Yet in the face of the ineradicably random, there is much we can do to hedge our risk and tip the odds of survival towards us.

We may never know exactly where a bolt will strike. Yet scientists who study storms say the atmospheric conditions that cause lightning have predictable patterns, making them particularly suited to probabilistic forecasts that show the range of future weather possibilities and their likelihood of occurrence.

Weather services will publish storm warnings, giving us time to act—time to prepare. We can see the clouds coming. Before the path of an electrical storm, we can find shelter in a building or a Faraday cage in a car. We avoid hilltops, seek low ground, and stay far from tall objects such as trees or telephone poles that would conduct lightning towards us.

Such simple steps can save our lives. They cannot solve the uncertainty of a storm strike, but they can limit the chance of catastrophe by reducing our exposure to risk. They replace the random with a hedge to protect—place parameters on downside destruction. When we shelter from the storm, we are strategizing in the face of the unknown. We are, perhaps without realizing it, using our intuition to risk think.

In some ways, *Risk Thinking* is a book about codifying common sense in a world of radical uncertainty. Our brains are wired to think forward, to imagine future situations, and to plan for the unknown. It is an ability ingrained in our genetic software but somehow lost in translation to a globalized society where corporations and governments depend on flawed forecasting to try to predict the unpredictable.

But the book is also far more than that. It advocates a new, more realistic approach to analyzing risk and strategizing for the future that is less dependent on the one simple solution or one unnuanced forecast and takes into greater account the need for flexibility and diverse approaches.

In the past, if an earthquake shook the ground beneath our ancestors' feet, our primitive huts slipped into the abyss. When the rains did not come, our crops failed. We learned to plan (hedge) for these events by storing grain in the good times because those who did not starved.

With our planning, we sought mastery over nature—to beat it at its own randomized game. We industrialized, building machines that brought us in from our agrarian existence to cities risen from the wilderness. We began to need fewer and fewer hands to feed more and more mouths. We became billions, and we abandoned the earth around us. Trees became commodities; wildlife became exotic. That green and blue that once enveloped us became no more than a holiday destination.

As we advanced, our ability to innovate and develop ever more amazing technologies has convinced us of our invulnerability. Our supply chains have grown cumbersome and complex, our communication worldwide and instant, our industries automated, our economies immediately reactive, our politicians uninhibited, and our greed for consumable resources gargantuan and unimpeded.

With the advent of statistics and probability now taught at school, we grow more confident in our planning. We make bolder and bolder predictions with a straight face, genuinely believing in our capacity for foresight—convincing ourselves that we know what is coming.

But there are events around every corner, ready to humble us: events that from infinitesimally small beginnings penetrate through our armor and tear our systems to shreds—the pandemics, financial crashes, cyberattacks, terrorist acts, geopolitical conflicts, and man-made disasters.

Paradoxically, our callous dominance over the environment and our distancing from it has made Mother Nature angry. We have strangled so much out of her that she reverts to the only thing she knows: bigger storms, stronger hurricanes, and deadlier diseases. And science, as wonderful as we have made it, has paled before her power.

As a species, we face increasingly interlocking worldwide challenges: climate change, water scarcity, population aging, resource depletion, and growing inequality. And as the world becomes more complicated, with nation-spanning corporations and worldwide financial webs, and as big data, machine learning, and artificial intelligence (AI) shift the decisions away from us, our vulnerability to radical uncertainty grows, and forecasting is proven increasingly ineffective. There is simply too much we must model over systems that are hypersensitive to disruption and rapidly reactive.

Yet every day, our governments and companies continue as though ignorant of risk. We construct buildings in identified flood plains. We bore into the ground for the carbon that is killing us. Our economists routinely get the forecasts they are paid to produce wrong by spectacular margins, and multibillion-dollar businesses plan manufacturing processes that collapse dramatically when minute disruptions break into their lines.

Our hubris has blinded us from seeing that our ability to plan amid uncertainty is weak; it is rendering the uncertainties of our world increasingly obvious. Now more than ever, we must remember our skill for risk thinking and recognize its use in contemporary times. We must adapt it to our business and social environment, enhancing it to cope with tribulations new and radically aggressive.

We need to work with nature. And we are starting to, slowly. But we also need to be able to survive as we quickly approach nature's tipping points and radically unpredictable events become commonplace. This requires rewiring how we think about the future—a revision to the way we teach aspiring managers in our business schools to make decisions about risk. We must free ourselves from our addiction to forecasts, realising their ineptitude in the face of uncertainty. Our predilection for wishful thinking must change.

We need to accept that in a radically uncertain world, we cannot ordain outcomes; we can only prepare ourselves for their potential occurrence. In our world, there is no single right or wrong answer to a question. There is only a multifaceted strategy. It is a better way of reasoning that we have dubbed "risk thinking," and the building blocks are scenarios.

Scenarios are our way to get our hands around an uncertain future. In their simplest form, they are narratives of the potential futures that could unfold around us. Importantly, however, scenarios are not predictions. They do not challenge the status quo of a business outlook with a single replacement vision of the future. Rather, they encapsulate and convey to stakeholders a range of possible future events with the intention of opening minds up to novel, uncomfortable, and unlikely signals of change and disruption. They are our way of asking, "What if?"

As we drive forward into a world of radical uncertainty, scenarios are our headlights in the dark. Just like headlights, they reach forward and capture a wide picture of the upcoming landscape as we navigate. More importantly, they only shine so far, and their beams fail to capture much of what is to the side of us. Objects ahead appear only as vague shapes in the distance at first, our headlights bouncing light onto them to reveal an outline, catch a movement, and cast unusual shadows. When something fuzzy comes into view, we might decide to slow down and place both hands on the steering wheel, providing ourselves greater time or maneuverability to react. Then, as we move forward and our beams of light become stronger, the object is illuminated more clearly, and we recognize it: a stray branch lying across the road or a child attempting to cross. Having been warned of the presence, we choose from a more informed, safer position: redirect or ignore, hedge or bet. That is the essence of the risk-thinking process and the scenario generation that supports it.

Our headlights do not cover the entire surroundings, and so occasionally, when we are travelling on a dark road at night, we might see something jump into view. If we are travelling too fast, then we will not have time to avoid it; this is what happens often in Eastern Canada when people run into a moose at night, often with fatal consequences. In principle, as we drive in the dark and set our speed, we are betting that whatever springs onto the road will leave us enough time to avoid a serious collision. Inexperienced or reckless drivers will simply take the risk, unhedged.

The metaphor of headlights in the dark lighting up our future works well for risk thinking. We can only illuminate a partial view of the future (the scenarios we generate). It is the scenarios we have ignored or missed that are the bets we are taking—the parts of the road we have left unlit with our headlights. So, in many cases of radical uncertainty, it behooves us to slow down (hedge) to be able to deal with the moose that will suddenly jump into view unexpectedly. Extending the metaphor, as we get closer to an object, our vision of it improves—just as in life, as we get closer to a future date, we often can improve our scenarios to better identify risk.

The opposite of this process would be our current mode of forecasting. We would flick the lights on once, assess the picture, and decide that the road ahead was clear. Then we would set the car on autopilot and turn off the lights. After all, what are the chances that a moose would burst out from the undergrowth right in front of us, right after we have just checked the road ahead?

There is not a day that passes when I do not see some other example of the need for a formalized, science-based approach to risk, especially since we have moved into a much faster-paced, data-driven world where recent wisdom regarding how to best manage has been shattered by the clear fragility of our economic systems. Recently, I received a series of articles regarding risk management from McKinsey, one of the foremost strategy companies in the world. And, once again, it was a lot about the problem, with a lot of vagaries about the solution. What they and others really need is to adopt a formalized, science- and mathematical-based method of analysis—risk thinking.

We need to rid ourselves of ad hoc approaches to our ever more fragile, risky world. This book is about why a change of approach is needed and how it can be achieved. It is written for the sophisticated, but not necessarily technical, individual charged with making complex decisions under uncertainty. Our goal is to codify and formalize this approach and create the necessary tools, algorithms, and data needed to do so in practice.

Toronto
February 2021

CHAPTER 1

QUANTIFYING UNCERTAINTY

Do you know if it will rain tomorrow? Take a guess, yes or no. Are you certain? Would you bet your umbrella on it?

Perhaps, like me, you look out the window and see what the weather has been like today to help you decide. You think about the weather over the past couple of days, about where you live, about the time of year—that sort of thing. Or maybe you check the weather forecast. That would be the smart thing to do. After all, there are professionals who are paid to figure this stuff out.

Say you flick on Channel 10 and watch the news report. And say you live in Toronto, Canada, and it is early April. The reporter might tell you there are few clouds on the horizon and that chances of precipitation are 20%. Do you still bet your umbrella on it?

I would not.

We deal with uncertainty all the time. And we strategize under uncertainty all the time as well, though we frequently do not realize we are doing it. Every time we cross the road, choose an insurance plan, or pick a stock, we think about the different possibilities on our horizon of interest—whether that is ten seconds from now or ten years—and we weigh up the risks.

But how can we quantify that process? I am not asking whether we can learn to predict what is coming. No one on this planet can look into the future and tell you with certainty what will happen tomorrow. What I am asking is, how can we look forward and assess what type of uncertainty we are facing? How can we know whether we are about to take a big risk or make a fairly safe bet?

Think again about the weather tomorrow. Now imagine we ask 100 weather forecasters (or their models) to choose one among five options for a possible tomorrow:

> No rain; a few drops; brief light rain; rain for a while; rain all day

After a bit of deliberation, we would end up with 100 answers. There is almost no way they would all pick the same option, despite the short horizon and the relatively advanced capabilities of statistical meteorology these days. Rather, we would end up with our answers spread over the five different options. Perhaps there would be more forecasters who picked one option than the others, or perhaps there would be no clear winner—just a mixed bag with more forecasters playing it safe and going somewhere in the middle.

This lump of answers, provided by experts in the field, represents future uncertainty. It is a selection of informed judgments about the future, and these judgments agree in some places and disagree in others. But this divergence does not mean our weather forecasters are useless; they disagree precisely because it is impossible to know for sure what will happen. And their answers are still very useful for giving us a picture of tomorrow's weather. We just have to know how to read that picture.

It is quite tricky to look at these 100 responses and figure out what is going on, but we can arrange them in a graph to get a clearer picture (figure 1).

QUANTIFYING UNCERTAINTY

Figure 1
100 Weather Forecasters Asked About the Possibility of Rain Tomorrow
It is difficult to look at these 100 responses and figure out what is going on, but we can arrange them in a graph to get a clearer picture. We call this graph a 'frequency distribution' or histogram.

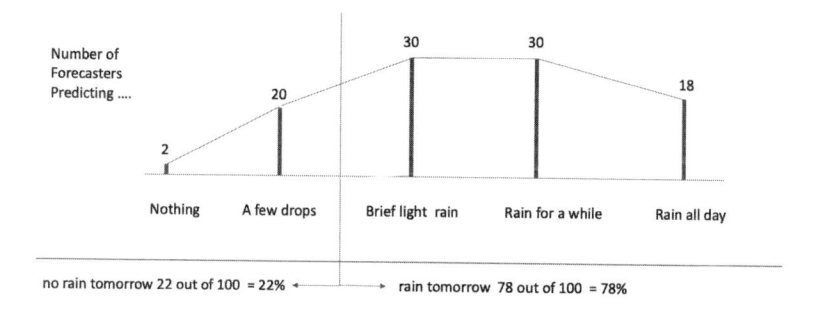

```
Number of
Forecasters                         30        30
Predicting ....                     |         |           18
                         20         |         |           |
              2          |          |         |           |
              |          |          |         |           |
           Nothing  A few drops  Brief light rain  Rain for a while  Rain all day
```

no rain tomorrow 22 out of 100 = 22% ←→ rain tomorrow 78 out of 100 = 78%

Source: Author

We call this graph a "frequency distribution." Along the bottom, running horizontally, are the different responses the forecasters chose (the *distribution* of possible answers). How high the vertical bars go represents the number of forecasters who chose that option (the *frequency* of selections). This graph gives us a really clear way to visualize the uncertainty around the weather tomorrow, and it shows us what the majority of our forecasters are estimating—either "brief light rain" or "rain for a while."

If we want to know whether or not we will need an umbrella, there is clearly an important dividing line on the graph between "a few drops" and "brief light rain." Anything to the left of that line, and we will be fine without an umbrella. Anything on the right, and we will need one.

To make it easy for people, we can represent this division as a single percentage. That is important because people understand percentages, and they find it easy to work with a single number rather than juggling many different scenarios. To the right side of our dividing line, our responses are for rain, and we can add up the numbers to give us our percentage: 30 + 30 + 18 = 78. So, 78 forecasters predicted some kind of rain tomorrow, meaning that the percentage out of the total number of 100 forecasters is 78%.

Armed with that percentage, we can make an informed decision about our strategy for tomorrow: umbrella or no umbrella.

Some of us (the risk takers) will risk getting wet. We will take a chance (or in other words, we will make a bet) that it will not rain, and we might get lucky. Of course, we could get unlucky and end up completely soaked. The risk averse will just stay inside, giving up on the idea of going out altogether. But the risk thinkers will hedge their bets and take an umbrella just in case. It is possible they will not need it, and they will still have to lug it around all day. But on the other hand, they might, and they will be properly equipped.

We all draw the line somewhere. I might hedge my bets by taking an umbrella only if the chance of rain is 40% or higher. You, on the other hand, might take an umbrella as a hedge if the weather channel says there is a 20% or higher chance of rain. That is because you are more risk averse than me. It is possible that even if the Weather Channel says it is 99% likely to rain that in fact it will not rain, and we need not have brought the umbrella. On the other hand, the distribution may indicate 10% rain, and we get caught in a downpour anyway.

And that is how to think about uncertainty and risk. It is about rejecting singular forecasts that present either a yes or no option (rain or no rain), getting your hands around the full spectrum of different possibilities for the future, and coming up with a strategy that can cope with a good range of possibilities. That is risk thinking in a nutshell.

As we will come to discover, learning to risk think involves knowing when forecasts can be useful and how we can use them to their full potential. For example, some forecasters will simply say it will rain and others will say it will not. A forecast is simply a single choice of one possible future—it often takes the form of simply throwing a dart at this uncertainty distribution and picking out a single point.

Clearly, that gives us a poor picture of tomorrow. It obscures the true range of uncertainty and means we miss out on comprehending all the possibilities. And if the distribution is wide (radically uncertain), perhaps with 30 people selecting rain all day and 30 selecting no rain at all, choosing just a single forecast to listen to is a crazy bet and tells us nothing about how to manage the future. If the distribution varies only slightly from one extreme to another, perhaps with 90 forecasters all selecting "rain all day," then a single forecast could be useful and may work well.

But a single forecast is never the best way to strategize for the future.

That is why the Weather Channel prefers the statement "a 78% chance of rain" (indicating something about the level of uncertainty) and leaves the decision of what to do about it up to us.

Is Anything Certain? Understanding Stochastic and Deterministic Processes

Considering whether it will rain or not is a fairly low-consequence affair. Get it wrong and you get a bit wet—so what? Perhaps you catch a cold a few days later if you are unlucky.

But what about getting struck by lightning?

Ranger Roy Sullivan of the Shenandoah National Park was a brawny man with a broad, rugged face who spent most of his life outdoors. He had a passion for freshwater fishing and was much loved for his affable nature. But Sullivan was also known for something else: being struck by lightning seven times during his career as a ranger.

This unfortunate feat earned Sullivan the nickname "The Human Lightning Rod," and he had the scars to prove it. Indeed, he became so suspicious of storms that he began carrying around a bucket of water everywhere he went in case lightning set him on fire.

On more than one occasion, this bucket came to his aid.

What are the chances? According to the US National Weather Service, the odds of getting struck once over an 80-year period are about one in 10,000. So, if the strikes were independent events, the probability of being hit seven times would be $(1:10000)^7$, or $1:10^{28}$—that is absurdly unlikely.

This kind of statistic is essentially meaningless, however. Take a risk thinker who, when she hears about a possibility of a thunderstorm in the weather forecast, stays indoors or in her car. Her chances of getting struck by lightning are effectively zero. Now look at the risk taker who hears about a thunderstorm but ignores it and goes out to the golf course. His chance of getting struck is much higher than one in 10,000.

In other words, your chances of getting struck depend heavily on whether you compensate (hedge) or take chances.

Look at Sullivan. For a start, the nature of his work as a ranger meant he was constantly outdoors and therefore more exposed to the weather. And he was also living in Virginia, which averages 35 to 45 thunderstorm days per year—much more than the national average. Also, when he was first struck in 1942, Sullivan was standing in a fire lookout tower with no lightning rod, which was located on a high vantage point. So, his odds of getting hit were actually much higher than average.

Clearly, averages are misleading!

But Sullivan is not alone. There are many people who, like Sullivan, regularly encounter mortal danger as part of their daily routine: firemen, astronauts, mountain climbers, fishermen, high-wire artists, rescue workers, and so on. What distinguishes them, unlike Sullivan who tempted fate, is the way and how well they prepare for their next event. The best, like the free solo climber Alex Honnold (chapter 5) who has the record for scaling the

3,000-foot vertical rock, El Capitan, in Yosemite Park, hedge their bets by trying to rid themselves of uncertainty. Facing huge risk, Honnold learnt every rock and crevice on his route up the rock. He choreographed his moves and practiced them endlessly until he could "dance" his way to the top, taking as few chances as possible. Honnold and all great risk thinkers hedge the bets they are taking as much as they can.

If there are two words that you need to know to understand this book and to categorize a future event, they are:

> Stochastic (STO-KAS-TICK): an event or data that is not known with absolute certainty.
>
> Deterministic: an event or data that is known with absolute certainty.

Like every situation involving risk, lightning strikes combine both uncertain (stochastic) and certain (deterministic) elements.

That lightning will strike in a thunderstorm is almost guaranteed (deterministic). That being inside your car keeps you safe from lightning in a thunderstorm is guaranteed (deterministic). But exactly where and when lightning will strike is radically uncertain (stochastic).

Likewise, that the middle of a golf course or the top of a lookout tower is dangerous in a thunderstorm is a given. That you might be struck in such circumstances is a significant risk with massive downsides—lightning can kill! But you can manage (hedge) your risk by simply getting into your car.

This is a metaphor for how you should think about any problem involving future uncertainty. Ask yourself, what is stochastic, and what is deterministic? Then act accordingly. Deterministic is when practice makes perfect. Stochastic is when your only option is to hedge your bets.

A great way to manage risk is to make your world more deterministic. We may never be able to predict where lightning will strike. But that does not mean we cannot make a few simple decisions to help us reduce the dangers of this risk.

If we know we can deal with the deterministic, then good strategy comes down to eliminating as much of the uncertainty as we can and dealing with the remaining, purely stochastic situation. Think about climate change. If we know burning fossil fuels will lead to higher world temperatures and more extreme weather, then whatever we can do to reduce carbon in the atmosphere with known technologies makes it easier to manage the remaining radical uncertainty, such as the consequences of a runaway climate.

Another example is drunk driving. If you are at a party, the risky thing to do is drive home—you do not know what is going to happen; it is entirely stochastic. But if you order an Uber, you reduce that uncertainty and turn the problem into a (mostly) deterministic one.

So, we do have some control over our future, and we can shift the odds in our favour.

Think also of mortgage rates: you can go variable or fixed. One of those is a deterministic choice; the other is stochastic. With variable rates, you take on uncertainty. Rates could go up or down in the future. But how much? And what is the cost of eliminating this uncertainty? Probably a few hundredths of a percentage point—but it reduces risk to almost zero (banks do sometimes go bust). That cost changes your future from stochastic to almost deterministic.

Weather forecasting (really, any forecasting) has improved greatly over the years. You can get one for 14 days ahead, and it is seldom wrong. That is thanks to massive supercomputers we now have doing modelling, which takes a lot of the stochastic parts out of the problem. As big data gets bigger and we get faster computers and better machine learning and AI, we will be able to reduce uncertainty even more.

Why We Have Been Getting Risk So Wrong

If there is one problem in our world of strategy and decision-making, it is mixing these two categorizations: stochastic and deterministic.

Every problem we encounter in business is essentially a mixture of stochastic and deterministic elements. We need to separate them and address them individually. But often we do not. We want, look for, and recommend one deterministic solution, falsely imposing a sense of security on a dangerously uncertain component. When we properly separate the stochastic and deterministic, however, we know that there is a single solution/action for the deterministic parts but that the stochastic will require reassessing and hedging from time to time.

We must learn to recognize when a situation is stochastic. And the solution to deciding on a strategy in the case of a stochastic event takes the form of a hedge (an action that mitigates potential downside, like getting wet). In our example, deciding whether to hedge is deciding whether or not to use an umbrella when you go out, just in case it rains.

Very often, we see a deterministic solution being offered to a stochastic problem. Saying definitively that it will not rain tomorrow (100% sure) is making a deterministic forecast for a fundamentally stochastic event. And deterministic forecasts lead to rash decisions and soggy shirts.

Consider the following example as well.

You are a government official in Singapore charged with managing the city-state's risk of flooding in case of sea level rise in the future. Well, we know that the level of the sea surrounding

Singapore in the year 2050 is radically uncertain—that is, it is a stochastic event.

To protect the city, you know you need to build a levee. But what height will it need to be to stop the sea level rise from causing havoc in the year 2050? Most scientists might say it will almost surely be below 3 feet, but some say, based on a valid scientific argument, that it could be as high as 20 feet. The science is uncertain. In the process of investigating the issue, you ask two construction firms for their proposals. This is what you might get.

>Proposal 1: Build a 3-foot-high levee because it will prevent a 1 in 100-year flooding event in 2050.
>Proposal 2: Build a 3-foot-high levee that could be extended to 20 feet in the future.

The price of proposal 1 is less than proposal 2, so initially, it looks attractive. But the first proposal is a deterministic solution to a stochastic problem. It has made a singular prediction of the kind of flooding that will happen in 2050, and it has created a solution based on that prediction being accurate. So, it inherently has the wrong form. You should not select it regardless of cost.

The second proposal has the correct form; it is a hedge against the sea level rising more than expected. So, it should at least be entertained. It admits that the future water level and the type of flooding to occur in 2050 are radically uncertain, and so it has created a solution that is adaptable to this future uncertainty. If we build an unmodifiable 3-foot levee and find it is inadequate much later, the cost of replacing it with a 20-foot wall might be much more expensive.

This might seem to be a simple example, but it reflects many of the endless strategic solutions executed at the highest echelons of government. For example, if we do not reduce our carbon output now and need to in more of a hurry later, the cost might be prohibitive.

Consider Premier McGuinty of Ontario in 2005, who stated this publicly: "We will eliminate coal-fired generation by 2009." Again, that is a deterministic solution to what is a fundamentally stochastic problem. There are so many uncertain factors when trying to eliminate coal—can this be done in time using alternative energy sources? If we replace it with gas, can we get the gas to the new plants in time? And there are many other factors.

McGuinty proposed a deterministic solution to a stochastic problem. It had the wrong form, and his advisors, had they used risk thinking, should have rejected it outright. An appropriate statement would have been: "We have a 70% chance of eliminating coal-fired generation by 2009. With careful planning and execution, we could improve our chances of achieving this goal, and that is what we intend to do."

Just look at today's newspapers. They are riddled with politicians proposing deterministic solutions to stochastic problems. Even as I write this section, politicians are making statements like, "All Canadians will be inoculated against Covid-19 by September." I wonder how they will fare when it does not happen. We need more risk thinkers managing our countries.

There is a lesson here. The very first question you should ask when facing a decision when managing a future situation is: What part of this is deterministic, and what part is stochastic?

Comparison in an Uncertain World

The risk thinking mindset works for any kind of future uncertainty. You can split any problem into its stochastic and deterministic elements; you can use forecasters or experts on a particular matter to help you gain forward-looking estimates of any uncertainty you face; you can represent their answers in a frequency distribution to get a clearer picture; and you can strategize based on the uncertainty before you, selecting hedges, and choosing when to take risks.

As we will explore in this book, the process works for massively complex issues such as climate change all the way down to simpler problems like choosing an insurance policy for your house. One of the most powerful abilities of risk thinking is its versatility in a world that is radically uncertain and increasingly complex.

It is also a great aid for choosing between two different uncertainties. Unlike comparing two deterministic quantities (such as asking, is the length of ruler A longer than ruler B?), two stochastic objects often do not have a simple comparison.

Say you want to invest in the automotive industry for the next year, and you are trying to decide between purchasing stock in Tesla or stock in General Motors. Both of those stocks have an uncertain future. But not the same uncertain future.

The risk factors affecting the profits for Tesla over the next year—like competition in the electric vehicle market, Elon Musk's leadership, and the cost and efficiency of electric batteries—are wildly different from a more traditional automobile company such as General Motors, which might depend more on fluctuations in fossil fuel prices and taxation or on their ability to fund research and development into, and retool factories to produce, electric vehicles.

Which is the better pick? Is Tesla stock a better investment than General Motors?

Asking this question is like asking whether there is going to be rain tomorrow. As we saw just now, saying either "yes" or "no," "Tesla" or "General Motors," is a very deterministic way to look at a problem that is clearly full of uncertainties.

In a world of radical uncertainty, we must think differently about how we might compare two companies, or portfolios, or one stock against another. We need some new metrics, new ways of benchmarking and conducting strategy.

As risk thinkers, we could survey many experts in the automotive industry to create a frequency distribution on the expected profits or losses of each company. Just like before with our weather forecasters, we could present these in a histogram to gain a clearer picture (figure 2).

Figure 2
Stock Picking, Tesla or GM? Comparison in a Radically Uncertain World
There is no simple answer when comparing two radically uncertain quantities. Sometimes one is better than the other and at other times worse.

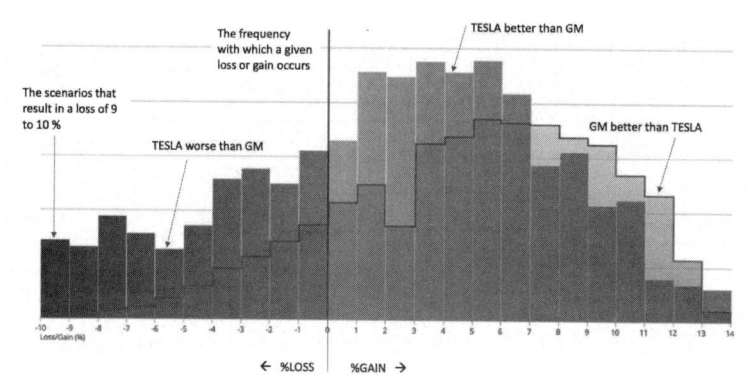

Source: Author

This histogram is identical to our graph for the weather, except we have laid our two options over the top of one another—GM in transparent grey, Tesla in solid light grey (upside) and solid dark grey (downside).

On the bottom axis, we have a set of possible scenarios from a 1% loss to a 10% loss and a 0% gain to a 14% gain. The bars are the number of times each scenario was picked by the experts. Sometimes we also weight the forecasts of experts by how accurate they might have been in the past.

Near the middle of the graph is a vertical line that splits the dark grey from the light grey. This line is very important. It is just like the line on our previous distribution that divides "rain" from "no rain." It is what divides our upside (on the right-hand side) from our downside (on the left-hand side). In this case, the line is the current price of the stock, with the horizontal axis being the deviation from today's price.

When you look at the two options here, it is impossible to say definitively which stock is the better option. Under some scenarios, one dominates the other and vice versa. Sometimes Tesla has more instances of gains than GM; in other cases, the reverse is true. Adding all the bars below zero gives the downside. Adding all the bars above zero gives the upside. So, one way to compare the stocks is to ask, does Tesla have more upside than GM?

Another way of comparing the two stocks is to look at the upside divided by the downside. This ratio is known as the risk-adjusted value of the upside (RAV). If RAV > 1 then the upside is greater than the downside on a risk-adjusted basis. Another way of saying this is that there is more likelihood of upside than downside. This is a great way to obtain a single figure that expresses the uncertainty of a stock, and we think it is far more helpful than a forecast of the exact value of the stock at a set future date.

As we can see, it is simplistic and misleading to say that one particular stock is better than another. That falsely imposes a deterministic mindset onto a fundamentally stochastic problem. The real picture is much more nuanced. And that is the true nature of a stochastic (or radically uncertain) world. What risk thinking can help us do is illuminate that more nuanced field of view by codifying uncertainty in a way that allows us to strategize effectively.

What Happens When Things Get More Complicated?

When we are dealing with the weather and deciding whether to take an umbrella, there is really only one risk factor: the rain. But what about if we were planning a multiday expedition into the Scottish Highlands?

Then, we would have plenty more risk factors that would influence our decision-making process. For example, in addition to the likelihood of rain, we would also need to think about temperature and wind conditions. When we set out, the actual future that we would experience would be a certain combination of all three of these risk factors, each of which is radically uncertain. About each we would have questions: Will it rain? Will the ground be frozen? Will high winds impede our progress? And for each, we will need to prepare our strategy accordingly.

As risk thinkers, we know that these risk factors can combine in a variety of ways to create an outcome, or what we would otherwise call a "scenario." A particular scenario is not a prediction of what *will* happen, but an expression of one eventuality that *could* happen. It is one possible story about the future. Scenarios are our way to get our hands around an uncertain future. In their simplest form, they are narratives of the potential futures that could unfold around us. They encapsulate and convey a range of possible future events with the intention of opening minds up to novel, uncomfortable, and unlikely eventualities. They are our way of asking, "What if?"

One of the key tools that we will discuss in this book is how to envision a complete set of scenarios that represents all the different possibilities from all of the risk factors involved in our problem. Just like we saw how we can understand the future uncertainty for a specific risk factor (such as rain) by representing it in a frequency distribution, we can represent the uncertainty of a more complex issue by creating a scenario tree that expresses possible multifactor scenarios and examining the likelihood of each coming true. Here is how this might look for the example of our expedition (figure 3).

Figure 3
The Scenario Tree
We can represent more complex uncertainty in the future using a scenario tree that expresses combinations of uncertain risk factors, together with the likelihood that they will occur.

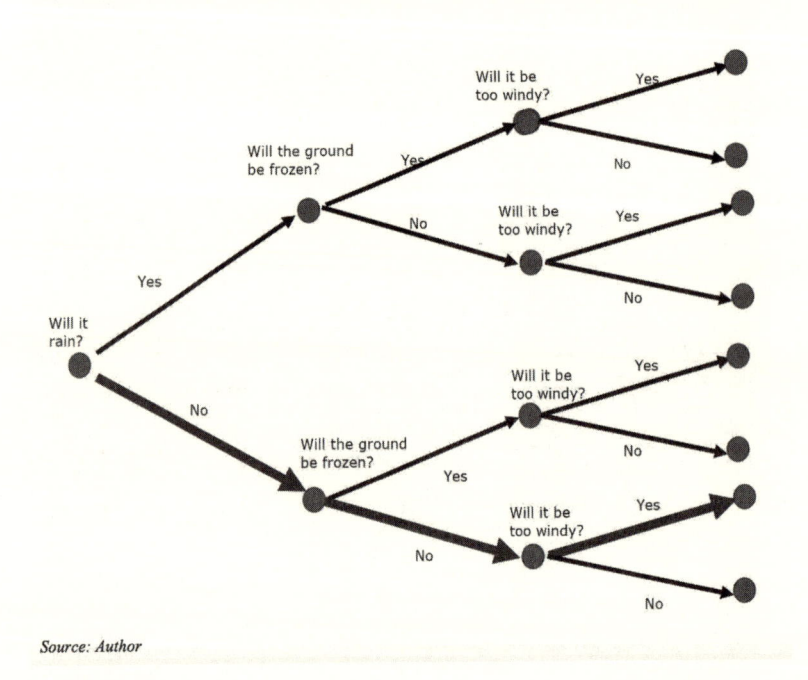

Source: Author

In this simplified example of a scenario tree, the risk thinker can see all the different possible futures by looking at a particular path, like the one in bold. In this scenario, it does not rain, the ground is not frozen, but it will be too windy.

Altogether, we would like the scenario tree to encapsulate *a spanning set of scenarios*, that is, a set of multifactor scenarios that contains the best and worst cases. We will see later in the book that in some cases, it is possible to generate a spanning set of scenarios—it all depends on how well your experts capture the uncertainty within the individual risk factors.

Of course, this is a highly simplified example of how we might represent the risks associated with a particular venture. But at the same time, these simple steps that we have just covered, from creating a frequency distribution through to a multifactor scenario tree, are the building blocks of the formal risk-thinking process. As we move through the rest of the book, we will examine each stage in more detail to learn about the applications of risk thinking in more complex situations. And we will also learn what to do once we have created our spanning set of scenarios; we will learn to navigate the future.

CHAPTER 2

ADDRESSING RADICAL UNCERTAINTY

Uncertainty clouds almost all the big decisions we make in our lives. Should we invest in the stock market? Are interest rates likely to rise or fall? How much exercise do I need? Should I buy that bigger car I want or save for retirement? If I change jobs, will my new company be secure and stable?

We do not know what the future will hold. But we must make decisions anyway. Humans are successful because they have adapted to an environment that they understand only imperfectly. Throughout history, we have developed a variety of ways of coping with the uncertainty that defines our lives. We stockpile, insure, anticipate—we are hyper-anxious animals with a level of realism that has a high survival value. And yet, as Ernest Becker proposed in the 1970s, by that same token we are also hypo-anxious, capable of denying our fear of tomorrow in order to act in the face of risk. We are capable of upholding the ultimate paradox: "the ever-present fear of normal biological functioning of our instinct of self-preservation, as well as our utter obliviousness to this fear in our conscious life."[1] And so we are survivors—natural-born risk thinkers.

---

[1] Ernest Becker, *The Denial of Death* (New York: Free Press, 1973), 16.

Yet a new kind of uncertainty floods the modern world, a kind that threatens to outfox our instinct for survival. As this chapter explores, we have entered a world of *radical* uncertainty that can trigger unexpected high-impact shocks from seemingly trivial events—that can flip markets, crash financial systems, and upturn natural environments—with the consequence that there is no guarantee tomorrow will look anything like today. And we are struggling to cope.

What Do We Mean by Radical Uncertainty?

The world is changing so fast and the consequences are so unpredictable that decision makers face complexity and change on a scale rarely seen before. Whereas the world was often predictable, today outcomes have become wildly uncertain. Unpredictable, high-impact events ("black swans") seem to be popping up more frequently, and we do not know how today's new technology will interact with tomorrow's unexpected problems or challenges. After all, just think of the world without the iPhone or the internet. If you are old enough to remember what it was like, you know how radically uncertain the effect the iPhone would have been when Steve Jobs first walked out on stage to present it.

This subject has been the focus of several good books lately. Margaret Heffernan's *Uncharted* (2020), John Kay and Mervyn King's *Radical Uncertainty* (2020), and Jens Beckert and Richard Bronk's collection of essays, *Uncertain Futures* (2018), are a few of the best.

Each of them, tailored to their very different audiences, draws attention to the spectrum of uncertainty we face today. Unfortunately, they all use different terms to do so. Heffernan talks about "complicated" versus "complex" systems; Kay and King write of "resolvable" and "radical" uncertainty (or "puzzles" and "mysteries"); Beckert and Bronk describe "ergodic" and "non-ergodic" economies; yet others suggest "stationary" and "nonstationary" processes. Importantly, at the outset of this book, we point out the need for some consistency in the terminology.

"Complicated" and "complex" are especially problematic due to their ambiguity and confusability. "Complexity" holds divergent meanings across different academic disciplines, while simultaneously "complicated" and "complex" hold dictionary-defined synonymity in a nonspecialized sense.[2] This is despite Heffernan's strong explanation of what she means by each.

As discussed in chapter 1, we find the pre-existing and thoroughly defined terms "deterministic" and "stochastic" to be appropriate; each has precise properties and technical meanings that bridge multiple disciplines.

A deterministic process is a system in which no randomness is involved in the development of future states of the system, so it will always produce the same output from a given starting condition or initial state. We may loosely conceptualize a deterministic process as a line of dominoes, each piece knocking over the one in front of it. We know that if we push the first, the last should eventually fall. You can describe a deterministic process with a set of equations that will tell you exactly what the outcome will be so long as you know the input—it might be difficult to discover this equation, but it exists no matter how complicated or intricate the process.

A stochastic process is a system that evolves in time while undergoing random fluctuations, and it is therefore impossible to predict an exact outcome. A stochastic process could be the flipping of a coin or the spinning of a roulette wheel. We may know the odds, but it would be impossible for us to say with certainty what the outcome of a particular flip or spin would be. Whether

---

[2] The Wikipedia article on "Complexity" illustrates this neatly.

or not we can model a stochastic process comes down to the level of uncertainty within it.

This highlights the fundamental difference between computers, as we know them, and the emerging quantum computers. Our current computers work with strings of zeros and ones and are deterministic in their methods of computation. Quantum computers work in a fundamentally stochastic way. In the world of the atomic and subatomic particles, quantities are not restricted to discrete values; they can be both particles and waves, meaning that they cannot be measured exactly. We see neither zeros nor ones but can identify only the probability of finding a quantity, like an electron, at different locations.

When we discuss the uncertainty within a stochastic process, we can split it between that which is measurable (and which therefore allows probabilities to be calculated) and that which is immeasurable (in which probabilities cannot be calculated because each situation is unique).[3]

The world of measurable uncertainty is one of logic and rules. It is based on unchanging scientific laws, it repeats in patterns, and it is therefore predictable. While its particular outcomes may not be knowable exactly, such as in a game of chance, they can be represented by a known probability distribution of possible outcomes. This world of measurable (or quantifiable) uncertainty is a rather comfortable (if utopian) one of equilibrium where you know precisely what your odds are because the factors determining them remain unchanged. This is the definition of a "stationary" (or "ergodic") stochastic process. It is the kind of measurable uncertainty that makes the casino a playground for mathematicians. We may not be able to say with certainty what the outcome of a particular dice throw will be, nor whether a roulette wheel will land on red or black, but we do know all the

---

[3] This distinction was first made by Frank Knight, but he used the terms "risk" versus "uncertainty."

possible outcomes and the frequency at which they would occur if we played over and over.

And because we know that we can measure and observe these probabilities accurately, we can plan with them in mind. We can manage, control, and occasionally even manipulate them at our will, and we can also maximize (or optimize) our outcomes via routine and efficiency. If our financial markets were completely like this, quantitative investment managers would be able to look for patterns that prevailed in the past, accurately predict that they would repeat in the future, and use them to make a lot of money without fear of losing capital. It would be a world with no unpredictable disruptions—no new technologies nor commodities, no pandemics nor political upheavals, and no revolutions either from without or within the financial system. There would also be no competition—no capitalism, even, because everybody would be able to accurately model the future. It would simply be a matter of making our economies efficient rather than robust—streamlined to the point of zero-waste, with no spare room for error or the unknown because there would be no such thing as either.

On the flipside, we have immeasurable uncertainty: nonstationary (or non-ergodic) stochastic processes—or what we have come to know as "radical uncertainty." This is the world of constant change, nonlinearity, fluidity, novelty, and endless disruption. It is the world where, as King likes to quip, "stuff happens"—where the future is not merely a puzzle waiting to be solved but is a mystery with undefinable parameters, where unknowns are unknowable and so cannot be captured using probabilities. It is the world of upstart technologies, disruptive politics, and unimaginable ideas, a world where threshold effects and compounding feedback loops mean tiny and seemingly insignificant changes can break out rapidly and snowball into massively high-impact events that are impossible to predict and that have consequences that cannot be guessed.

This uncertainty can be endogenous (generated from within a system), for example created from innovation, competition, and even miscalculation. Or it can be exogenous (generated from outside a system), like a virus from Wuhan that fells an entire economy or an extreme weather event that destroys a factory at the heart of a complex global supply chain. It is a world wherein randomness rules and chaos wreaks havoc on any attempt to create comprehensive lists of possible outcomes with precise numerical probabilities attached. It is a world that requires robustness and resilience rather than streamlined efficiency: one for which there is no rulebook, forecast, or knowable equation with which to model it.

What Heffernan, Kay and King, and Beckert and Bronk all agree on, despite their differing terminology, is that we currently inhabit a world that is a mixture of the measurably and immeasurably uncertain, and yet we have absolutely no idea how to deal with the latter. We prefer to use the more precise language *deterministic*, to indicate something that could be determined precisely, where data is known or could be found exactly, and *stochastic*, where data is random and where the outcome of a process or event is random or presumed not to be known with certainty. *Radical uncertainty* will refer to situations in which it would be impossible to know the outcome with certainty. Any situation we encounter will most likely be part deterministic and part stochastic and possibly radically uncertain. How we tackle the problem will be a function of whether it is mostly deterministic or mostly stochastic. The decisions we take to address it will differ in each case.

In a deterministic situation, we must execute well, but we can plan our actions in advance. Thus, a deterministic situation suits five-year plans that streamline for efficiency, target zero waste and maximum upside, and to which we stick firmly.

In a stochastic situation, we still target the upside, but we must also hedge our bets to limit risk. And we must constantly re-evaluate our strategy as we discover more information and our scenarios become better approximations of the future.[4]

The risk thinker's starting position is to accept that, in most cases, you simply cannot predict accurately what will happen. It is difficult to predict an earthquake, and who knows what climate change will change. But that is not an insurmountable obstacle. For example, even something so impossible to predict as experiencing sudden blindness while you hurtle through space, as did Canadian astronaut Chris Hadfield (chapter 5), can be overcome when a risk-thinking mindset is adopted.

To cope, a risk thinker constantly practices for new situations, learning what it is possible and prudent to hedge against, how to deal with the unimaginable when it crops up, and, ultimately, what they must simply gamble on going to plan. They show that, while living lives of radical uncertainty, unable to forecast what will happen during the next mission, it is possible to prepare for the unknown with the appropriate scenario generation and practice. They show that, even when faced with incomplete information, it is possible to strategize actively and take imperfect action that improves your odds. Such practice, and the realization that the unexpected will undoubtedly occur, makes it possible to be calm and level-headed when extreme events hit.

How Do We Measure Uncertainty? Turning to the Experts

In the face of uncertainty, scenarios are the fundamental blocks with which risk thinkers build their strategy. They do this either explicitly or implicitly. A useful set of scenarios needs to span the whole range of possible future states and contain the very best and worst that we may reasonably expect at some future horizon. If it can do this, then, when we come to plan our strategy, we

---

[4] Dembo, R. "Risk Thinking," TED Global University 2010. Accessible at: https://youtu.be/KQ_I0KEeeFY.

will be able to make informed decisions about which scenarios we think we can ignore and which we should hedge against.

As risk thinkers, the very first thing we do when we want to generate scenarios for a particular issue is identify the individual risk factors that affect this issue's future.

Any issue is the result of several risk factors acting simultaneously. For example, if we want to understand the uncertainty of forest fires in Australia, we need to understand the uncertainty in combinations of three factors: drought, heat, and high winds. If we wish to understand the effects of climate change on Miami, we need to uncover the uncertainty in the combination of sea-level rise, high tides, category four and five hurricanes, and precipitation in Miami at the chosen horizon. If we were looking at the effectiveness of lockdown measures on the spread of a pandemic, we would look at three risk factors—social distancing, hygiene, and mask-wearing in closed spaces—since it is the variation in these factors that determines how fast a virus spreads through the population.

To understand the uncertainty in each single risk factor, we must derive the appropriate data. It may not exist anywhere. The existence of radical uncertainty means we cannot look to historical patterns to reliably inform us of long-term future trajectories; too often, a black swan will foil a forecaster's attempt to extrapolate prior trends into tomorrow (we will explore this more in chapter 3).

So that leaves us in need of forward-looking data. To get true forward-looking information on a risk factor and the uncertainty that surrounds it, we must find what the most trusted scientists, politicians, engineers, economists, academics, and industry authorities are saying and writing about the factors they specialize in. As leaders actively engaged in their field, experts have their fingers in all the right pots of up-to-date knowledge to be able to provide informed—though not always accurate—answers about what might be around the corner. We call these individuals our "experts," and their views, when we ask them to opine on risk factors, we call "expert judgment" or "crowdsourcing from experts."

On a large enough scale, we can use artificial intelligence (machine learning and natural language processing) to search the writings and presentations of experts worldwide to understand the uncertainty in their views on the subject. Or we can simply ask them directly using intelligent polling (structured expert judgment), and artificial intelligence can help us there as well. The use of structured expert judgment was pioneered by Professor Roger Cooke and his associates.[5] In this method, they use polling of experts to get their views on an issue. The polling combines a way of understanding the expertise of the respondent and then weighs the response accordingly. We extend this by doing the "polling" either directly or by using machines to "read" the written words of experts.

But expert judgment is also useful on a small scale, for each of us every day who need to make difficult life decisions.

Say we are looking to purchase a house as an investment over 20 years. Obviously, we would like to get the best return possible. To understand this issue, we can break it down into some simple risk factors. The first risk factor that we might consider is the structural integrity of the house. If the building remains in a good condition and needs minimal repair work over 20 years, we will make more money on our investment. However, if the structure deteriorates, and we need to spend money on costly repairs, then we will make less money on our investment. The second risk factor is the direction of the overall housing market. If the housing market slumps, we can assume the value of our house will slump as well. If the housing market booms, the equity in

---

[5] Cooke, R. M. *Experts in Uncertainty: Opinion and Subjective Probability in Science* (New York Oxford: Oxford University Press, 1991).

our house will rise too. The third risk factor is development in the local area. If there is a lot of positive development during the 20-year period (a nearby park is built, a new school opens up), then the value of our house will increase. If there is negative development (a noisy bypass is constructed nearby or new, more affordable residences are built in the area), then the value of our property will decrease.

To gain forward-looking data on our first risk factor, we might ask a surveyor for an estimate on the structure's quality and the repair work that might need doing over the 20-year period. During their inspection of the property, our surveyor would look for signs of rot in the woodwork and any subsidence (sinking of the land that could destabilize the house). They might climb up into the loft and check the integrity of the roof, go down into the cellar and study the foundations, and walk about the building checking out the quality of the insulation and drainage while noting any fire safety hazards.[6] Then, in their report, the surveyor would list potential maintenance issues that could develop and provide an estimate of the future costs.

We would consider this an expert judgment. But do we rely solely on this single surveyor's assessment? Most people would. But what if we asked for a second opinion? Say we brought in another surveyor to undertake an assessment, and they notice something that the first did not. Perhaps, as they clamber up into the loft, they see that the timber in the overhead beams is starting to warp in a similar way to a house they surveyed a few years back, the roof of which ultimately collapsed. When they come to write up their own report, the second surveyor makes a note

---

[6] All these individual components are what we call micro factors, and they can combine in various ways to influence each other and the larger macro factor of "structural integrity." Very usefully, when our surveyor provides their expert judgment on the macro factor, they neatly capture all of these micro factors within their evaluation.

of this and provides an estimate of the future maintenance and repair that is much higher.

That is useful information. It adds to our picture of possible futures. So, by asking more than one expert, we have gained an additional valuable insight. But what would happen if we asked ten different surveyors, or a hundred? We would get a distribution of answers, some high, some low—most likely clumped together around a middle value.

Already we can begin to see that this distribution of answers, from those experts who are in a good position to provide them, could be useful for creating some scenarios about the future. Now, there are many ways that we can combine the different values our surveyors have given us to achieve a singular, middle-of-the-road prediction. We could even just calculate the average. But that is precisely the opposite of what we want to do as risk thinkers. To try to obtain a singular value would eliminate all the little nuances—the uncertainties—in the data (such as the highly valuable opinion of the one surveyor who had seen that type of warping before). Indeed, only by embracing these disagreements in the data—by incorporating them within the scenario generation process rather than eradicating them from it—is it possible usefully to employ expert judgment.

Who Counts as an Expert?

Many people would call the American economist and Nobel laureate William Nordhaus an expert. Author of more than 20 books, he is widely lauded for using quantitative modelling to integrate climate change into long-run macroeconomic analysis (he examines how the climate impacts the economy). Most famously, Nordhaus claims that a 4°C increase in global temperature would reduce gross domestic product per capita (a country's economic output per person) by between 2% and 4%.

That does not seem very much.

Nordhaus's research has made a big splash: his fairly sanguine forecasts about the economic impact of climate change have heavily influenced the blasé political response in recent years as his and his supporters' views infiltrated government policy making.

However, among climate scientists and left-field economists, Nordhaus's reputation is found wanting. His most outspoken critic, Steve Keen, for example, gave a damning presentation at the OECD Conference "Averting Systemic Collapse" in Paris on September 18, 2019.

Examining Nordhaus's claim from a physical environment perspective, Keen quickly demonstrated its absurdity. A 4°C increase in world temperature means most of the tropics and subtropics would be uninhabitable. Great stretches of currently cultivatable land would be unusable for agriculture. The sea level would rise by 20–40 meters, drowning coastal cities and destroying infrastructure worldwide. And approximately 6.7 billion people (about 90% of the global population) would die.

That is hardly commensurate with a 2–4% decline in economic output. Or, as Keen asked with just a hint of derision, "Now how on earth can you square those two visions of the future?"[7]

Keen found several flaws with the laureate's "spurious methods," including the assumption that climate change will leave about 90% of GDP unaffected *simply because it happens indoors*.[8] He also said Nordhaus "misrepresented the scientific literature"—quite a hefty accusation in academic circles. And Keen argued that

---

[7] Keen, S., "Flawed Approaches (and a New Approach) to Environmental Challenges" at the *OECD Conference Averting Systemic Collapse*, Paris, September 18, 2019. Accessible at: https://youtu.be/EtKW3OK2_lk.

[8] In other words, Nordhaus and the flock of economists who followed in his footsteps had incorrectly equated the climate with the weather and suggested that jobs that were performed under a roof would be largely unimpacted.

Nordhaus made several basic miscalculations using faulty models and also diluted extreme warnings from scientists who specialized in climate change with optimistic expectations from economists.

It is that last charge in particular that interests us since it refers to how Nordhaus gathered and used expert judgment.

As we know, acquiring expert opinions is a great way to obtain forward-looking data. And it is particularly useful for bringing the current understanding of complex scientific research about physical risk to bear on the financial variables with which policy-makers and economists are particularly concerned, like GDP (more on this in chapter 8).[9]

When acquiring expert judgment, so long as you are hearing the views of respondents who are experts in the specific area about which you are asking them, the more you have of them the better.

But in one of Nordhaus's foundational studies from 1994, he asked just 22 people—of whom only 18 fully complied, and one partially—to opine on the economic impact of climate change.[10] Ten were economists, four were "other social scientists," and five were "natural scientists and engineers."

Furthermore, this small group also contained members it should not have. Eight of the economists came from subdisciplines that had little or nothing to do with environmental economics. Thus, they were categorically *not* experts in the field about which they were being asked. Keen humorously illustrates this by highlighting one of their responses when asked about the existence

---

[9] Lenton, T. M., Held, H., Kriegler, E., Hall, J. W., Lucht, W., Rahmstorf, S., & Schellnhuber, H. J., "Supplement to Tipping Elements in the Earth's Climate System," *Proceedings of the National Academy of Sciences*, 105:6 (2008), pp.1786–1793, at 1791. Accessible at: https://doi.org/ 10.1073/pnas.0705414105.

[10] Nordhaus, W. D., "Expert Opinion on Climatic Change," *American Scientist*, 82:1 (1994), 45–51.

value of species of animals: "I don't care about ants except for drugs."[11]

Nordhaus received wildly varying responses to the questions he asked. The economists who were not experts in environmental economics unsurprisingly dismissed climate change's ability to damage the economy. Their average response was that a 3°C rise in global temperature by 2090 would result in a 0.4% hit to GDP.

The natural scientists' average was 12.3% (more than 30 times higher!). Quite rightly, some wondered how it was even possible to make an estimation using such a basic measure of climate change as global temperature. As the one participant who refused to answer put it,

> As [one] who has spent his career worrying about the vagaries of the dynamics of the atmosphere, I marvel that they can translate a single global number, an extremely poor surrogate for a description of the climatic conditions, into quantitative estimates of impacts of global economic conditions. (Nordhaus, 1994a, 50–51)

The economists, on the other hand, wondered with equal dismay how the scientists could have such a pessimistic view of the human capacity to adapt to changing circumstances. They thought that, with enough energy and brainpower, humans could "adapt or develop new technologies so as to prevent any significant economic costs."[12]

This extreme disagreement may not have been an issue in and of itself (although using nonexperts certainly was) so long as

---

[11] Nordhaus, "Expert Opinion," quoted in Keen, S., "The Appallingly Bad Neoclassical Economics of Climate Change," *Globalizations* (2020), 1–29, at 9. Accessible at: https://doi.org/10.1080/14747731.2020.1807856
[12] Nordhaus, 1994, 49.

Nordhaus had examined why it was that his participants disagreed so much. But, astonishingly, he simply decided that the views of the non-economists were invalid and *excluded them entirely*. He then presented the finding that expert judgment suggested a 3.6% fall in GDP for a 3°C rise in global temperature.

So, not only did Nordhaus exclude the respondents who were perhaps most qualified to speak to the impact of climate change; he also veiled the uncertainty and disagreement in the study to produce a singular forecast of the future. This forecast subsequently went on to inform government policy in the form of reports by the Intergovernmental Panel on Climate Change (IPCC)—in other words, it is shaping our global (lack of) response to climate change.[13]

These claims are not just "useless," says Keen in his presentation, "they're worse than useless—they've distracted us from the important challenge we face."

As Cooke explains, to be accepted as scientific data, expert judgments must adhere to the principles of the scientific process, including accountability, neutrality, fairness, and the ability for empirical control, the last of which is possible through validation. Validation of expert judgments means both that the judgments reflect the beliefs of the experts and that those beliefs reflect reality.

When collecting expert judgment, it is therefore essential to

---

[13] As Keen goes on to explain, Nordhaus made an equally important exclusion in one of his later articles published in 2017, where he was garnering his expert judgment from literature. Originally searching Google, Google Scholar, and the economics-specific database *Econlit* for expert judgment, Nordhaus decided to ignore the first two because there were too many results and once again only focus on the articles in *Econlit*, which were almost exclusively written by economists and, consequently, were void of disciplinary diversity. See Nordhaus, W. D., & Moffat, A., "A Survey of Global Impacts of Climate Change: Replication, Survey Methods, and a Statistical Analysis," Discussion Paper No. 2096 (Cowles Foundation 2017).

find *experts*, for a start. But just as essential is then to *listen* to those experts when they give you diverging judgments.

Birds of a Feather

The primary issue with experts is that they are human. And humans exhibit bias. They are emotional, hold preconceived values, act irrationally and with prejudice, have friends, enemies, and rivals, falter under pressure, and generally remain unable to calculate impartially in a way that a machine might. Because humans have what we call these "interests," their judgment cannot be impartial or disinterested. Their background (such as their education, their experience, their personality) and their current situation (such as their professional reputation, their stakeholders, their bosses) influence their evaluation process and consequently the judgment that they will provide.

Ideally, we would be able to have a machine generate scenarios completely automatically, with as little bias from humans as possible. Paradoxically, the most valuable intelligence and sentiment regarding the future rests with the experts who are very involved or care deeply about the event that is about to unfold, which leaves them unable to remain impartial and unable to think truly independently.

These interests become an issue when they overlap and intersect with one another. Asking a pool of experts to produce judgments can often result in similar patterns of thought characterized by self-deception, forced manufacture of consent, and conformity to group values.[14] In layman's terms, we call this groupthink. Judith Curry's more entertaining name for it is "mutually assured

---

[14] Cooke, R., Kraan, B., & Goossens, L., "Rational Consensus Under Uncertainty: Expert judgment in the EC-USNRC Uncertainty Study," in K. Andersson (ed.), *NEI-SE—308* (Sweden, 1999). Accessible at: https://inis.iaea.org/collection/NCLCollectionStore/_Public/31/016/31016470.pdf.

delusion (MAD)."[15] What we frequently see in groups of people—such as a selection of surveyors, a slew of government analysts, or a clutch of academics at a conference—is an unconscious desire for harmony or conformity overriding rational evaluation. This peer pressure produces shared illusions and faulty rationalizations. And that is dangerous since it can lead to distributions that are clumped too closely together and that fail to capture the more extreme possibilities. The result, when we generate our scenarios, is that we miss possible outcomes.

Two different surveyors who provide us with expert judgments on our house might be contracted by the same agency. They might share common conceptions about houses in the local area based on the conversations they have had with work colleagues, bosses, or each other. Or perhaps they gained their qualifications from the same university, being taught by the same tutors. What this means is that our surveyors may all be thinking similarly. They may be using overlapping cognitive resources to provide their judgments. And it is impossible to somehow quarantine or remove these experts from their interests: too many are inherent or ingrained over a lifetime.

This type of groupthink can happen to any pool of experts. And unfortunately for us, it is particularly prevalent in experts whom we might initially consider to be bastions of independent thought—our most valuable sources of expert judgment: academics. A group of climate scientists, no matter how widely dispersed across the globe, will typically all be reading the same literature, talking to one another at conferences, and applying to the same funding bodies. And sometimes they find themselves within a box. Just like any academics, most of them need to "publish or

---

[15] Judith Curry, "Mutually Assured Delusion (MAD)," November 5, 2013. Online blog post on *Climate Etc.*, available at: https://judithcurry.com/2013/11/05/mutually-assured-delusion-mad/.

perish," and so to avoid the latter, they subscribe to the groupthink that is currently in vogue and shun those who contest it.

As a young, promising researcher interested in climate studies, Wallace Broecker was on track for a cushy academic career filled with conventional scientific experiments, dull administration, and a neat crop of august academic papers. But one afternoon in the early 1950s, a distinguished and unusually fiery Austrian nuclear physicist by the name of Hans Suess gave him some advice. Under no circumstances, said Suess, try to climb the academic career ladder. "Be a dynamic incompetent," he exclaimed. "Do at least three outrageous acts a year. Then no one will want you to be an administrator."

And so Broecker did just that. He began a lifetime of outlandish practical jokes on his colleagues, spent hours dreaming up wild experiments, and undertook a remarkable array of idiosyncratic adventures—mixing ocean current surveys, coral reef studies, and glacier research. On his adventures, Broecker became interested in the flora that glaciers and ice caps left behind millions of years ago. And, with radiocarbon dating all the rage in the fifties and sixties and an academic community that largely left him to his own devices, he started analyzing debris at lots of different sites.[16]

He found, remarkably, that the recession of the last Ice Age had happened in "a geological instant"—just a few hundred years, in fact. For Broecker, the implications were huge. He realized that global climates could shift far more rapidly than previously believed, and in 1975, he made the following prediction:

> The exponential rise in the atmospheric carbon dioxide content will tend to become a significant factor and by early in the next century will have driven the mean planetary temperature beyond

[16] Robin McKie, "Warning Science," *Arts & Culture* (June 5, 2008), accessible at: https://www.thenational.ae/arts-culture/books/warning-science-1.229705.

the limits experienced during the last 1,000 years.[17]

Broecker's views were decried at the time and his prognostication discounted. Such was the groupthink of his colleagues that they simply could not conceive such a radical conclusion.

But Broecker was correct. He described almost exactly what we are experiencing now.

So, as risk thinkers, our task is to acquire and then preserve the uncertainty in our data. However, we must add some components. First, we must solicit views from actual experts. Then we minimize groupthink by diversifying our group of experts as much as possible to obtain the widest range of views we can. And lastly, we must ensure that we pay the most attention to the more extreme views—taking them into account even though in traditional statistical modelling, they would be discounted as "outliers." The risk thinker's key insights come from the voices on the far ends of the spectrum—the wild cards, the oddballs throwing curveballs, the traditionally ignored. As risk thinkers, not only do we find the disagreement to be the most important part of our expert judgment, we also avoid using such expert judgment to make a simple forecast. Instead, we use the views we have gathered to read and gain an understanding of the range of uncertainty of a particular risk factor, organizing it on a distribution graph.

Building Up a Picture through Data

When we are working through an issue that is individual in scale, such as the decision to purchase a house or perhaps the best strategy for investing in education, we may acquire our expert

---

[17] Broecker, W. S., "Climatic Change: Are We on the Brink of a Pronounced Global Warming?," *Science*, 189:4201 (1975), 460–463. Accessible at: https://science.sciencemag.org/content/189/4201/460.

judgment manually—either through research online or by soliciting the opinion of knowledgeable people in the industry in person. To help us make the best decision, instead of asking five surveyors for their view on the structural integrity of our investment property, we would diversify our pool of experts. We can consequently bring in a plumber, an architect, a realtor, etc. With such small numbers, it is fairly easy to conceptualize the uncertainty around the issue simply by listening to their views and responses.

However, for more complex issues where we are acquiring the judgment of perhaps several hundred or even thousands of experts through polls or machine learning, we need a way to organize their responses and display them visually. Only by doing this may we appreciate the majority and minority views, the groupings, and, most importantly, the level of uncertainty that exists among them. We do this through a distribution graph, as the following example will show.

To hinder the advance of Covid-19 as it spread around the world in early 2020, governments enacted lockdowns that shuttered businesses, limited social activity, and stalled the global economy. The long-term impact of the virus was yet to be fully realized, but companies forced to shut down temporarily faced an immediate and pressing question: How long will the lockdowns last? With staff members in limbo, supply chains blocked up, and revenue dwindling to a trickle or extinguished entirely, decision makers were forced to confront radical uncertainty.

Between March 26 and April 9, 2020, Riskthinking.AI, the company I founded, conducted a global survey of 303 experts in the finance community, ranging from risk managers to consultants to bankers, to ascertain their perspectives on the crisis. Alongside several questions on how the situation would impact the global economy over the next six to eight months, we also asked them to estimate how long they thought the lockdowns would last in their region.

ADDRESSING RADICAL UNCERTAINTY 39

The responses we received from our experts were highly varied, ranging from a minimum of one week all the way to a maximum of a full year. To organize and display this data, we can plot it onto a distribution graph, laying the possible values (the weeks of lockdown) along the horizontal X-axis and the frequency (the count of the occurrences of the value, i.e., the count of people who predicted each value) along the vertical Y-axis. We can observe this below (figure 4).

Figure 4
Global Risk of Lockdown Duration
The responses we received from our experts were highly varied, ranging from an anticipated minimum of one week all the way up to the expectation of a maximum of a full year.

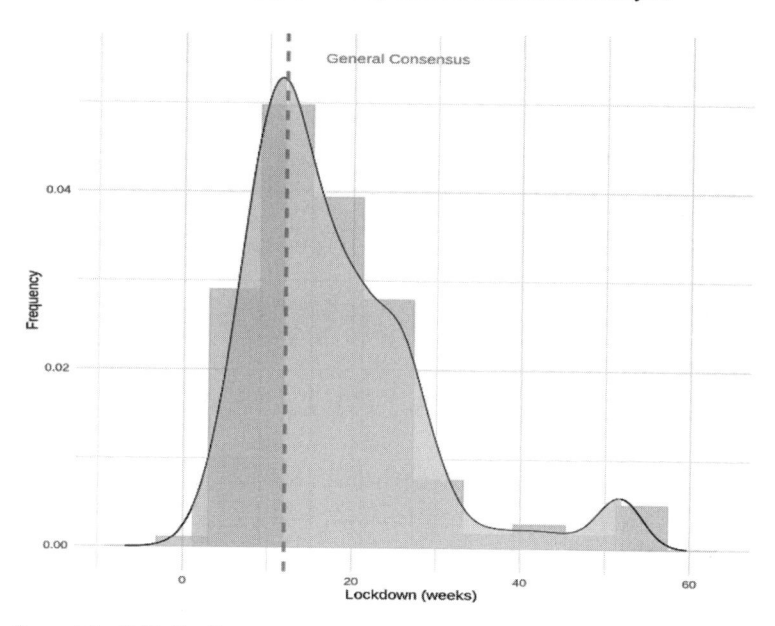

Source: Author, Riskthinking.AI

Crucially, this distribution captures uncertainty over the particular issue at the moment in time when the survey was taken. In this instance, it portrays something very clearly: radical uncertainty.

As we see, the responses were highly varied, ranging from a small number of participants who rather optimistically anticipated only three weeks of lockdown, to a large number who expected it to be around 12 weeks, through to another small number, the pessimists, who believed that the lockdown would last much longer—up to 52 weeks, even. In other words, the graph shows that people thought the lockdown could last anywhere between three and 52 weeks. Imagine trying to plan for that as a business—there would be almost no impact if it is the lowest value, and almost certain bankruptcy if it is the highest. Now looking back, 52 weeks was not a crazy result, and it captures what actually occurred.

The second thing we observe is that this does not look like a normal distribution (we will understand why that is significant in the next chapter). It is not symmetrical like a normal distribution, and it seems to be skewed to the right, with a sharp peak on the left, and what are called "fat tails," that is a significant number of people who voted for the extremes. We can see that a lot of people seemed to think the lockdown would be between 10 and 20 weeks—that is where most of the mass is—but there were a few people who thought it was going to be more than 30 weeks. How do we understand that asymmetry?

Running vertically down the graph, we have a grey dashed line, which is the consensus view, reading 12 weeks. We can think of that as the most common view of the lockdown length or some widely accepted forecast. The area underneath the curve on the right of the dashed line, we can think of as the likelihood that the lockdown will be more than 16 weeks. And we can think of the area to the left of the dashed line as the likelihood that it will be less than 12 weeks. The more weight you have to the right, the more likely it is going to be more than 12 weeks. The more weight you have to the left, the more likely it is going to be less than 12 weeks.

The key thing to take away from this graph is that we are viewing the global uncertainty around Covid-19 lockdowns at the end of March 2020.

When asking our experts for their judgment on lockdown length, we also asked for their judgment on what effect they thought Covid-19 would have on several financial benchmarks, including the S&P 500, over the next six months, relative to its closing level on Thursday, March 26 (2,630). As we can see (figure 5), the prevailing view was that it could go either way, and the middle value sat around −15%. Once again, the level of uncertainty was extraordinary, ranging from a minimum prediction of −84% to a maximum prediction of +72%.

Figure 5
Global Uncertainty Around the S&P 500
Experts gave a wide range of predictions for the S&P 500 over the next three months, ranging from a fall of 84% to a gain of 72%. The middle value was a fall of 15%.

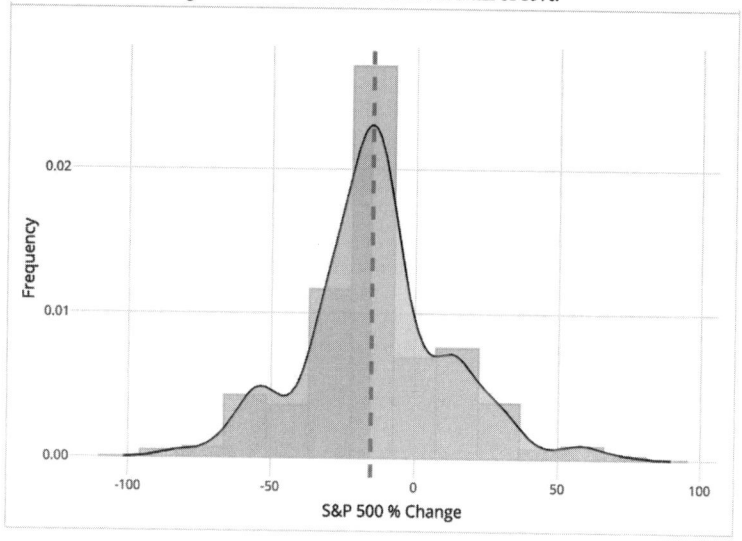

Source: Author, Riskthinking.AI

Now, if we go and look at what actually happened in the S&P 500 during the period (figure 6, below), we see that the middle value our participants gave (–15%) was way off. The S&P 500, to everyone's surprise, shot back up to levels seen before the outbreak. That is why it is crucial, as a risk thinker, to avoid just taking the middle value as a forecast when facing a radically uncertain future. Quite often, the middle value is meaningless.

More importantly, if we took our uncertainty distribution and laid it over the S&P 500's actual movement (as we have done with the shaded box in figure 6), we find that the actual movement was fully contained within the minimum and maximum projected values of our respondents. The first "box" shows the ranges for the S&P for the first 3 months, and the second "box" resulted from a new set of scenarios that were generated after 3 months to cover the next 6 months. Curiously, the market sentiment was that the second 3 months were more uncertain than the first 3 months.

Figure 6
YTD S&P 500 and Projected Min/Max Fluctuations, a Backtest
The S&P 500's actual movement was fully contained within the minimum and maximum projected values of our respondents for two consecutive, different periods.

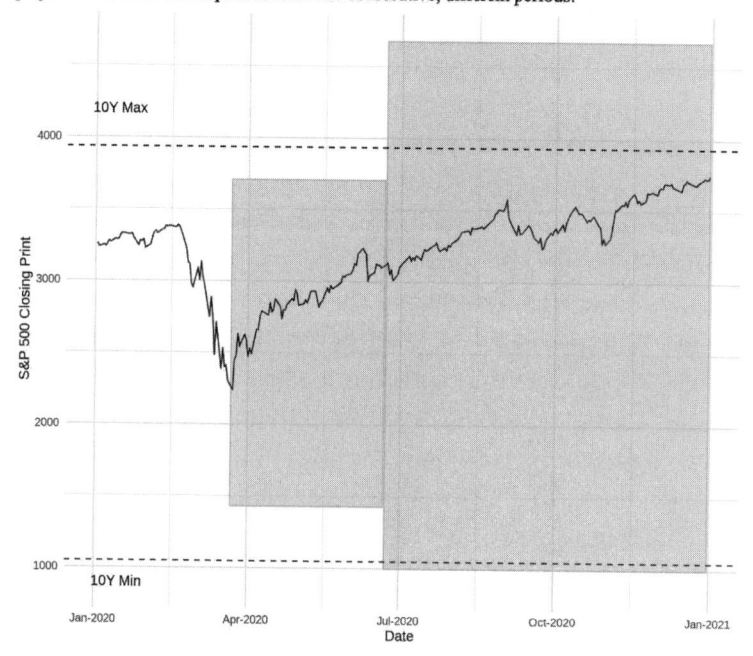

Source: Author, Riskthinking.AI

If we were to manage risk in the range that our experts predicted, we would have performed well. This range is extreme, however, compared with any kind of risk management that would have been done at the time with standard risk tools. And that is one of the most important benefits of obtaining expert judgments: they provide us with a good indication of both the extreme upsides and the extreme downsides that are possible—they have a strong ability to encompass the full range of possible futures.

Although only a small number of participants suggested extreme values, as risk thinkers, we pay the most attention to these tails of the distribution. After all, when we are dealing with radical uncertainty, we know that it is the extremities of the distribution—the multiple-digit standard deviation values—that have the greatest impact despite being the most infrequent. That is where the nastiest and the best possible events occur, so that is where we must focus.

Harnessing Collective Knowledge

Although the above example is based on the distribution of an opinion survey, in a radically uncertain world, we mainly have to rely on science or some other means of extracting the causality that governs the events we are modelling. Correlation does not mean much in a radically uncertain situation. Neither do probabilities.

We must also capture the uncertainty in the range of predictions these models produce. This is the clue to how we can model radical uncertainty and how we may generate reasonable scenarios that capture the uncertainty and that we can use to measure risk.

The future we see in any radically uncertain situation is in the heads of the experts, be they traders in investment banks, epidemiologists in a research center, data scientists in a mathematics institute, or mathematical modelers at a university. Yes, they are influenced by their experience set, by the past to some degree, and by the current state of knowledge. But they have views informed by years of study and experience. Their views could be poor at first, but they do get better as science gets better, as mathematical knowledge grows, and as computers get faster and handle more data. And it is precisely capturing the uncertainty in their views that leads us to understand the risk of radically uncertain situations. Their collective intelligence is the secret sauce to managing radical risk.

In all these cases, one could summarize the first task of any radically uncertain problem as:

> Using the collective intelligence of experts, find the risk factors that drive the uncertainty.

As we will explore with another example on Covid-19 in chapters 6 and 10, this translates to social distancing, handwashing, and wearing masks—the risk factors that prevent the spread. For climate change, explored in chapter 8, this translates to macro factors like manmade GHG in the atmosphere and climate modulators like El Nino all the way down to micro factors like individual droughts or floods in one region.

It is important to note that the risk factors we examine are related to the issue at hand. Previously we looked at how the length of lockdown might affect economic factors. In this section, we are discussing the risk factors that might affect the spread of Covid-19. Hence the focus on compliance with government suggestions and restrictions.

The second task is to:

> Understand the range and uncertainty that is justifiably possible for these risk factors.

This captures the idea that radical uncertainty may be expressed as a distribution of possible values for each of these risk factors, as seen by the latest science and mathematics from a trusted, broadly chosen, set of experts.

For Covid-19, this would be affected by how many people, in each region, comply with mask wearing, handwashing and social distancing. Notice that it is often combinations of factors that cause issues.

Another example is climate change where the combination of the risk factors—heat, drought, and high winds generated by rising greenhouse gas concentrations in the atmosphere—causes massive fires such as those in California and Australia.

And so, ultimately, we need to:

> Understand the uncertainty in combinations of factors.

This is the primary challenge that we address later in this book.

CHAPTER 3

WHY FORECASTING IS OVERUSED

So far, we have learnt what radical uncertainty is, why it is so dangerous, and how we can start conceptualizing it by turning to experts and creating uncertainty distributions. Already, by embracing this uncertainty, we have taken an important leap away from the current, dominant mode of risk management, which is based on forecasting. In this chapter, we examine forecasting as a process to understand why it is problematic and how it should be used (with caution and over short horizons).

Humans are hardwired to think ahead. From as young as six months, we can make generalizations about data to estimate probability—not that we know at the time that we are doing something so complex.[18] As we take in the world around us, our brains unconsciously represent the sights, sounds, and smells as statistics, asking, always, what will come next? Parsing patterns and projecting probabilities are ingrained even in the learning of language, psycholinguistic scientists have found. We acquire our words and phrases not through some innate biological grammar

---

[18] Kayhan, E., Gredebäck, G. and Lindskog, M., "Infants Distinguish Between Two Events Based on Their Relative Likelihood," *Child Development*, 89 (2018), 507–519. Accessible at: https://doi.org/10.1111/cdev.12970.

or genetic endowment—as we once thought—but through perceiving repetition, frequency, regularity, and pattern. From our first cry to our final syllable, we wonder about the upcoming moments and express them to our peers.

This future-thinking was our ancestors' greatest gift. It ensured our survival alongside species that had an evolutionary head start of millions of years and that were many times faster and stronger than us. And our ability for prospecting and planning has created around us a complex society that thrives on forward-looking data. Doctors take our family history and blood samples to predict our longevity. Standardized tests tell us at which jobs we will excel, while algorithms map traffic so we can get to appointments on time. Artificial intelligence, once the villain of sci-fi, now tracks our digital movements to predict our predilections—from movies to restaurants to lovers—and present them at our fingertips. And we use well-known formulas to save for retirement.

We have built entire industries around guessing ahead. Banks calculate our creditworthiness a decade from tomorrow; insurance companies cast lots on our chances of survival; school systems predict grades that pigeonhole our career paths. Everywhere we go, we are inundated with forecasts. From watching weather reports on TV to the newspaper headlines spelling triumph or disaster, a deluge of forward conjecture determines our mindset on each and every event we conceptualize. For every eventuality, it seems, in systems no matter how complex, we reduce our outlook to a singular, deterministic value. Want to know the future of the global economy in the wake of Covid-19? GDP will contract 5.2%, according to the World Bank as of June 2020.[19] Need a specific region, say, sub-Saharan Africa? That will contract 2.7%. What about the UK economy in the wake of Brexit? The Office

---

[19] World Bank. *Global Economic Prospects, June 2020* (Washington, DC: World Bank, 2020). Accessible at: https://openknowledge.worldbank.org/bitstream/handle/10986/33748/9781464815539.pdf.

for Budget Responsibility, coincidentally, landed on a contraction of 5.2% for that one as well in March 2020, assuming a "typical" free trade agreement was struck.[20]

Where did this belief in our powers of prediction come from? Primarily, statistics.

Around the beginning of the last century, in Britain and America, there emerged a profession of statisticians—masters in inference—who spread their tools for experimentation and analysis into almost every academic discipline and beyond into the public sphere. Their workings became all-powerful and ever present in our dialogue, our businesses, our politics, and our newspapers. They created a defining hallmark of the modern lexicon that expresses the "logic of uncertainty."[21]

Statistical thinking has taught us how to avoid talking in the absolute, but it has simultaneously left us dependent on percentages to express the world around us. A recent study commissioned by the BBC found that 22% of news stories run in the UK, whether on television, radio, or the internet, now reference statistics. In economic news, that figure jumps to 75%. Significantly, the paper found that these statistics, while prevalent, were typically "vague, patchy, and imprecise." They were dropped into stories by political and business elites who lacked any statistical training, and yet the claims were not questioned by anyone who had a clue how to do so. The two sides of an argument would simply fling them at each other in the hopes of winning.[22]

---

[20] "Economic cost of Brexit laid bare in OBR forecasts," *Financial Times* (March 11, 2020). Accessible at: https://www.ft.com/content/72938c66-638f-11ea-a6cd-df28cc3c6a68.

[21] Porter, T. M., "Probability and statistics," *Encyclopedia Britannica* (February 3, 2020). Accessible at: https://www.britannica.com/science/probability.

[22] Cushion, S., Lewis, J., Callaghan, R., "Data Journalism, Impartiality and Statistical Claims," *Journalism Practice*, 11:10 (2017), 1198–1215. Accessible at: https://doi.org/10.1080/17512786.2016.1256789.

This inability to understand or utilize statistics effectively may be fairly unproblematic when we buy knockoff Bluetooth headphones on Amazon at the direction of fake 5-star ratings (which is reputedly 66% of them).[23] And the consequences are trivial if we step outside of the house without a rain jacket based on a 5% precipitation warning from the Met Office and subsequently get soaked. But our inability becomes a problem when we are trying to direct (and predict the direction of) entire economies.

We mistakenly believe that any issue, no matter how complex, can be whittled down into a singular forecast—a statistical prediction. Bloomberg recently created a Brexit Barometer that expresses their outlook for the UK's economic response to the departure from the European Union. Updated daily, it bundles a variety of different indicators—based on 22 data sets in total, each with its own underlying assumptions—into an aesthetically pleasing, instantly understandable weather icon. Sunny is for a healthy, above-average prediction and comes with values of 80 and above, rainy for below 0, and thunderstorms for below −40. For most of February 2020, the predictions were ticking along at a not-unhealthy "windy" icon at an average of 2, indicating a mildly positive outlook. Anyone looking to invest in the British economy at that point may well have felt themselves on relatively stable, though not fortuitous, ground.

Then on March 11, the World Health Organization declared Covid-19 a pandemic. And Bloomberg's outlook hastily corrected itself. By April 1 it was at −150, and the prospective investor of February was perhaps feeling a bit chafed.

And that is the problem. We are profoundly bad at this type of forecasting. Prakash Loungani at the IMF analyzed how accurate

---

[23] Dwoskin, E. & Timberg, C. "How Merchants Use Facebook to Flood Amazon with Fake Reviews," Washington Post (April 23, 2018). Accessible at: https://www.washingtonpost.com/business/economy/how-merchants-secretly-use-facebook-to-flood-amazon-with-fake-reviews/2018/04/23/5dad1e30-4392-11e8-8569-26fda6b404c7_story.html.

economic forecasters were and found the results appalling: they had predicted just 2 of the previous 150 recessions. "The record of failure," he said, "is virtually unblemished."[24]

A recent study of the euro-dollar exchange rate found that tossing a coin would have been as effective as the experts who attempted to forecast even general trends.[25]

The outbreak of Covid-19 only emphasized this inability. In the face of myriad questions about the future of health care systems, the employment status of millions, the development of a vaccine, and the safety of essential workers, forecasters have been found wanting in accuracy and wildly at odds with one another. In April 2020, the most optimistic among the 28 institutions that the *Harvard Business Review* surveyed predicted that the US economy would contract 8.2% in Q2, 2020. The most pessimistic said it would do so by a whopping 65%.[26] In the end, it was 32.9%.

Following the publication of a 60-page government document setting out the possible economic advantages of a UK trade deal with the United States that forecast a potential 0.07–0.16% GDP boost, cabinet office minister Michael Gove provided a sage warning to the House of Commons: the problem with these types of economic impact assessments, he said, is that "people think they are predictions."[27]

---

[24] Shaw, A. "Why economic forecasting has always been a flawed science," *The Guardian* (September 2, 2017). Accessible at: https://www.theguardian.com/money/2017/sep/02/economic-forecasting-flawed-science-data.

[25] Gigerenzer, G. *Risk Savvy: How to Make Good Decisions* (New York: Viking, 2014), 86–93.

[26] Pohlman, P., and Reynolds, O. "Why Economic Forecasting Is So Difficult in the Pandemic," *Harvard Business Review* (May 18, 2020). Accessible at: https://hbr.org/2020/05/why-economic-forecasting-is-so-difficult-in-the-pandemic.

[27] "Economic cost of Brexit laid bare in OBR forecasts," *Financial Times* (March 11, 2020). Accessible at: https://www.ft.com/content/72938c66-638f-11ea-a6cd-df28cc3c6a68.

And he is right. Forecasts give people a false sense of security. They offer a misplaced comfort in the numbers, enabling decisions to be made based on probability analysis that is too reductive to be useful, that skips over too many unknowns in search of a stylized mathematical model that can provide a sense of precision. This is not only unhelpful, as Kay and King point out, but it is actively misleading: it creates probabilities that disguise uncertainty rather than provide useful information, and it allows decision makers to shift the onus of a decision onto risk professionals who provide spurious statistics.

It is as if people believe they can throw a dart at the future and hit the one event that will occur. In a world as uncertain as ours, they might as well be throwing a dart at the surface of Mars and trying to hit a specific rock.

Importantly, even those who use forecasting not to attempt to predict the future but instead to establish a temporary basis for an action plan contingent on incoming information still misuse the data they generate. The traditional use of forecasting entails creating a distribution of estimated potential outcomes surrounding the central forecast, but then ignoring all those other possible futures in favour of establishing an action plan based solely on the middle-of-the-road projection. Also, since models underlying forecasts are based on history, no thought is given to possible future outcomes that lie outside the bounds of historical experience.

Why do forecasters often get things so wrong? In brief, it is because they assume deterministic and tame stochastic processes for their modelling and remain blind to the very pressing existence of a radically uncertain macroeconomy. They willfully ignore the fact that "stuff happens" that is impossible to predict. In search of a singular figure from which readers might hang the future of their companies—such as the percentage the economy will shrink in the next three months—forecasters must cut a lot of corners and contend with competing pressures. Of course, there are many sensible-sounding words for this. "Extrapolation," "leading indicators," and "informal models" (otherwise known as "guessing") are but a few. These shortcuts, necessary to complete the calculations, frequently ignore the devils in the detail. And as an astute observer at the OECD in Paris summed up, "We are getting worse at making forecasts because the world is getting more complicated."[28]

Simply put, there are now too many devils to take account of. Globalisation has created supply chains that are deep and complex. Communication has become pervasive and instant. Our industries have become automated, our economies lightning-reactive, our politicians uninhibited, our geopolitics volatile, and our technology rapidly advancing and increasingly disruptive. All of this means that tiny changes can have disproportionately massive effects on entire systems, and that the tools of the forecaster must be impossibly sensitive and unrealistically comprehensive.

And yet the problem is that we keep on insisting that forecasting is the only way to go about preparing for the future. We cling to standard economics and finance theory that choose to ignore immeasurable uncertainty and that frequently conflate the deterministic and the stochastic. Time and again, unexpected shocks demonstrate for us that economies do not progress in patterns in which every sequence or sizable sample is equally representative of the whole. We know that history does not, in fact, repeat itself in any measurable or predictable way. The future is not "merely the statistical shadow of the past" because its parameters are neither

---

[28] Shaw, A. "Why economic forecasting has always been a flawed science," *The Guardian* (September 2, 2017). Accessible at: https://www.theguardian.com/money/2017/sep/02/economic-forecasting-flawed-science-data.

"predetermined" nor "immutable."[29] Because of this, we cannot base our expectations on calculated probabilities.

And yet many current forecasters, despite their recurring errors and the frequent and evidenced rebuttal of their abilities, still possess the kind of "will to believe" in their abilities that is more akin, as Oliver Pilmis has provocatively suggested, to how magicians "keep faith in their own ability to perform magic because they believe in the magic of others."[30]

They often use the very existence of immeasurable uncertainty (and the resultant unexpected shocks) to convince their audiences that errors are not their fault. Forecasts can always be updated. They concern themselves with holding to the standards of their profession and, following an apparent miscue, will point back to their correct identification as if it were a narrative that could help us understand what is going on.

Forecasting in Historical Context[31]

Planning has always been one of our greatest strengths as a species. Never were we alone in doing it, however, as the Bischof-Köhler hypothesis would have us believe; monkeys,

---

[29] Davidson P. "Risk and Uncertainty," in Skidelsky R., Wigström C.W. (eds) *The Economic Crisis and the State of Economics* (New York: Palgrave Macmillan, 2010), 17. Accessible at: https://doi.org/10.1057/9780230105690_2.

[30] Pilmis, O. "How Forecasters Deal with Errors," in Beckert and Bronk (eds). *Uncertain Futures: Imaginaries, Narratives, and Calculation in the Economy* (Oxford: OUP, 2018), 125.

[31] The section relies heavily on the excellent book by Moore, P. *The Weather Experiment: The Pioneers Who Sought to See the Future* (London: Chatto & Windus, 2015). Other sources are: Foresightr. "A Brief History of Forecasting," *ForesightR: Trends and Forecasting Strategies* (May 6, 2016). Accessible at: http://foresightr.com/2016/05/06/a-brief-history-of-forecasting/; Hyndman, R. "A Brief History of Forecasting Competitions," *International Journal of Forecasting*, 36:1 (2020), 7–14.

dolphins, birds, and other intelligent creatures use flexible cognitive prospection beyond the needs of their present, just like we do.[32] Great apes such as the orangutan, for example, have demonstrated the ability to plan by weighing up their current drives against a mental pre-experience of upcoming events—they practice self-control, imagine future gratification, and then prepare for it.[33] They even, like us, craft tools to undertake their work. And the New Zealand kea (*Nestor notabilis*) can perform statistical inference, integrating knowledge across different cognitive domains to flexibly adjust their predictions of sampling events.[34]

But when it comes to human cognition, complex planning was our shining advantage. In an environment beset by creatures with sharper senses and stronger and faster bodies, our ability to out-anticipate them has been the key to our survival and, unfortunately, to their demise.

Each crucial stage in our evolution has relied upon our ability to think ahead: the highly organized, communal enterprise of hunting large prey with specialized tools; the mental mapping of bushes and trees and the anticipation of their fruit in seasons to come; and even the fieldwork of agriculture for the grains of tomorrow. All of it over time reduced our labour and secured us the leisure to construct advanced civilizations.

But this desire for future knowledge, numerous though its boons have been, has led us astray on almost as many occasions as

---

[32] Osvath, M. "Great Ape Foresight Is Looking Great," *Animal Cognition*, 13 (2010), 777–781. Accessible at: https://doi.org/10.1007/s10071-010-0336-7.
[33] Osvath, M. & Osvath, H. "Chimpanzee (*Pan Troglodytes*) and Orangutan (*Pongo Abelii*) Forethought: Self-Control and Pre-Experience in the Face of Future Tool Use," *Animal Cognition*. 11 (2008), 661–74. Accessible at: https://pubmed.ncbi.nlm.nih.gov/18553113/.
[34] Bastos, A. P. M., Taylor, A. H. "Kea Show Three Signatures of Domain-General Statistical Inference," *Nature Communications*, 11:828 (2020), 1–8. Accessible at: https://doi.org/10.1038/s41467-020-14695-1.

it has helped us. In search of better clues from nature, we began by animism, shamanism, totemism, mysticism, and many other isms to augur spurious details about the days ahead—about the fertility of crops or the movements of the rains. For a thousand years in Greece, young priestesses would undertake the role of the Oracle at Delphi, breathing in volcanic fumes and hallucinating the will of Apollo to counsel on matters of war, colonization, and religion.

Unanimous testimony from classical sources tells us that, at least in the West, augury—divination from the flight of birds—was the most ancient and venerated of this search for the future. Even before the Romans, its practice was widespread, but it was they who laid out a fixed system of interpretations and established the fundamental rules for the reading of auspices. Rome herself was, according to the legend of Romulus and Remus, located by the taking of auspices (*avis-* bird; *-spex*, observer). And these augurs soon operated at the apex of imperial governance, extracting divine will from the sky to guide military, political, and social endeavours.

Where nature was not looked to, many civilizations predicted their future from sortition—or lottery, as we would call it. This was to draw randomly from a collection of sticks, stones, beans, or other small items to divine from them the will of supernatural deities. In the Judeo-Christian tradition the "casting of lots" frequently appears—as when, in the book of Joshua, the Hebrews cast lots to know God's will for the division of the land of Israel. The Chinese tradition of divination from the *I Ching* (or the *Book of Changes*), which guided government officials for thousands of years, was made by casting coins, dice, marbles, and other items to generate a hexagram that offered a reading.

These ancient practices, though certainly chance and probability were involved, were absent any sort of mathematical interpretation of the symbols and circumstances surveyed. We created no numerical laws governing the random events we encountered.

But during the Renaissance, humans turned their minds to the stars with new and determined precision. Astrology, though by no means born during this period, was at once transformed by the publication of Nicolaus Copernicus's *De revolutionibus orbium coelestium* (1543). This treatise swept away the old Ptolemaic model of the universe (with the Earth at the centre) and in its place established by careful, empirical observation of the heavenly bodies the heliocentric model of planetary motion. The Western world accepted for the first time that it was they who moved around the sun—and not the sun that moved around them.

Science soon became its own discipline distinct from philosophy and technology, and the Scientific Revolution was born. Across mathematics, physics, astronomy, and biology, a new appetite for change and improvement disposed of the reverence of the past so carefully carried up through the Middle Ages. The scientific method was conceived as a research tradition of systematic experimentation alongside empirical observation. Together, the two massively expanded our predictive powers as we learned to observe, hypothesize, and test. And the great movement these methods began culminated in Galileo Galilei's summa that the laws of nature were "written in the language of mathematics, and its characters are triangles, circles, and other geometric figures."[35]

Like never before, we could map the movements of the planets, but the greatest leap forward for our forecasting ability came from two quarrelling geniuses, Isaac Newton and Gottfried Leibniz, who developed what the former called the "science of fluxions" but which the latter gave the name more recognisable to us: "calculus." By calculus, we studied change. We gained a new mathematical system that could model how variable quantities changed conditions and, importantly, we could deduce their consequences.

---

[35] Drake, S. (ed. and trans), *Discoveries and Opinions of Galileo* (New York: Doubleday, 1957), 237–8.

Probability theory emerged in the 17th century when John Graunt and William Petty started thinking about populations. Together, they developed human statistical and census methods that allowed them to produce the first life table, which gave the probabilities of survival to each age. Soon Graunt was also making estimations of the population of London based on analysis of mortality rolls. At the beginning of the 18th century, the notion of probability was given scientific treatment in volumes such as Jakob Bernoulli's *Ars Conjectandi* (The Art of Conjecting, 1713) and Abraham de Moivre's wonderfully named work, *The Doctrine of Chances* (1718). Soon we were putting probabilities on the human sex ratio, and we began studying the theory of errors in observation and created methods for estimating unknown quantities like the libration (or wavering) of the moon. By 1791, the word "statistics" formally entered the lexicon thanks to Sir John Sinclair, and not long afterwards, Adolphe Quetelet introduced the idea of *l'homme moyen* (or the average man) and the variances thereof.

Modern statistics burgeoned in the late nineteenth and twentieth centuries alongside an uncomfortably long brush with eugenics. The Victorians Francis Galton and Karl Pearson transformed the study of statistics into a mathematical discipline that could be used not just for science but for political and industrial purposes too. From the former, we received the concept of correlation, standard deviation, and regression towards the mean; from the latter, the Pearson product-moment correlation coefficient, which is still widely used today. Other bright sparks like British statistician Ronald Fisher developed the null hypothesis, maximum likelihood, and many other key concepts that have become integral to modern data science, machine learning, and predictive analysis.[36]

With each leap forward, we became better at systematically

---

[36] Rao, C. R. "R. A. Fisher: The Founder of Modern Statistics," *Statistical Science*, 7:1 (1992), 34–48. Accessible at: www.jstor.org/stable/2245989.

observing, collecting, analyzing, presenting, and interpreting the numerical data of the universe and relating it into probabilities. And with that information, we began our battle with uncertainty renewed, hoping to measure it, avoid it, and on the odd occasion, even control it. None of this, however, quite captured the public imagination so spectacularly as the innovations of a single man—the man who gave birth to the very word "forecasting."

Robert FitzRoy's Invention of Weather Forecasting

On the epic voyage of HMS *Beagle* around the South American coast and the Galápagos Islands in the 1830s, Charles Darwin was not the only man who would change the world. Though we know intimately the story of how the biologist collected material for his groundbreaking theory of evolution, eventually published in *On the Origin of Species* (1859), we often forget the ship's captain—the taciturn but ingenious Robert FitzRoy. Yet it is to FitzRoy and his achievements in later life that we owe the word "forecast" in its current sense.

FitzRoy was just 23 when appointed commander of the 240-ton *Beagle* in 1828, a cramped vessel with three masts and a measly ten guns. Yet FitzRoy, despite his youth, was an innovative captain; he outfitted the masts and booms of the vessel with lightning conductors, protecting it from the ravages of storms. Over the first five years of the ship's life at sea, he lost not one mast or yard, suffered no split sails, and, despite the attempts of the weather, lost none of his sailors overboard. He led his crew with style, courage, and skill on two dangerous voyages, the first in 1828 surveying the South American coast around Patagonia and Tierra del Fuego, and the second with Darwin in 1831 to visit the Cape Verde Islands, the South American coast, the Strait of Magellan, the Galápagos Islands, Tahiti, New Zealand, Australia, the Maldives, and Mauritius before returning to England in 1836.

Though staunchly religious, FitzRoy also believed in the advances of science and empirical measurement. He was the first captain to adopt Sir Francis Beaufort's now-famous wind scale to log conditions as he commanded the *Beagle*.

He retired from active duty in 1850. On the recommendation of the Royal Society's president, he was appointed chief of an experimental government department in 1854 intended to amass and analyze weather data collected at sea to protect mariners. As Meteorological Statist to the Board of Trade (his new title), he and his staff of three set to work.

Soon, however, FitzRoy realized that with the data coming into his office, he could use his understanding of the weather to do much more than cut sailing times—he could predict storms. FitzRoy knew that around the coasts of Britain between 1855 and 1860, 7,402 ships were wrecked, and 7,201 lives were lost. After a particularly devastating storm in 1859 caused the loss of the *Royal Charter* and 450 of its passengers as well as 200 other ships about the Welsh coast, he convinced Parliament to set up a storm warning service.

This elaborate system made use of 15 newly established land stations and revolutionary telegraph technology to collect live weather data from land and at sea at set times and transmit it to him. He quickly developed charts that allowed him to make predictions of upcoming weather, and in these charts was his first use of the term "weather forecast."

The government agreed this work was essential for shipping, but FitzRoy thought the information ought to be available to the public. At that time, fishermen and farmers were still reliant on the appearance of clouds or on biological weather warnings—they kept frogs in jars or took note of the behaviour of swallows in hedgerows to give them early warnings of the weather. So, the pioneering predictor opened up his work to the public, publishing his forecasts in *The Times* for the first time in 1861.

FitzRoy's work during the late 1850s was controversial. Often his forecasts were wrong, or late, based as they were on skimpy and often sporadic data; many a ship that heeded an incorrect warning and kept from the waters lost their profits for the day. During his early attempts, FitzRoy also faced skepticism. When Parliament considered the idea that gathering weather observations from sea and land could one day mean that "we might know in this metropolis the condition of the weather 24 hours beforehand," such raucous laughter broke out that proceedings stalled. But FitzRoy was always insistent on the science behind his work. "Prophecies and predictions they are not," he once said. "The term forecast is strictly applicable to such an opinion as is the result of scientific combination and calculation."[37]

To many farmers and fishermen, FitzRoy was a hero. His weather observations, capturing the popular imagination, garnered him celebrity status. *Punch* christened him "The First Admiral of the Blew" and "The Clerk of the Weather," to the public's great amusement, and even when he made errors, the response from them was often humorous, as one newspaper report of 1862 demonstrates:

> Admiral FitzRoy's weather prophecies in *The Times* have been creating considerable amusement during these recent April days, as a set off to the drenchings we've had to endure. April has been playing with him roughly, to show that she at least can flout the calculations of science, whatever the other months might do.

FitzRoy's response was often in jest, mocking "those whose hats have been spoilt from umbrellas being omitted."[38] Over time,

---

[37] Moore, P. "The Birth of the Weather Forecast," *BBC News* (April 30, 2015). Accessible at: https://www.bbc.co.uk/news/magazine-32483678.
[38] Ibid.

his engagement with the public earned him a reputation in the media as a daring scientist, and he had both ships and racehorses named in his honor—as well as a request from Queen Victoria herself for a prediction about a trip to the Isle of Wight she planned to undertake.

FitzRoy could not have known it at the time, but his forecasting spawned an entirely new paradigm for thinking about the future—a fascination with forecasting—that would expand outward from the narrow confines of the weather and into almost every aspect of society.

Prophecy and the Club of Rome

It is not just economists and weather forecasters who have a hard time forecasting. Even computer gurus and other modern wizards find it difficult to foresee the future.

For example, a cabal of MIT computer gurus, technocrats, and businessmen in an "invisible college" who called themselves the Club of Rome published in 1972 one of the boldest predictions of the future the world had ever seen—a "rediscovery of the laws of nature," their publicists claimed, through the medium of the computer.

And the prognosis was not good.

Italian industrialist Aurelio Peccei had invited the group together under the noble intention to save humankind from a growing ecological threat. They had built a computer model called World3 that was able, they claimed, to track industrialization, food, population, resource use, and pollution up to 1970, and they extrapolated from these trends a range of different scenarios out to 2100. Their ambition was to probe into the problems of humankind—poverty, environmental degradation, monetary disruptions, and more—which they called the "world problematique." Their goal was to communicate its trajectory to the public.

It was a discipline-spanning doomsday prophecy with a damning message: growth will soon outstrip resources, and when it does, civilization will end.

Like a virus, the prophecy spread around the globe. On its release, some claimed it was "likely to be one of the most important documents of its age"; others said it was simply "a rediscovery of the oldest maxim of computer science: garbage in, garbage out."[39] Whatever their beliefs, the media could not get enough. Headlines included: "A Computer Looks Ahead and Shudders" and "Scientists Warn of Global Catastrophe." Over its lifetime, the book sold some 30 million copies and was translated into 30 languages, catalyzing public debate about the end of days that still continues.

According to their modelling, as technology gave diminishing returns and pollution rose unchecked, a dearth of raw materials would stifle population growth and reduce the world to worse than nineteenth-century living standards. Vital metals such as gold, silver, tungsten, copper, tin, and mercury would disappear within a lifetime. By 2020, we would experience a fall in per capita income, and then just 20 years on from that, malnutrition and a failing health service would cause populations to plummet.

What was their answer to this predicament? We should put a cap on prosperity and economic expansion. We simply had to make do with what we had.

But the analysts, as advanced as their computational chicanery and technical lingo most certainly were, were blinded by the magnitude of their forethought. So vast was their ambition, so expansive their reach for tomorrow, that corners had to be cut and guesswork had to conquer comprehensiveness.

---

[39] Passell, P., Roberts, M., & Ross, L. "The Limits to Growth," *New York Times* (April 2, 1972). Accessible at: https://www.nytimes.com/1972/04/02/archives/the-limits-to-growth-a-report-for-the-club-of-romes-project-on-the.html.

Ultimately, however, their greatest failure was not to reveal a limit to resources but to impose their own arbitrary limit on human endeavour.

The Club was not alone in failing to envision the advances in computing technology. Thomas Watson, the founder of IBM, supposedly said in 1943, "I think there is a world market for about five computers." There are now many more computers than people, and in 2015, his company's revenue was approximately $100 billion, all from computer hardware and software. With computers at the time taking up whole rooms, it must have been impossible to imagine that today each of us would have dozens of computers at home and hidden in everything from our cars to our washing machines and doorbells.

Even while teaching at Yale in the seventies, I remember an active debate on whether there would be a computer in every home. Now we have supercomputers in our pockets.

We talk similarly today about whether every house will be a solar generator. Given the rate of price decrease of solar (down 99% over the past four decades, according to an MIT study, and faster than Moore's law)[40] and the material science improvements for solar generation, this green alternative could be ubiquitous in the future—every roof tile, window, wall, sidewalk, or can of paint might be a generator of electricity.

The Club also missed a few other important details that even skeptical reviewers at the time pointed out. The *New York Times* argued that demand would drive resource innovation to replace the scarce with the plentiful: plastics for metal or synthetic fibers for natural materials, which in many instances, it has. Renewables are replacing fossil fuels; silicon fiber is replacing copper; and

---

[40] Chandler, D. "Explaining the Plummeting Cost of Solar Power," *MIT News* (November 20, 2018). Accessible at: http://news.mit.edu/2018/explaining-dropping-solar-cost-1120.

digital has replaced material consumption in industries such as photography.

On other matters, the Club was simply wrong: we have yet to exhaust vital minerals; food prices remain low despite finite arable land; pollution has yet to choke global health (much). We live longer today than ever before, and, generally, most pollutants in Western cities are declining thanks to technological leaps and a global movement to protect the environment. As we have grown wealthier, population growth—which the authors of *Limits* claimed would rise steadily until cut off—has declined from 2.2% per year in 1962 and 1963 to 1.05% per year today of its own accord. Recent research points out that even before *Limits* was published, our population growth had peaked and was declining.[41] But the Club failed to catch that one. As a recent column in *Foreign Policy* summed up, "The Club of Rome's doomsday prophecies of global starvation are now starved for credibility." Perhaps it was an idea that ought immediately to have been consigned to the "dustbin of history."[42]

In recent years, predictive models have become common in virtually every data-based discipline, from biology to marketing to criminal justice. Even in radically uncertain situations, prediction is now the language of our future.

But simple forecasting is often unsuited for the current complex and uncertain world because of its focus on a single number instead of a range of possibilities.

---

[41] Roser, M., Ritchie, H., & Ortiz-Ospina, E. "World Population Growth," *Our World in Data* (2013) Accessible at: https://ourworldindata.org/world-population-growth.
[42] Lomborg, B. Rubin, O. "The Dustbin of History: Limits to Growth," *Foreign Policy* (November 9, 2009). Accessible at: https://foreignpolicy.com/2009/11/09/the-dustbin-of-history-limits-to-growth/.

Why Forecasting May Miss the Mark

Forecasting has become a billion-dollar industry, compounded by the response to the Global Financial Crisis of 2008 and no doubt set to expand further in response to the 2020 pandemic and its aftermath. In the banking sector, risk management has become the number one priority. Currently, banks' risk function operating models dedicate about 15% of their workload to analytics. By 2025, that number will have grown to 40%.

And yet errors mean forecasting often costs more than it saves. One large Asia-Pacific bank, according to the McKinsey Institute, lost $4 billion because it applied interest-rate models that contained incorrect assumptions and data-entry errors.[43] Modeling is used now even where it is unhelpful, and it has become a crutch for companies trying to make the best use of their exponentially growing pool of data and their rapidly expanding computing power. Quite often, not only do these models fail to predict crises, but they increase exposure to risk by duping companies into believing that the potential downsides of a decision are within an acceptable range.

But as the world becomes more complex, with globe-spanning supply chains and worldwide financial webs, and as big data, machine learning, and AI leave us increasingly automated, vulnerability to radical uncertainty grows. There is simply too much that must be modeled across systems that are hypersensitive to disruption and rapidly reactive.

Despite this, at least a few times each year, the Bank of Canada, the US Federal Reserve Bank, the Bank of England, the European Central Bank, and their counterparts in the G20 make

---

[43] Härle, P., Havas, A., & Samandari, H. "The Future of Bank Risk Management," *McKinsey & Company* (July 22, 2016). Accessible at: https://www.mckinsey.com/business-functions/risk/our-insights/the-future-of-bank-risk-management.

forecasts on the future of their economies to which we give the same devout reverence as our ancestors did their soothsayers. A classic example is the Bank of Canada's forecast in October 2018 for the following March. The bank predicted that the Canadian GDP would be 2.4% in March of 2019. The actual number was 0.4%, a huge difference with huge implications. How could it be so wrong over such a short period?

One of the biggest mistakes that forecasters make is to believe that they can predict black swans. These are your radical uncertainties renamed. They are events that are outliers, located beyond our ability to conceive because, so far, no evidence can even point to their probable existence. They are also events that carry an extremely high impact despite being so unlikely. And, from a psychological perspective, they are events which, after they have happened, we believe we could have predicted if only we had taken certain things into account. The term itself is derived from the ancient world, when orthodox thought maintained that black swans did not exist, and the story of their discovery is a metaphor for how an unexpected event can fundamentally undermine the logic in a system of thought.[44]

Time and again, we have proven that we cannot predict black swans—trying to do so is a contradiction of the very term itself since black swans are by definition unpredictable. Yet there is a common but fatal arrogance among forecasters and analysts that there exists some divine model that accurately describes the data-generating process of the real world, and that it is their job to find it. But there is not. There is no Platonic form for the messy particulars of the real world—no ideal model that can generalize the specifics of such a complex and random reality.

For every black swan we think we can imagine and account

---

[44] Taleb, N. N. *The Black Swan* (London: Random House, 2007).

for, another lies in wait unseen. And yet in trying to predict one after the other, we waste valuable resources, we neglect other possibilities, and we become more vulnerable. It is far more effective to focus on consequences. Instead of trying to guess the details of radical uncertainty, betting on a central forecast among a distribution, we should be preparing to deal with a potential range of impacts. For example, instead of guessing from which country a cyberattack might come and which operating system it might strike, risk thinking would focus more on the consequences. It would ask, "What would be the impact if every computer running the latest Mac OS suddenly crashed?"

The immemorial mantra of investment literature is that "past performance is not a guide to future returns," yet another of our greatest follies is believing precisely the opposite to be true. We are enamored by the precedence set by data, beholden to the belief that it can pinpoint the future. In fact, recent brain imaging studies have shown that when we are asked to recall past events and imagine future situations, identical areas of the brain light up.[45] It is as though we are hardwired to use the past to predict tomorrow.

Yet black swans have no precedents. As our economy develops, it looks increasingly unlike the economy of yesterday. It is massively interconnected, rapidly responsive, and highly sensitive to change. And so, it is volatile like never before. As the *Harvard Business Review* points out,

> Less than 0.25% of all the companies listed in the world represent around half the market capitalization, less than 0.2% of books account for approximately half their sales, less than 0.1% of drugs generate a little more than half the pharmaceutical

---

[45] Suddendorf, T. *The Gap: The Science of What Separates Us from Other Animals* (New York, NY, United States: Basic Books, 2013), 94. Cited from Beckert and Bronk. *Uncertain Futures*, 107.

industry's sales—and less than 0.1% of risky events will cause at least half your losses.[46]

This is why standard deviation, the most common tool in the forecaster's tool kit, fails us time and again. When forecasters want to predict risk, they look to past data and measure the amount of variation in the set of values. This is standard deviation, or sigma (σ). It is a way to know how much a series of numbers—like the number of goals in World Cup football matches or the price of a stock on different days—varies around its mean, or average.

A set of data that does not move around much and has most of its values closely grouped near the average (like the daily high temperature in Hawaii), has a low standard deviation. A set of values that varies greatly (like the daily price of silver, which is notoriously bumpy), has a high standard deviation because its values are spread over a bigger range. In finance, standard deviation works as an expression of volatility. The higher the standard deviation, the higher the volatility. Project that value forward, and you ostensibly have an expression of risk.

In an economy of tame randomness—with no radical uncertainty—about two-thirds of the variations should fall within −1 and +1 standard deviations. Variations above three standard deviations should happen only 0.03% of the time. And above seven standard deviations should be for all intents and purposes considered impossible. This is what we call normal distribution. We can see it as the normal distribution or bell curve on the graph below.

---

[46] Taleb, N. N., Goldstein, D. G., & Spitznagel, M. W. "The Six Mistakes Executives Make in Risk Management," *Harvard Business Review* (October 2009). Accessible at: https://hbr.org/2009/10/the-six-mistakes-executives-make-in-risk-management.

Figure 7
Normal Distribution
When forecasters express their visions of the future, they often do so by assuming that most of the world operates on a normal distribution. 68% of the population lies between +1 and -1 standard deviation from the mean. A full 99.7% lie within 3 standard deviations from the mean.

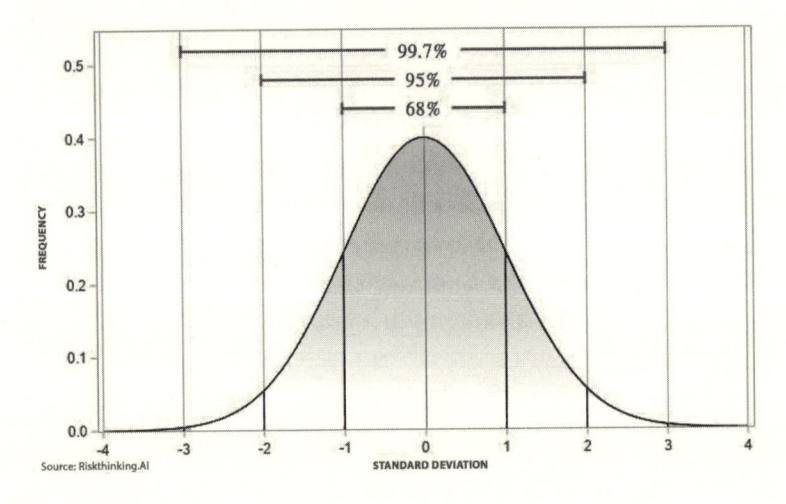

Source: Riskthinking.AI

Source: Author

When forecasters express their visions of the future, they often do so by assuming that most of the world operates on a normal distribution. They assess the risk of a future endeavour by looking back at past data and calculating the standard deviation. Based on the past data, they say, this is a safe bet—no big bumps ahead.

This is almost exactly what happened in the 2008 financial crash, which was due to faulty risk models and credit ratings practices in collateralized debt obligation (derivatives) markets. We know now that agencies assumed they were dealing with stationary stochastic uncertainty—the kind of risk that can be measured and manipulated, the kind that repeats in patterns—when they created their financial products. They were not. They had confused it with radical uncertainty. In doing so, they deployed many models that incorrectly assumed that relevant probabilities followed a normal distribution while using historical data to calculate the probability of future default—something it could not do. This gave them a false sense of security, and they began behaving as though their models could accurately forecast objective probabilities. As Beckert and Bronk put it, "The results were devastating."[47]

When modelling complex processes with hundreds of components all acting upon one another to influence the outcome, it is mostly a fundamental mistake to assume a normal distribution. There are too many moving parts, too many unknowable quirks or external influences, and too many potential chain reactions that can disrupt the distribution. In real life, variations above seven standard deviations happen frequently—they can even exceed twenty or thirty standard deviations, leaving investments in turmoil and forecasters scratching their heads. The 2010 Flash Crash and the 1987 Black Monday Crash were both examples of unprecedented downswings in the market that were greater than twenty standard deviations. Another example is in 2015 when the Swiss National Bank stopped trying to cap the Swiss franc exchange rate to the euro—the franc jumped 19% in value, a 180-sigma movement.[48] If the distribution of the Swiss franc-Euro exchange rate would have been normal, such an event would have been as likely as a particular meteor in the solar system hitting a particular grain of sand on a particular day in the future.

Forecasting only works if the world is extremely stable for the period observed—that usually means for very short periods ahead.

---

[47] Beckert and Bronk. *Uncertain Futures*, 19.
[48] Harwood, V. "High Sigma Events—They're Not All Black Swans," *Six Figure Investing* (February 6, 2021). Accessible at: https://sixfigureinvesting.com/2016/07/understanding-interpreting-high-sigma-events-black-swans/.

CHAPTER 4

RISK THINKING: A DIFFERENT WAY TO LOOK AT THE FUTURE

Forecasters have, for at least the past 40 years, had the "deplorable effects" of their trade pointed out by Nobel prize-winning economists.[49] Indeed, even Keynes admitted that "our knowledge of the factors which will govern the yield of an investment some years hence is usually very slight and often negligible." The result, he said, is that market valuation "cannot be uniquely correct, since our existing knowledge does not provide a sufficient basis for a calculated mathematical expectation."[50] Nothing has changed since then despite advances in probabilistic analysis.

In writing this book, I intend to disrupt our dependency on deterministic statistical fortune-telling. But rather than simply pull the rug from underneath the feet of forecasters as Heffernan, Beckert and Bronk, and Kay and King have already successfully done, this book offers a codification of radical uncertainty that as yet is missing: it offers a way for us to translate uncertainty into

---

[49] Shaw, A. "Why economic forecasting has always been a flawed science," The Guardian (September 2, 2017). Accessible at: https://www.theguardian.com/money/2017/sep/02/economic-forecasting-flawed-science-data.
[50] Keynes, J.M. *The General Theory of Employment, Interest and Money* (London: Palgrave Macmillan, 1936), chapter 12.

risk, and from there to create strategy that allows us to navigate the unknowable future we face. This codification is particularly important because, while these authors offer up useful suggestions, they provide no structured framework in which to actually apply their ideas in a risk management setting.

Heffernan, for example, suggests that rather than running our economies as finely tuned production lines that are efficient but brittle, we ought instead to aim for robustness via preparation. Illustrated through a series of well-evidenced examples, Heffernan tells us we must explore, experiment, and empower. We must show "genius and creativity in preparation."

We need "just-in-time thinking that maximizes the efficiency of any aspect of the work that can be standardized, measured and predicted, such as manufacturing." In other words, we must overcome deterministic problems with increased efficiency—automation, technology, etc. And where a problem is complex (or, to us, stochastic), we must build up resiliency measures. We must also become "trusted participants," "invest in a dynamic ecosystem," and ensure that "cultural translation articulates, reinforces and adapts insight and experience."[51]

We must replace solutionism with exploration, open strategy up to everyone in an organization because insight and intelligence can exist anywhere, use imagination to extrapolate from early warning signs, and recognize how interconnected our global systems are and how quickly change can spread throughout them. Above all, we must "kick our addiction to planning, making more time to pay attention to the details, contradictions, and paradoxes all around us" so that we can identify threats and opportunities.[52] As a review in the *Financial Times* points out, Heffernan "stands in the pulpit quietly admonishing us to be a

---
[51] Heffernan, M. *Uncharted: How to Map the Future* (London: Simon & Schuster UK, 2020), 304.
[52] Heffernan, *Uncharted*, 314.

little wiser, reflect a little more, to do the things that deep down we already know we should be doing."[53] How we put this into practice remains obscure. Where are the economic trade-offs to guide decision-making? Where are the models to replace traditional economic models that are no longer valid? We receive a multitude of enlightening examples but no semblance of a formal approach to this type of risk preparedness.

Kay and King's *Radical Uncertainty* does a similarly excellent job of critiquing the standard approach to uncertainty in finance and economics. It is a well-made point that forecasters frequently confuse "the vast range of possibilities that lie in between the world of unlikely events which can nevertheless be described with the aid of probability distributions, and the world of the unimaginable." Rather than banks and businesses that rely on models claiming impossible knowledge of the future, Kay and King suggest, like Heffernan, that we must adopt policies and strategies that are adaptive and robust to many alternative futures. We must use experienced judgment informed by credible and consistent "reference narratives" (that we must accept may be wrong when empirical evidence reveals alternatives) in a collaborative process. These are good ideas, yet again we are left without a starting point or a structured process with which to apply this advice. Kay and King suggest that in a radically uncertain environment we must be willing to throw up our hands and say, "I don't know." But then what do we do?

Our answer to this question is "risk think." Risk thinking can help guide decision makers in a systematic, formalized modelling framework, as we will show.

As a whole, this book offers a revision of the way we think about the future. In many ways, it does so with a similar emphasis

---

[53] "Uncharted: How to Map the Future Together—A Plea for Fresh Thinking," Review, *Financial Times* (February 19, 2020). Accessible at: https://www.ft.com/content/0401d240-4f43-11ea-95a0-43d18ec715f5.

on dismantling our dependency on forecasting that previous books have had. And in many ways, it also takes on board a lot of the ideas that Heffernan and others elucidate. It argues for a way to embrace uncertainty rather than run from it or mask it beneath the language of scientific calculation. In a world that is becoming increasingly subject to radical uncertainty—whether in the form of climate change, pandemics, cyberattacks, or some as yet unforeseen systemic disruption—risk thinking offers a way for us to get our hands around our possible futures without shrinking them into a singular forecast.

But, crucially, our difference from past studies on uncertainty is to provide a codified approach through risk thinking's method of scenario generation for us to map risks and strategies so that, when we have to decide whether to bet or hedge, we do so equipped with the best knowledge available. Building on a step-by-step process, we must constantly reassess and re-evaluate our strategy based on new data through an iterative process.

Our Step-by-Step Process

Laid out step by step, risk thinking can be formalized, for large institutions, in this fashion:

1. Split your problem into the deterministic and the random or stochastic parts.
2. Eliminate the deterministic parts through planning, practice, and efficiency.
3. Gather forward-looking data to measure the uncertainty on each of the individual radically uncertain risk factors that affect what is being measured through structured expert judgment, using polling or machine learning (if you have the luxury of time and a team of data scientists).

4. Generate consistent, forward-looking scenarios for combinations of these risk factors that span possible futures (those that include the best and worst outcomes).[54]
5. Evaluate the impact on you or your institution under each scenario.
6. Decide which scenarios you will ignore (take a bet on) and which you will mitigate to hedge possible negative outcomes, regardless of their likelihood.
7. Constantly re-evaluate your strategy, updating scenarios at regular intervals towards the horizon, accounting for new information produced within the scientific community or elsewhere.

This is the kind of risk thinking that we imagine large businesses or institutions executing. But we will also show that risk thinking can be practised by every one of us without all of this formality. Steps 3, 4, and 5 may be estimated or used with poetic licence. And, when you think about it, we often solve problems involving future uncertainty in just this way using nothing but our intuition—a valuable resource that this book hopes to highlight.

The first step, separating the deterministic and stochastic elements, is the risk thinker's defining trait, and a theme to which we will return throughout this book. Being able to identify the deterministic from the stochastic—and splitting a problem into these two parts accordingly—is a way for us to reduce the seemingly insurmountable challenge of strategizing in the face of large, complex uncertainties. A large part of most problems that initially appear to contain a high degree of radical uncertainty can be compartmentalized into smaller, deterministic processes that are solvable through well-known management techniques: project management, proper staffing, efficient processes, contingency

---

[54] This is quite technical and is described in the appendix.

planning, routine practicing, and securing the correct equipment, which is step 2. In doing these simple steps, the decision maker will be left with a minimized and much more comprehensible form of uncertainty, and it is then that the real impact of the risk thinking process can be brought to bear on some of our biggest issues.

The nature and form of the solution are what matters, not the amount of manpower or computing power you can throw at it. We can even reverse engineer whether a given solution is appropriate, even if we do not understand the domain. An example is how El Al solved its hijacking problem versus the approach by the US Department of Homeland Security, mentioned in chapter 5.

In the third step, we turn to our experts, the only true source of forward-looking data. The fourth step, how one generates scenarios automatically, contains the primary innovations of risk thinking. We will show how it is possible to generate these scenarios with an algorithm that enables consistency and mitigates human bias. Once the set of scenarios is created, we walk through the process of evaluating their impact. It is sometimes onerous for companies to do valuations under stress. They are simply not equipped to do so without major internal work. However, this is less and less the case since stress testing is now widely accepted. The algorithm is important because ad hoc scenario generation can never achieve the consistency markets will require when pricing uncertainty. And, consistency, comparing apples to apples, is paramount to investors and decision makers.

Risk thinking's scenario generation is almost the antithesis of most forecasting. Risk thinkers do not believe in forecasting, except, of course, when the time period into the future is so small that forecasting can do well. Even our weather forecasters would not dare try to forecast the temperature in Toronto at noon on July 14, 2035! Risk thinking presumes that the best we can do is generate a spanning set of scenarios, one that captures the possible science- and data-based futures with the best, most trusted information available. We have no choice but to describe the possible space in which the future lies. And, as the future approaches, our view of it narrows and gets more accurate.

A risk thinker would not stop at the generation of scenarios but would focus attention on the best and worst possible cases to develop a strategy today. That is a fundamental reversal of the forecaster's view. Forecasters work within the parameters of the probable—they model what they believe should happen, not what could happen. But it is precisely the improbable that concerns the risk thinker—the outliers, the extremities, the twenty-sigma eventualities. By ignoring those, you fail to appropriately conceptualize the multifarious nature of the future. By ignoring the possible and maybe improbable scenarios, you are simply betting against the future.

With our scenarios in hand, we measure their impact (step 5). Then we move to the action phase (step 6). This is a business decision. Scenarios with a large impact may sometimes be very unlikely, but these are potentially the pandemics waiting to pounce. In executing risk thinking, we ignore the likelihood of scenarios at first glance and focus on their impact. Two firms with the same or similar outcome under a given scenario might react differently, and that is legitimate. However, the important thing is that they will know the bets they are taking explicitly: the scenarios they ignore.

The risk thinker admits that there is no magic "solution" in the face of radical uncertainty—no single answer to the multiple possibilities of tomorrow; there is only a strategy with one or more hedges to protect us from the magnitude of extreme downsides—or to exploit the benefits of the upside. The form of a solution using risk thinking is an action and a hedging regime. The expectation is that events will occur that will cause the risk thinker to modify the scenarios and change tack. That is another key difference from forecasting. The form of a solution derived from forecasting is a single action. It gives you a deterministic solution to a stochastic problem. It is to point the ship towards a port, lash a rope around the wheel, and head below deck to take cover from the storm.

Where forecasting leaves you unable to adapt, risk thinking has you at the helm and ready to react. And crucial to that reaction is the final step, number 7, constantly acquiring new information with which to update your scenarios and adjust your strategy.

While this book is primarily intended as an instrument for decision makers to manage risk, we also hope that there is something to gain for the individual. For individuals making those decisions and wanting to practice risk thinking, the process need not be so formal—we do not advise you to run algorithms on your way to work. But we do hope to instill a beneficial mindset: a way to look at a course of action, think of some scenarios and their impacts, and decide whether to bet or hedge. To recognise when a solution to a problem is proposed and it has the wrong form. This kind of mental analysis should be ongoing, a reflection on the scenarios when situations change and a re-evaluation of the path chosen through uncertainty. It is about getting away from the single instance forecast. It is also about understanding why we naturally hedge our bets in some cases.

To put it in layman's terms, it is the act of spreading your eggs into more than one basket or setting aside funds for a rainy day. These common-sense adages are lessons that our forefathers learned from experiencing uncertainty the hard way. Curious, though, that major corporations and governments often fail to practice them.

What we want to show is that in many ways we are all natural risk thinkers. We just have not formalized it. This book is that formal process.

CHAPTER 5

REAL RISK THINKERS (OR NOT)

Training for risk can produce gratifying results and save lives; failing to grasp all the risks can be catastrophic. Some, like astronaut Chris Hadfield, trained for every eventuality except the one that happened. But his preparation helped him overcome the unexpected. Others, such as the airline El Al, thought more carefully than their competitors about what they were trying to achieve (in this case, airline security) and came up with a nonconventional but better solution.

Failing to think comprehensively about the risks to any venture might leave your expensive building flooded in Manhattan or your global supply chain shattered by an earthquake. As part of our examination of risk, in this chapter, we look at a few didactic real-world stories of risk thinking in action (or not). We explore risk thinking in space, risk thinking on the rock face, risk thinking on the ground, risk thinking in Manhattan, and risk thinking after an earthquake as examples of how to think better about risk in a world of radical uncertainty and how we might apply the lessons.

Risk Thinking in Space: How to Prepare for the Unpreparable

Travelling at 29,000 km/hr and equipped with a jetpack and joystick, Chris Hadfield stood in the airlock of the Space Shuttle *Endeavour* and stared out into the vast nothingness of space. Before him, the sun rose over Earth, as it did every 92 minutes at that speed, and bathed the mountains and valleys, the rivers, lakes, and oceans, with the glistening light of a new dawn. Beyond, infinite darkness beckoned.

The mission was to install a Kevlar-clad titanium robotic arm, the Canadarm2, onto the International Space Station, and Hadfield was lead spacewalker—the first Canadian ever to undertake extravehicular activity (EVA) beyond the confines of Earth's atmosphere. As he clung to the shuttle, hurtling through the vacuum of the universe, Hadfield checked one final time the tether that ran from his suit to that of his partner, Scott Parazynski, and on to the structure.

Secure, he thought, and he stepped out into the void.

Five hours later, drill in hand and the engineering work well underway, Hadfield noticed his left eye begin to smart. It was a tingling at first, the kind that a bit of grit or an eyelash might cause. But then it became a burning sensation, and no amount of blinking would rid him of whatever contaminant was in there. Then tears welled up, and, in zero gravity, they sat right there over his cornea instead of falling down his cheek, partially blinding him.

Puzzled, but not alarmed, Hadfield continued with the installation. But as the salty liquid pooled and crossed the bridge of his nose, bringing with it whatever had been irritating his left eye, he gradually lost sight in his right one as well. Now, still floating outside the space station, still holding the drill and midway through engineering work on the most advanced construction tool ever built, he was totally blind.

Hadfield had encountered radical uncertainty.

Back at Mission Control in Houston, engineers, medical biologists, and every array of NASA personnel erupted into a frenzy of theorizing, hypothesizing, and scenario generation. Was there a leak of the highly caustic lithium hydroxide in the air-purification system? How many minutes would that give him before his lungs gave out? What did the rest of his vitals look like?

Two hundred and fifty miles above them, Hadfield contemplated the same possibilities. Training for this mission had begun four years before blastoff—before the International Space Station even existed. Each and every five-minute segment of the spacewalk had been choreographed to perfection. The astronauts had covered countless conceivable problems and every potential solution, and they had worked through the scenarios endlessly. But nobody had prepared Hadfield for this one.

Blind, hurtling through space—it is enough to make anyone panic. Yet Hadfield felt no fear. NASA had eradicated that instinct in training; they had taught him how to react to the unknown with focused curiosity instead. And, most importantly, they had taught him the fundamentals of risk management, to create an optimal strategy that minimized the impact of unfortunate events—like lithium hydroxide seeping into his lungs, corroding membranes, and causing an agonizing death—and simultaneously maximized the realization of opportunities—like completing the installation.

NASA deemed lithium hydroxide to be a high-impact event (obviously, dead astronauts tend to be), and it was also one of their first thoughts, a seemingly plausible scenario. So, it was high loss, high likelihood. What is more, this downside risk was fairly easy to hedge against. All Hadfield had to do was begin venting oxygen, of which he had plenty. Absent sight, in a practiced motion, he opened the purge valve on his suit to dump any contaminated air into the void, mitigating the potential presence of toxic fumes.

Then he waited, slowly leaking oxygen, wondering, if he did not die, when he might get back to work on the station. He slowly worked through possible scenarios and solutions.

Twenty minutes, later Hadfield's vision returned. He checked in with his partner. Parazynski had seen no need to come to his assistance since he would have been unable to do anything—the opportunity cost of him stopping work was too high ($450 million too high, to be precise)[55] against a practically absent mitigation effect. So, he had instead made valuable use of the time by furthering the installation. Now clear-sighted and together, they had optimized their strategy and could complete the engineering.

Only later did Hadfield find out that the culprit had been the anti-fog liquid with which he had (a little too liberally) cleaned his visor the night before. It was dishwasher detergent, essentially. Yet remaining calm had allowed him to sweat through the issue, to think logically about the scenario and, ultimately, to finish the job he had set out to do.[56]

NASA is comprised of risk thinkers. They prepared Hadfield for radical uncertainty, and they had no choice but to do so. Not every eventuality can be accounted for when you launch astronauts beyond the reaches of Earth; not every twist and tumult of

---

[55] This is what it costs NASA every time it launches a space shuttle, according to their FAQ. Bray, N. "Space Shuttle and International Space Station FAQ," *NASA.gov* (August 4, 2017). Accessible at: https://www.nasa.gov/centers/kennedy/about/information/shuttle_faq.html.

[56] Hadfield, C. *An Astronaut's Guide to Life on Earth* (New York: Little, Brown and Company, 2013), 1–2, 31–33, 86–96.

space exploration can be imagined in advance. This was a lesson they had learned already on numerous occasions.

Risk Thinking on the Rock: Make Your World More Deterministic

A scrawny kid with big ears and wide-set, dark eyes, Alex Honnold burst onto the global rock-climbing scene in 2007. His achievement was astounding: free soloing (that is ascending with no safety ropes or harness) Yosemite's Astroman and the Rostrum in a single day—two demanding routes both more than 800 feet that even fully roped-up elite climbers face with trepidation. A year later, he free soloed the 1,200-foot, 5.12d finger crack that splits Zion National Park's Moonlight Buttress. As told by the *Alpinist*, "The ascent was reported on April 1. For days, people thought the news was a joke."[57]

A few months after that, he became the first person to free solo the 2,000-foot regular Northwest Face of Half Dome, also in Yosemite—acclaimed at the time as the most impressive rope-less ascent ever completed.

But Honnold was not happy with this feat. In the face of an overwhelmingly large climb, he had not known how to prepare. There were simply too many moves, too many potential risks, he thought. And so, he had skipped the preparations and, as he said, decided to "go up there and have an adventure."[58]

Unsurprisingly, this was not the best strategy. Halfway up, he got stuck on an unfamiliar route. "Imagine being by yourself," he

---

[57] Lowther, A. "Less and Less Alone: Alex Honnold," *Alpinist*, 35 (2011). Accessible at: http://www.alpinist.com/doc/web17s/wfeature-alp35-alex-honnold-profile-less-and-less-alone.
[58] Honnold, A. "How I Climbed a 3,000-Foot Vertical Cliff—Without Ropes," *Ted Talks*, hosted on Youtube.com (October 28, 2018). Accessible at: https://youtu.be/6iM6M_7wBMc.

later recalled, "in the dead centre of a 2,000-foot face, wondering if you are lost." And each moment of indecision costs you valuable energy—energy that, if it fails, means you plummet to certain death on the valley floor below.

On an imposing, near-vertical blank slab of granite with no handholds, he had to trust the friction in his shoes alone to grip the surface. But then he reached a foothold that looked perilously unstable. "I started to panic," he said, retelling the event. "I could hear people laughing on the summit above me. I wanted to be anywhere but on that slab ... I knew what I had to do, but I was too afraid to do it."

Eventually, Honnold summoned up the willpower, accepted the bet he was taking, and made the step. The foot held, and he did not die.

News of his successful ascent brought him widespread fame among the climbing community. However, Honnold was disappointed. In his diary that night, he put a frowny face next to the entry and wrote, "Do better?" When asked why he was disappointed, Honnold said, "I didn't want to be a lucky climber. I wanted to be a great climber." He was frustrated that his lack of preparation meant he had had to take an unnecessary risk.

Intuitively, Honnold had struck on one of the key facets of the risk-thinking process. He had understood, and highlighted in extremely clear terms, the two sides to a problem: the deterministic and the stochastic.

Honnold faced radical uncertainty and extreme risk while he was climbing the rock face—a sudden gust of wind that could blow him from the surface, an acute cramp in his arm causing him to seize up, falling debris striking him as he climbed. These were things that he could be aware of, but which he could not predict. There was no way to know when or how they would strike. They were the stochastic half of the equation, and to be a great climber, he would have to acknowledge and accept those.

But there was also the deterministic half. These were the things that were not subject to uncertainty: the shape of the rock face, the security of each foot and crevice, his endurance on the day. These were elements of the problem—risks—that he could have eliminated through careful planning and repeated practice. His disappointment stemmed from the fact that he had failed to minimize the risks arising from the deterministic aspects of the problem.

Honnold took a two-year break from free soloing after the Half Dome. But in the back of his mind, his desire to achieve "true mastery" ticked over, and he began to think about the unthinkable: free soloing El Capitan, a 3,000-foot vertical granite rock in Yosemite that is the jewel of the global rock-climbing community, a rock that had only ever been ascended with ropes.

It took him seven years to build up to it.

This time, he knew that his preparation and his dedication would have to be perfect. He would have to eliminate every single deterministic aspect of the climb by practicing each move over and again with ropes until they became automatic. He would have to know the exact route he would take years in advance and ensure that it was thoroughly mapped and in good condition before he began. His level of preparation was such that days before the event, he would climb the route with a partner using ropes and spend hours removing loose rocks from the way and checking and rechecking each foothold.

Even his diet would have to be consistently perfect to give him both the fuel he needed and avoid stomach bugs in the months around the event. He even banned chocolate: "It might have helped a few percentage points," he said, "but maybe not." Yet by taking these measures and others, he was reducing the likelihood for failure down to its minimum—he was hedging against the downside risks.

As a risk thinker, Honnold intuitively used scenario generation to help him visualize the different dangers and opportunities he faced. He imagined the climb, with all its different pitfalls and hazards, learning to identify the risks that lay ahead and categorize them as either something he could mitigate or something he would have to bet on going to plan. It was about "feeling the texture of each hold in my hand and imagining the sensation of my leg reaching out and placing my foot just so. I'd imagine it all like a choreographed dance thousands of feet up."

The most difficult part of the climb was called the Boulder Problem. It was about 2,000 feet off the ground and comprised the hardest physical moves on the whole route: long pulls between poor handholds with very small, slippery feet. These handholds were, he said, "smaller than the width of a pencil, facing downwards, that I had to press up into with my thumb." But it got worse. "The crux culminated in a karate kick with my left foot over to the inside of an adjacent corner, a maneuver that required a high degree of precision and flexibility."

In that moment, Honnold faced the most extreme risks, and he was most exposed. Yet by generating scenarios in his mind about what could go wrong and how he should approach the problem, he was able to mitigate the deterministic aspects of this karate kick move. He began a nightly stretching routine for a full year in advance of the climb to ensure his leg was limber and could perform the kick under duress automatically. For the stochastic elements—the sudden gust of wind, for example—he knew that it would be a risk that he would have to take on. All he could do was choose a day with low-wind conditions. The point was that he was able to identify these elements of the equation in advance, and this allowed him to mentally prepare for the climb.

"I had to consider every possibility while I was safely on the ground," he said. "I had to visualize and rehearse enough to remove all doubt."

The result of this risk thinking was that Honnold was able to complete the climb absent fear. In fact, he was confident, and he enjoyed it. When he had climbed Half Dome before, he said, "I was hesitant, afraid, and it wasn't the experience that I wanted." But up El Cap, "I climbed with a smooth precision and enjoyed the sounds of the birds swooping around the cliff. It all felt like a celebration. And then I reached the summit after 3 hours and 56 minutes of glorious climbing. It was the climb that I wanted, and it felt like mastery."

To the uninitiated, Honnold's feat looks like madness—a crazy risk for a foolhardy kid. And indeed, even his sponsors saw it that way. In 2014, about three years before his climb, Clif Bar announced that they would be withdrawing their sponsorship of the climber along with several other free soloists. "We concluded that these forms of the sport are pushing boundaries and taking the element of risk to a place where we as a company are no longer willing to go," the company wrote in an open letter.[59]

But what they failed to realize was that, while Honnold certainly was taking a risk, it was one that was minutely calculated and minimized. His grand achievement, as much as making it to the top, was to implement intuitively a cohesive risk-thinking process in the face of radical uncertainty. As his film crew summed up, "Part of being a professional climber is identifying and acknowledging the risks, assessing them, minimizing them, and then moving on."[60] And it is that approach that will help businesses, individuals, and governments survive in today's

---

[59] Branch, J. "A Sponsor Steps Away from the Edge," *New York Times* (November 16, 2014). Accessible at: https://www.nytimes.com/2014/11/16/sports/clif-bar-drops-sponsorship-of-5-climbers-citing-risks-they-take.html.

[60] Vasarhelyi, E. C., & Chin, J. "What if He Falls? The Terrifying Reality Behind Filming 'Free Solo,'" *New York Times*, hosted on Youtube.com (November 2, 2018). Accessible at: https://youtu.be/3-wjmIFlnNo.

risk environment—you do not have to be a statistician with a multimillion-dollar computer to apply this stuff.

Risk Thinking on the Ground: Create the Right Form of a Solution

Often a system fails because it mistakenly attempts to apply a deterministic solution to a radically uncertain or stochastic situation. Take airport security, for example. The American solution is to have a rules-based system that tries to mitigate potential risks with a set of questions and processes out of a guidebook. They have a low-grade employee with a rule book who mindlessly applies instructions: "No liquids. Take off your shoes and put them on the conveyor," etc. It does not matter if you are quite obviously tramping around in flat shoes—the rules say take them off. The notion is that with enough rules, we can solve the problem.

When US Homeland Security officials evaluated the Transportation Security Administration (TSA) in 2015, they pretended to be terrorists and tried to smuggle guns and bombs onto planes 70 different times. And they succeeded 67 of those times despite the TSA's lengthy screening process. That is a failure rate of over 95%.[61]

The Israeli airline El Al has a very different approach, one that I would classify as risk thinking. The 1960s and 1970s saw Palestinian terrorist groups commit a large number of hijackings. El Al and others quickly developed a risk-thinking approach to the problem. They have a psychiatrist who interviews every passenger before boarding. And they look at you on cameras to examine

---

[61] Fishel, J., et al. "Undercover DHS Tests Find Security Failures at US Airports," *ABC News* (June 1, 2015). Accessible at: https://abcnews.go.com/US/exclusive-undercover-dhs-tests-find-widespread-security-failures/story?id=31434881.

your body language as you enter the airport. They start generating scenarios about you from the moment you walk into the terminal.

The Israeli notion is that because there is no solution, they have to hedge against the unknown and the uncertain. If a terrorist could be anyone and look like anyone, a rule book will not cut it. But a trained behavioural analyst might. The Israelis' ultimate hedge, however, is to stick a guy on the plane in plain clothes—looking just like a passenger—armed and prepared to counter any threat, just in case all else fails. And their solution works well. The first and last successful hijacking of an El Al aircraft took place in 1968.

The nature or form of the solution is what matters, not the amount of manpower or computing power you can throw at it. In a radically uncertain world, there is no single solution; there is only a strategy for hedging your risk to guide you through.

Risk Thinking on Wall Street: Broaden Your Scope

Some risks you do not see because you are looking in the wrong direction.

During the ten years I spent as a professor at Yale, I would often discuss mathematical problems with Stephen Ross, a famous finance professor and office neighbour. He would tease me with my consulting on large engineering projects, saying I should shift my focus to finance. Being a child of the sixties, that seemed like anathema to me. But in the summer of 1986, he prevailed and introduced me to Goldman Sachs, and I accepted a summer job, which later turned into a 14-month assignment.

I discovered that finance was a treasure trove of interesting mathematical problems, and at that time, Wall Street was beginning a renaissance as a mathematically driven profession. To my surprise, I really enjoyed working there with the 40 other first-rate academics they had hired. It was like being at a great university and earning 10 times as much.

Back then, Goldman was not at the top of the heap in the investment banking world. It was a relatively small, flat, and nimble organization headquartered at 85 Broad Street—across the road from the biggest investment bank, Solomon Brothers. At one stage, I asked the co-CEO, Bob Rubin, who had called me in to discuss a problem, why they had hired me—an applied mathematician who did not know what a bond coupon was.

He told me a story that has stuck with me ever since.

There were a few generals back at the beginning of the last century who were taken to see an unusual manufacturing plant in Detroit. They saw these funny-looking horseless carriages rolling off a noisy production line. Upon leaving, one of them turned around to the others and said, "Well, there we have it, the next war will be fought with tanks not faster horses." Little did he know, but the general was a risk thinker. He did his scenario generating while watching the line, and one scenario stuck out. If horseless carriages could be made to work and be produced en masse, then, if not now but at some point, they would outpace horse-drawn carriages in war. And he was right. Rubin and his co-CEO Friedman believed that the "next war" on Wall Street would be fought with mathematics and models. So, he hired 40 of the best minds he could from academia and let them innovate. How right he was!

As it happens, Bob Rubin is probably one of the most natural risk thinkers I have ever met. The story goes that one day Jon Corzine, his head of fixed income, came to him with a trade. It could bring huge value to Goldman Sachs, more than $1 billion. Rubin asked, naturally, what was the risk and downside. Corzine responded that it could possibly bankrupt Goldman if the US defaulted on its Treasuries. "Well," said Rubin, "we are not doing it. The risk may be minuscule, but the downside is extreme. We have no need to take such risks."

I had another encounter with Goldman Sachs in 2005. I had the good fortune of meeting the then CEO, Hank Paulson, at a New York cocktail party. Hank began telling me of his pride and joy, a new building that would house all of Goldman's now many employees in one state-of-the-art location next to the World Trade Centre in Battery Park.

This 43-storey $2.1 billion steel and glass building was going to be impregnable, said Hank—it was in the wake of 9/11, so security was top of everyone's risk-management checklist. The new skyscraper was going to have 11-foot guard posts, multiblock security zones, instant police response. It would be a fortress capable of withstanding basement, grade-level, and airborne threats.

At the time, I had just started Zerofootprint, a cleantech company designed to help communities combat climate change, and I had a different kind of risk at the forefront of my mind. I said, "Henry, have you thought about the fact that Battery Park will probably be underwater at some point in the next few years? It's not like you're building in Zone C, up near Broadway. Zone A, where you're talking about, is right down low on the waterfront. Did you ever consider the fact that there's a scenario in which part of your building could be partially submerged? Because you're in the flood zone if New York gets hit.

"And this isn't exactly unlikely," I continued. "You're running one of the best risk-management institutions in the world—you guys are known for this. But have you ever taken into account the climate change risk here?"

He said, "Hmm, I didn't think about that."

And there is why risk thinking could have helped him. Had he done a deep dive in preparing scenarios for futures that would inform him of the risks such a building might face over the next 50 years, surely climate change scenarios would have entered the picture. Yes, it was pre-Al Gore but not early for climate change as a risk. And examining climate change and its consequences for sea-level rise would have surfaced scenarios where Battery Park would be underwater.

As it happened, not so long after, New York was battered by Hurricane Sandy, and Goldman Sachs's building, even with a heroic effort to protect it with sandbags, came within inches of being underwater. Had that happened, it would have caused havoc for the firm.

I find it amazing that even the best risk managers in the world can miss out on simple scenarios that, very often, do not even come under the "extreme" category. Even they could learn a thing or two from risk thinking. There is value in a broad crowdsourcing of opinions about the radical uncertainties that lie before us.

But the reason was that climate change was not Hank's business. Nor was it that of his planners and architects. But if they had gone out and done some risk thinking—the structured kind we are talking about in this book—if they had solicited some expert judgment and gone wide enough in terms of whom they asked, someone would have cropped up with the idea to look into climate change.

Risk Thinking for Disasters: Balance Cost with Resiliency

Natural disasters can have a devastating effect on even the best-laid business plans, often because they are "unforeseen."

At 2:46 p.m. on March 11, 2011, a magnitude-9.0 earthquake struck off the northeastern coast of Honshu, the main island of Japan, about 18.6 miles below the floor of the western Pacific Ocean. Caused by a rupture of the Japan Trench, separating the Eurasian Plate from the Pacific Plate, the violent underwater tectonic upheaval and its subsequent aftershocks generated massive tsunami waves that climbed as high as 40 meters and raced at speeds of up to 800 kilometers per hour towards the shores. In a matter of minutes, the first wave reached the coast and swept in, tearing apart coastal towns and inundating the city of Sendai. According to reports, the wall of water coursed some 10 kilometers inland, carrying ships with it, destroying thousands of buildings, and, on its retreat, ripping hundreds of tons of debris— houses, cars, and trucks—and thousands of victims back out to sea. Low-lying lands were left entirely submerged, while further inland, the earthquake caused fires to break out in petrochemical plants and oil refineries and destroyed roads, rail lines, electricity supplies, and great swaths of industrial infrastructure. Damage to the reactors at a nuclear power plant in Fukushima operated by Tokyo Electric and Power Company created the second-worst nuclear disaster in history, as radioactivity flooded into hundreds of square miles of land, forcing tens of thousands of people to evacuate and contaminating the soil and sea. Conservative estimates place the death toll of the Great Sendai Earthquake at 16,000.[62] It was probably closer to 86,000.[63]

---

[62] Pletcher, K. and Rafferty, J. P. "Japan Earthquake and Tsunami of 2011," *Encyclopedia Britannica* (March 27, 2020). Accessible at: https://www.britannica.com/event/Japan-earthquake-and-tsunami-of-2011.
[63] Park, Y., Hong, P., Roh, J. J. "Supply Chain Lessons from the Catastrophic Natural Disaster in Japan," *Business Horizons*, 56:1 (2013), 75–85. Accessible at: https://doi.org/10.1016/j.bushor.2012.09.008.

Figure 8
Geographical Distribution of Losses and Damage in Northeast Japan
The tsunami tore apart coastal towns and inundated the city of Sendai, flattening tens of thousands of buildings and triggering a meltdown at the Fukushima nuclear power complex.

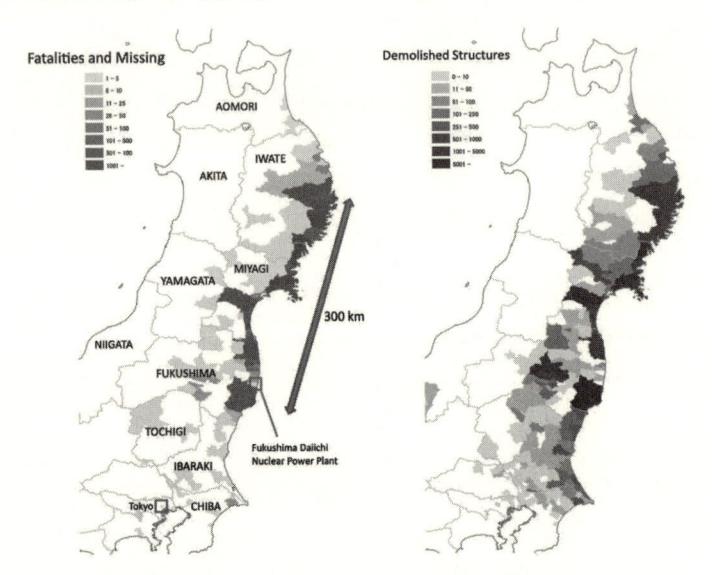

Source: National Research Institute for Earth Science and Disaster Resilience (2011)

The disaster in Japan mobilized international relief efforts. Yet as organizations such as the Red Cross and Doctors Without Borders swung into action, industries in countries halfway around the world were rudely awakened to a bet they had unwittingly taken, and which they had just lost.

Tokyo, and much of eastern Japan, where the tsunami hit, operates as a central nexus of complex, interlocking supply chains that spread their brittle fingers across the globe to feed some of the world's largest companies. Two Japanese companies were responsible for producing 60% of the world's supply of silicon wafers, the raw material from which computer chips are made. The earthquake damaged Shin-Etsu Chemical Corporation, the largest, shutting down production in their factory. And on the other side of the world, in California, vice president of operations for Hewlett-Packard, Tony Prophet, awoke to the startling realisation that his $65-billion-a-year supply chain had a chink in its armour.[64] He was not the only one.

Japan, at the time, was the largest supplier of dynamic random-access memory and flash memory, which plays an integral role in supplying standard logic controllers, liquid crystal display (LCD), and LCD components. After the disaster, prices for these parts soared by 20% around the world.

The auto industry was particularly hard hit. Ford, Volkswagen, BMW, Toyota, Chrysler, and GM had to place a hold on the production of some cars because they depended on paint pigments made only in Japan. Many big Japanese names had the majority of their plants in the affected zones, which had to close, and this impaired vehicle output drastically. Suzuki lost 60% of its production for a month, Nissan 52%, and Honda and Toyota 63% each.

As parts could no longer be produced, shutdowns spread along the supply chain abroad. Toyota plants in Europe, North America, and China seized up for almost three months, while Honda cut production in the UK by 50% for seven weeks. Three Nissan plants in the US shut down completely. Renesas, which supplied about 40% of the global automotive industry's computer chips, was badly damaged, which had similarly devastating consequences.[65] Peugeot-Citroën cut back production by 40–70% at most of its European plants because it lacked an engine airflow sensor imported from Japan.

Across the world, automotive and technology manufacturers

---

[64] Lohr, S. "Stress Test for the Global Supply Chain," *New York Times* (March 19, 2011). Accessible at: https://www.nytimes.com/2011/03/20/business/20supply.html.

[65] Park, Y., Hong, P., Roh, J. J. "Supply Chain Lessons from the Catastrophic Natural Disaster in Japan," *Business Horizons*, 56:1 (2013), 75–85. Accessible at: https://doi.org/10.1016/j.bushor.2012.09.008.

suddenly realized how fragile their production line was. But how could they have let it get that way?

Globalisation has brought with it supply chains that are complex, deep, long, and therefore vulnerable. Japan, in particular, has pioneered the concept of just-in-time manufacturing through the Toyota Production System, which reduces times within production systems as well as response times from suppliers. Its primary philosophy is to produce goods to meet customer demand exactly—in time, quantity, and quality. In other words, it aims to have zero excess, or "minimum waste," whether that is in the form of spare inventory, in-built delay times, overstocking, or a diversified rather than narrow set of suppliers or purchasers for a good.

This is a philosophy of efficiency, and it works well. In a controlled environment such as a single factory floor, we can streamline and automate to our heart's content with comparatively few upsets. And for a while, it works with supply chains too. Most products today comprise thousands of parts manufactured all over the world in a complex system of interdependent supply lines that has been whittled down to deliver maximum speed with minimum cost. Businesses that successfully implemented these lean, global models saw huge improvements in margins and were able to quickly surpass their competition.

But that philosophy fails us in a world of radical uncertainty. These models are infrequently calibrated to risk exposure, and, as the Great Sendai Earthquake or the Covid-19 pandemic of 2020 underline, they are highly vulnerable to disruption. The answer, seemingly obviously, is to make supply chains more robust. We ought to hold more inventory, create additional production lines, build in redundancy across suppliers, practice near-shoring, reduce the number of unique parts we rely on, and regionalize supply chains rather than let them spread across the globe.

But all of that costs money. Put your weight too heavily

towards resiliency, and you will lose out to a competitor with a leaner model. Too efficient, and you will find yourself floored by the next hurricane or rampant pandemic. It is about striking a balance between the upsides and downsides, and that is where risk thinking comes in. It can help you map your supply chains by creating scenarios that reveal weaknesses, improve the end-to-end transparency, and take targeted measures to reduce your exposure to the shocks with the highest impacts.

CHAPTER 6

HOW DO WE CREATE SCENARIOS?

Scenarios are our way to get our hands around an uncertain future. In their simplest form, they are narratives of the potential futures that could unfold around us. Importantly, however, scenarios are not predictions. They do not challenge the status quo of a business outlook with a single, replacement vision of the future. Rather, they encapsulate and convey to stakeholders a range of possible future events with the intention of opening minds up to novel, uncomfortable, and unlikely signals of change and disruption. They are the key to navigating the uncertainties that we face.

The metaphor mentioned in the foreword of headlights in the dark lighting up our future works well for risk thinking. We can only illuminate a partial view of the future (the scenarios we generate). It is the scenarios we have ignored or missed that are the bets we are taking. So, in many cases of radical uncertainty, it behooves us to slow down (hedge) to be able to deal with the moose that will suddenly jump into view unexpectedly.

The opposite of this process would be our current mode of forecasting. We would flick the lights on once, assess the picture, and decide that the road ahead was clear. Then we would set the car on autopilot and turn off the lights. After all, what are the chances that a deer would burst out from the undergrowth right in front of us, right after we have just checked the road ahead?

Scenarios are the fundamental building blocks from which risk thinkers form their strategy. They do this either explicitly or implicitly. A useful set of scenarios needs to "span" the whole range of possible future states and contain the very best and worst that we may reasonably expect at some given future horizon. If it can do this, then, when we come to plan our strategy, we will be able to make informed decisions about which scenarios we think we can ignore and which we should hedge against. But at the very least, we need to know how "good" a set of scenarios is before we apply it, and that is a major challenge. Scenario evaluation is a significant problem in the generation process today, but there are ways to overcome it.

Royal Dutch Shell and the Beginning of Scenario Generation

Scenario planning originated as a military tool, but the idea to apply it in a corporate setting began with Royal Dutch Shell after the repeated blunders of a very expensive computer-driven forecasting system called the Unified Planning Machinery (UPM). Its quantitative, model-based methodology was great at suggesting a vision for "business as usual," but by its deterministic, middle-of-the-road forecasting, it tended to suppress discussion of different perspectives. And after it led the company in the wrong direction for the last time in the early 1970s, Shell's head of economics and planning for the exploration and production division, Jimmy Davidson, finally dumped the thing and turned to company veteran Ted Newland for an alternative.

The problem was that neither Davidson nor Shell had much of an idea of what the alternative could be. They simply named it Long-Term Studies. Newland, a senior planner known for his unemotional, incisive views of global politics, was brought to the London headquarters, stuck in a cramped cubicle on the 18th floor, and told to "think about the future."

Unfazed, Newland began by coming up with a "Year 2000" study report, and he brought on additional colleagues to help dream up long-term outlooks in the form of alternative futures. But Shell executives were uninterested in complex, stuffy analysis. What he needed, Newland realized, was a good story to capture their interest. So, he turned to Pierre Wack, then the head of planning for Shell France—more importantly a former magazine editor with a penchant for Eastern philosophy and mysticism. Wack had a knack for weaving a good yarn, and the pair focused on telling plausible, easily understandable narratives about events that might unfold.

One of their first projects looked at tensions in the Middle East. Most oil executives at the time were under the impression that the geopolitical strife there would ultimately abate, allowing Western-dominated stability—and thereby cheap oil prices—to triumph. But Newland and Wack examined more closely the pressures on the ruling governments of Iran and Saudi Arabia and came up with a different scenario. What if tensions failed to abate? What if they worsened? If global events conspired in such a way, the oil market might swap from one driven by consumers to one where the power lay in the hands of oil-producing nations. And if it did, an energy crisis could emerge. One of their scenarios, which they presented between 1972 and 1973, was simple: the oil price could shoot up from its current $2 per barrel to what was then the inconceivable price of $10.

It was not the numerical estimate of this scenario that was important. That was, in fact, of the least concern to Wack and Newland. What their scenario intended to do was invite Shell's top dogs to devote some attention to some of the most deeply held assumptions about the industry in which they were operating.

The Shell executives, curmudgeonly and reluctant, eventually began to listen to Newland and Wack and put in place a few hedges: some commonplace insurance policies that had been forgotten in the pursuit of their business-as-usual outlook during the fifties and sixties. And when prices hit $13 per barrel in 1975, and then soared again in 1979 to $37 off the back of the Iranian revolution, Shell found themselves in an enviable position.

Newland and Wack suddenly had the ears of everyone in the company.

Shell's approach to scenario generation was unique at the time, but its success meant corporations across almost every industry copied it. One US government report estimated that up to 85% of scenario studies were at one time derived from or based almost entirely on the process that Wack and Newland began.[66] And in 2011, a Bain survey revealed that 65% of companies expected to deploy some form of scenario planning that year.[67]

But what Shell and everyone who followed their approach are currently missing is a way to formalize the method of scenario generation and scale it up. And that is what this book is all about.

Shell scenarios work excellently as one-offs for Shell—filled as they are with "Shell speak"—but they are difficult to transfer. They are very dependent on the quality of a few minds sitting around a table and discussing the future. Also, developing scenarios is currently a tediously long and prohibitively expensive

---

[66] The study is reported in Wilkinson, A. & Kupers, R. "Living in the Futures," *Harvard Business Review* (May 3, 2013). Accessible at: https://hbr.org/2013/05/living-in-the-futures.

[67] Rigby, D. & Bilodeau, B. "Management Tools & Trends 2011," *Bain & Company* (May 11, 2011). Accessible at: https://www.bain.com/insights/Management-tools-trends-2011.

endeavour for many companies. Before any modelling can even begin, analysts must understand complex assumptions about things like population growth, technology evolution, and international politics.

You need to be able to press a button and get a scenario, and you also need to know how good those scenarios are.

This seems impossible. You never know whether a scenario is good or bad until you have run it or applied it to a problem. And that currently takes considerable resources. Besides, having to bring people around a table is too time intensive; you can never generate a comprehensive range of up-to-date scenarios by the time radical uncertainty strikes or new knowledge needs integrating into the model. Lastly, it could never be consistent across companies.

Another issue is that inconsistencies too often arise depending on who is entrusted with creating the scenario, and there is no algorithm available for eliminating bias. Inconsistency is a huge issue if you are a marketplace trying to price risk. Take climate change for example. Everyone, especially governments and corporations, is a stakeholder in its progression. In December 2015, the folks on the Financial Stability Board of the G20 established the Task Force on Climate-Related Financial Disclosure (TCFD) to find a way for governments, businesses, banks, and other entities to measure their financial risk with respect to climate change. Sensibly, after several years, everyone agreed that measuring risks would require the generation of credible forward-looking scenarios that would encompass future downside and upside risk. But that is about as far as they got. In fact, they quickly realized they had absolutely no idea how to do it.[68]

Presently, the way that the TCFD and others such as the US

---

[68] Even as recently as 2018, there was still no agreement as to how these scenarios should be generated. "Task Force on Climate-related Financial Disclosures," TCFD Conference, New York (May 1, 2018).

Federal Reserve generate scenarios to test portfolios is completely unsubstantiated by any mathematical theory. When a scenario is imagined, no one has any idea where it sits on the spectrum of possible scenarios, and they have absolutely no idea how good or bad it is. They are, simply put, taking a shot in the dark.

There is a name for this type of scenario generation (which is the norm today): BOGSAT[69]—a Bunch of Guys/Girls Sitting Around a Table dreaming about the future.

The TCFD started on the right track. Risk thinking begins with the realization that the essence of any forward-looking risk assessment relies on the ability to generate scenarios of the future. But not just any scenarios. We require scenarios that have particular properties to be able to price risk consistently across financial markets and within sectors in a market. In particular, they need to form a spanning set of scenarios so that we know that extremes are captured. Because it is the extremes that are the key to understanding radical uncertainty.

How Do We Codify Scenario Generation?

Imagine if we could automate scenario generation: span the range of possible future events, find some "black swans," understand the potential for "white elephants" (good futures), and account for a full range of market sentiment. That is the holy grail. We will approach this, but first we must address an important problem.

So far, attempts at automated scenario generation and risk modelling have been misled by the general misperception that financial markets are "complete" as opposed to "incomplete." In a complete market, transaction costs are negligible, and all participants have perfect and instantaneous knowledge of all market prices, their own utility, and their own cost functions. In addition to this, a complete market requires a knowledge of all possible

---

[69] Ascribed to Professor Roger Cooke.

HOW DO WE CREATE SCENARIOS?

future states of the world and a way to hedge against them. In short, a complete market is one where perfect hedges exist.

We can illustrate this with a simplified example. Suppose we are betting on the outcome of a coin toss. For this to be a complete market, it has to be free to place the bet, and the dealer always has to be willing to take the bet. The coin can only land on either heads or tails. In other words, there are only two states of the world at the outcome, and we can identify both of them. If we were to make a bet on the outcome, that would be called a "state claim"—we are making a claim on one future state of the world. Let us say we bet a dollar on heads. The payoff is $1 if heads is the outcome, and –$1 if tails is the outcome. Now, the simple hedge against loss would be to place another bet simultaneously on tails in addition to our one on heads. That way, no matter what state of the world we end up in, heads or tails, we both win and lose and therefore neither gain nor lose money overall. Our two bets would always cancel each other out, and we would always walk away no poorer or richer than we began. We have eliminated all risk, but note that there is no upside either!

On such a grand scale as the global economy, things are more complex—not that such complexity has ever stopped economists from attempting to model it as a complete market. As humans, we are hardwired to think that there is an answer to every puzzle, and so economists make massive assumptions about the way markets and market participants behave to square away their math. After all, the advantages would be immense: to know all possible future states of the world and be able to bet and hedge against them would render market participants invulnerable to loss. If markets are complete, you can arrange your portfolio so that, whichever state of the world comes up, your payoff is known and protected. It would be a dull world, though, with no gains either. Taking some risk in the face of uncertainty can have an upside!

But radical uncertainty significantly undermines any hope

of modelling markets as complete. There are just too many unknowns—too many sudden, unpredictable disruptions—to identify a concrete, objective answer that captures and mitigates against all possible future states of the world.

There can be no perfect hedge because markets are incomplete. That is the risk thinker's first and most fundamental admission.

It is also their greatest strength. By acknowledging that there cannot be a single, perfect answer to the uncertainty in the world, we abandon the fruitless search for it and instead learn to navigate with a set of imperfect but nonetheless useful tools.

If we think back to the structured elicitation of expert judgment that we performed earlier, we acknowledge this as imperfect. We ask for the judgment of as many of the best experts that we can, knowing that perhaps we have missed that one lone wolf who might have provided the perfect piece of forward-looking data. But that is life. Our best option is not to pretend our data is perfect but to optimize this process and learn how to strategize with the knowledge that it is flawed. We must seek a characterization of the future that is weaker than the one available in a complete market model, but which is also possible to achieve. And we always know that whatever strategy we may adopt, we will have to review it periodically to update scenarios on the future and to potentially change direction.

A useful set of scenarios will span the whole range of possible future states and contain the best and worst that we may reasonably expect in a given time frame, including what appears at first glance to be extreme or unlikely.

In this chapter, we show how to systematize the generation of scenarios to enable them to be generated automatically, without any prior assumptions about the underlying probability distributions. The only inputs required are the future macro events, natural, financial, or otherwise, that trigger the request for forward-looking scenario analysis.

Our methodology has one other important feature in that we can show that in a significant number of cases it guarantees the generation of spanning sets of scenarios relative to the uncertainty captured by the distribution graphs for each risk factor.[70] That is, the worst and best scenarios are guaranteed to be in the generated set for some common types of problems. More importantly, it minimizes the bias introduced when humans design scenarios.

To our knowledge, at the time of writing this book and certainly at the time the ideas in this chapter were first discussed publicly, there were no other known methods we are aware of for generating multifactor scenarios algorithmically. The advantages of algorithms are clear—they enable consistency, something needed for the general use of stress testing in financial markets and elsewhere. Furthermore, the mathematics allows one to know in advance the qualities of the scenarios that will be generated—for example, under what conditions they span the range of future possibilities.

The Benefit of Using Algorithms

A key benefit of the algorithms we will describe is that the same methodology applies to a very wide variety of disparate problems and organizations while allowing for their unique, different physical and organizational details. In this way, we guarantee that the risks of all parties may be measured in the same way, thereby creating the possibility for an apples-to-apples comparison—something essential for investors.

Moreover, many radical uncertainty problems are a mixture of disparate disciplines. For example, say we wanted to stress test financial institutions prior to the US elections to see how well

---

[70] It is "spanning" under the assumption that our estimate of uncertainty for each individual risk factor captures the extremes. For a more detailed explanation, including the mathematical proofs, please see the appendix.

they could handle the possible financial outcomes of the elections. Or if we wanted to stress test the financial stability of a country in the early days of Covid-19 based on the length of lockdown that might ensue. In both these cases, there are multiple disciplines involved—political, financial, epidemiological, etc. So, any scenario would have to include multiple risk factors drawn from disciplines that infrequently communicate with each other. I will address this issue as well.

The algorithm I have developed follows the logic we have outlined above. To describe it in the least technical way possible, let us review an example. A more technical description with some mathematical results is in the appendix to this book. This simplified presentation, however, does capture the essence of the method.

We will use the uncertainty of Covid-prevention regimes to show how it might work.

We are back in the early part of 2020. Covid-19 has been declared a pandemic by the World Health Organization. It is ravaging Northern Italy and has just begun to appear in Canada with a handful of known cases. The way it is spread, through aerosol transmission, has been verified. To prevent the virus spreading, it is also determined that proper masks, handwashing, and social distancing, if properly applied, reduce the spread in the population by more than 95%.

Compliance then becomes critical to the effectiveness of preventive measures. Key risk factors are:

- compliance with mask-wearing
- compliance with social distancing
- compliance with regular handwashing

The government orders the population to voluntarily follow mask wearing with proper masks, handwashing, and social distancing of at least 2 meters in any encounter. The risk is that the population will not comply with these measures, and spreading will occur.

Epidemiological models show us just how quickly spreading can occur, depending on how well people comply with the combination of these measures.

So, the first task is to obtain estimates for how many people will comply with each of these measures and then develop scenarios on the combinations of compliance. To do this, we go out to the population at large to estimate how well the population compliance would be. This could be done through structured expert judgment, a fancy way of saying polling done scientifically, which we discussed in chapter 2. The result is a distribution of values for each risk factor shown in figure 9 below. These distributions below come from an actual study of the uncertainty of the risk factors in a poll done on 300,000 Canadians at the end of March and beginning of April 2020.

Figure 9
Social Distancing Uncertainty Distribution
We go out to the population at large to estimate how many people will comply.

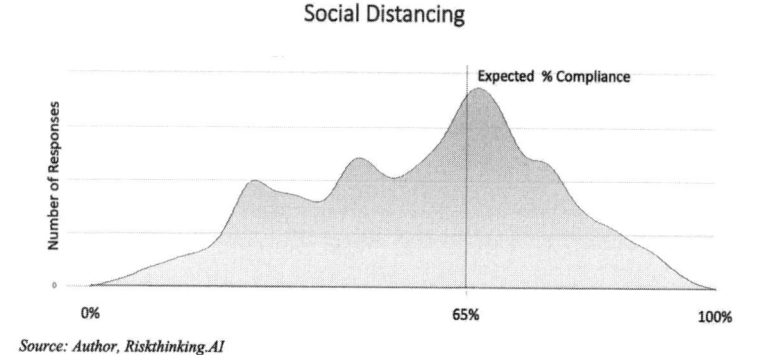

Social Distancing

Source: Author, Riskthinking.AI

The original expectation was that 65% of the population would comply with social distancing, but the results showed that the percentage compliance was much lower, with a few people not complying at all and most people complying less than expected. But what is clear from the social distancing frequency distribution is that the percentage compliance could vary wildly.

Figure 10
Mask Wearing Uncertainty Distribution
The original expectation was that 60% of the Canadian population would comply, but the results showed that the percentage compliance would most likely be lower.

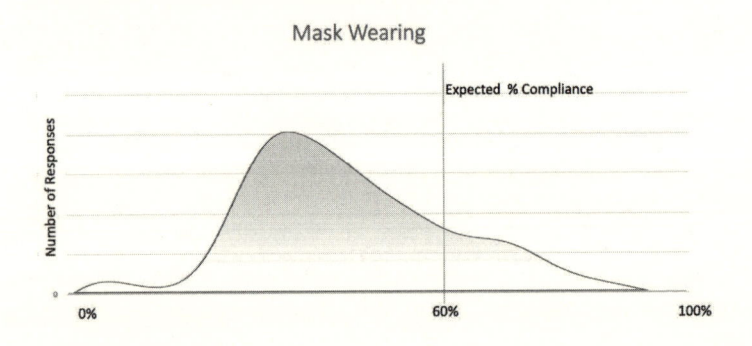

Source: Author, Riskthinking.AI

For mask wearing (figure 10), the original expectation was that 60% of the Canadian population would comply, but the results showed that the percentage compliance would be much lower, with many people not complying at all and most people complying less than expected. But, once again, the range of people complying varied a lot.

For handwashing (figure 11), the original expectation was that 60% of the population would comply, but the results showed that the percentage compliance would be much greater, with some people not complying at all and most people complying more than expected. There was still much uncertainty, but the distribution shows a skew toward larger compliance than expected.

Figure 11
Hand Washing Uncertainty Distribution
There was still much uncertainty, but the distribution shows a skew toward larger compliance than expected.

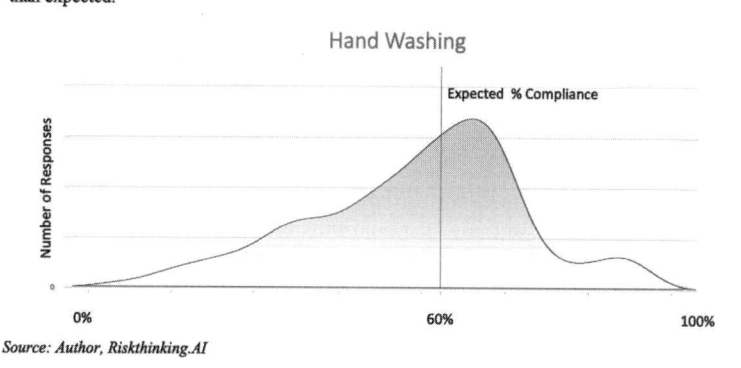

Hand Washing

Expected % Compliance

0%   60%   100%

Source: Author, Riskthinking.AI

It is all very well to know the uncertainty in each risk factor individually. But what if a radically uncertain event was dependent on a combination of risk factors. Some people will wear masks religiously and socially distance, but they may be negligent in handwashing on occasion. Others may wash their hands religiously after every encounter but sometimes be lax regarding social distancing. Yet others might keep living with all three compliance orders as much as possible.

As you can see, there are many possibilities for these different risk-factor combinations. In fact, there is an infinite number of possibilities.

But, what if the numbers that scientists expected for compliance were wrong? Given the radical uncertainty surrounding Covid-19, they almost certainly would be. How could we generate scenarios that could capture the extreme, but not completely unlikely, combinations of these three factors?

This is where the distributions reflecting the future uncertainty in these risk factors come in. The area to the right of the expected percentage compliance figure on the graph is the likelihood of getting more compliance, and the area to the left of the consensus view of compliance gives us the likelihood of less compliance. Notice I use the word "likelihood" and not "probability." This is a mathematical nuance since, in a radically uncertain situation, probabilities do not strictly exist.

The range of values we have seen with the results of strategic expert judgment that produced these individual uncertainty distributions is also available. Whereas it is feasible to extract the single-factor future uncertainty distributions from experts, getting distributions on combinations of these factors would be almost impossible.

A significant insight that allows us to find distributions of combinations of factors from the individual uncertainty distributions comes from the scenario tree, which we first saw in chapter 1.

To reflect the different possibilities, we draw a scenario tree that allows for the extreme uncertainty that we are faced with in capturing the range of values we could expect. To start, let us assume that the compliance with handwashing and social distancing and mask wearing are independent of one another.[71] Then, a scenario tree that captures the extreme possibilities can be drawn and is shown in figure 12 below.

---

[71] It is possible to treat a case where there is dependence among these factors. For example, if someone complied with washing their hands, they would be more likely to social distance.

HOW DO WE CREATE SCENARIOS?

Figure 12
A Scenario Tree for Covid-19
To reflect the different possibilities, we drew a scenario tree that allowed for the extreme uncertainty that we faced in capturing the range of values we could expect.

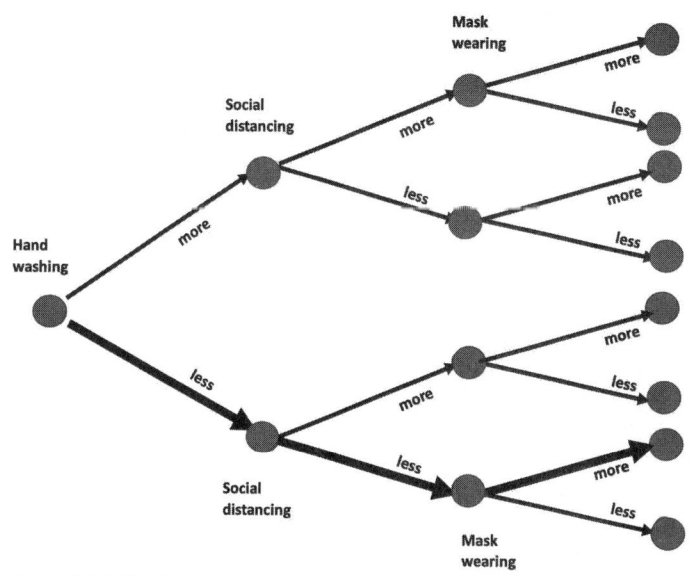

Source: Author, Riskthinking.AI

The scenario tree may be expressed as we would in any language statement of the possibilities. Handwashing might be greater than the consensus view or less. Just as social distancing may be complied with more or less than experts expect. The same is true for mask wearing, which could be complied with more or less than expected. The tree takes into account all the possible combinations of these factors. A particular multifactor scenario is given by the path highlighted in bold. The "plain English" translation of this path is:

> Handwashing in the future is less than experts expect, so is social distancing, but mask wearing is much better than we expect.

Every path in the tree is a similar story about a possible combination of factors that could occur. There are 8 different paths, each one of which is a multifactor scenario. If there were 4 factors, the number of paths would be $2^4 = 16$ paths (multi-factor scenarios), and if there were 5 factors there would be $2^5 = 32$ paths (multifactor scenarios), and so on.

We now know the form of the multifactor scenarios. So far, however, the tree is a bit lifeless. We do not know how likely each of these scenarios is, and we also do not have a good idea of the possible values of the "higher than expected" and "lower than expected" branches—in other words, we know neither the uncertainty around each factor nor the possible impact that such uncertainty could have.

That is where our uncertainty distributions come in handy. The innovation of our method is to marry the data gleaned in uncertainty distributions with the causal scenario tree. These distributions give us estimates of four critical values that we need to develop scenarios that combine all factors material to the issue, namely, the possible range of upside and downside movements in the factors and their likelihood of occurrence. From the single-factor distributions, we extract the tail values and the weights that the ensemble of experts attributes to the upside and downside values, and we use this to evaluate our scenario tree.

Although this is a simplified explanation of the actual detailed process that Riskthinking.AI, which produces forward-looking climate scenarios, uses to generate scenarios algorithmically, it captures the essence of the process.

Here is where it gets interesting: not only can we generate multifactor scenarios automatically this way, but we can say that the best and worst scenarios will be among them even before we have seen the situation in which they will be applied.[72] When

---

[72] This is shown for a technical reader in the appendix.

you think about it, this is an amazing result. It does not hold in all possible situations we will encounter, but it does for a vast majority of them.

We now have everything we need to stress test the future. I will give some examples later in the book of how this may be applied in practice, but let us first see if this could be applied to artificial intelligence to "teach AI" how to risk think.

CHAPTER 7

CAN WE TEACH AI TO RISK THINK?

One thing is clear. AI will be playing an ever-growing role in our lives, from driving us around to writing our emails, translating our speech and beating us at complex games—even performing operations on us in hospitals. Of course, much of this is already happening, but we have only seen the tip of the iceberg. AI will revolutionize our lives and the way we live.

For some, this is scary—but no scarier than it was for some when the first automobiles appeared *en masse* at the beginning of the twentieth century. People always struggle to accept change. But just like you knew the world was changing when cars first arrived, or personal computers were first discussed, or the internet was born, we see the future often because its embryo is here already. Ubiquitous AI is coming, so we had better get used to it. It will change our lives radically in ways we cannot predict.

One of the glaring shortcomings of AI so far (although things are changing fast) is its inability to reason and assess risk as fully as humans can. Humans are natural risk thinkers, generalizing from small amounts of data, trading off upside with downside and regret[73] as we navigate through life.

---

[73] Dembo, R. and Freeman, A. *Seeing Tomorrow: Rewriting the Rules of Risk* (New York: Wiley, 1998), chap. 4.

Every complex decision we make is our way of dealing with some future uncertain event, balancing risk and return, even if it is not explicit. This chapter shows how we might provide AI with the ability to manage risk as we do. There is no doubt that we must make AI smarter before it starts running our world.

Humans are wired from childhood to use probabilistic reasoning to deal with uncertainty and to reason in situations that are not exactly like anything we have seen before.[74] This is often evident in practice.

A significant shortcoming (as of early 2021) of artificial intelligence is the inability to make decisions that take into account the risk of future events. As Jeff Dean, current lead of Google AI, commented:

> Today in machine learning, we tend to train models to solve particular problems, or perhaps we do small-scale multi-task learning of a few related tasks, or transfer-learning from one related task to a few other related tasks. We do this separately for many different problems. Those systems can do impressive things, like translate English to Japanese, or categorize what is in an image for tens of thousands of different categories of objects, but they can't do anything outside their narrow domain in which they have been trained. I contend that this is not the right approach for building truly flexible systems. Ultimately, we need to be building machine learning systems that simultaneously solve thousands or millions of different problems in the same system, and that can leverage their expertise at solving these other

---

[74] Xu, F. & Garcia, V. "Intuitive Statistics by 8-Month-Old Infants," *Proc. Natl Acad. Sci. USA*, 105:13 (2008), 5012–5015.

problems in order to flexibly learn how to solve new problems on their own.

Source: Google

An example from Uber demonstrates this inadequacy.

Uber in Arizona: What Happens When Autonomous Vehicles Cannot Risk Think

The current shortcomings in AI technology's ability to assess and think about risk was demonstrated tragically in March 2018 when one of Uber's new autonomous vehicles, a fleet of which the company had been trialling in Arizona, struck and killed 49-year-old Elaine Herzberg in Tempe—the first pedestrian death associated with self-driving technology.[75]

Uber's vehicles use light detection and ranging (Lidar), a way to measure distances by lighting up the target with a laser and measuring the reflection with a sensor. As the name implies, it is very similar to radar, but with light, and the AI uses differences in laser return times and their wavelengths to create digital three-dimensional representations of the view in front of the vehicle.

The Uber vehicle, a Volvo SUV, was travelling at 40 miles per hour late on a Sunday night on a wide suburban road. The drive was an unremarkable one until it "saw" an unrecognized object on the side of the road a few seconds up ahead at current speed and decided to ignore it.

---

[75] Wakabayashi, D. "Self-Driving Uber Car Kills Pedestrian in Arizona, Where Robots Roam," *New York Times* (March 19, 2018). Accessible at: https://www.nytimes.com/2018/03/19/technology/uber-driverless-fatality.html.

Six seconds later, it ploughed into Herzberg, who was running with her bike to cross the road.

An experienced human driver might have reasoned (in milliseconds) that there is a scenario in which the object on the side of the road might be a living being that was about to cross.[76] The driver would have "hedged" their risk by slowing down to reduce the chances of a collision until they had gathered additional information.

By the time the Uber vehicle recognized the object as a woman with a bike, however, it was too late. It had not reduced its speed, and at that point, if the woman decided to run across the road, there was going to be a collision—and it was almost surely going to be fatal. Perhaps the autonomous vehicle had never encountered a situation like this before. Still, if we are to have autonomous vehicles on the road, they need to be able to manage risks like these—they need to be able to strategize and make decisions even when presented with incomplete information.

The next accident will also be a case that was never in the AI training set because there is an infinite number of possibilities in such situations.

Uber's autonomous vehicle was not the first to cause an accident. Tesla Motors disclosed a fatality involving a self-driving car in 2016 when the sensors of a Model S driving on autopilot failed to pick up an 18-wheel truck and trailer crossing the highway. The car drove full speed under the truck's trailer, killing the driver.[77] What happened to Tesla and Uber could happen to any autonomous vehicle company because AI has still not been imbued with risk thinking.

---

[76] In fact, there was a backup driver behind the wheel at the time, though it is unknown why they failed to act.

[77] Yadron, D. & Tynan, D. "Tesla Driver Dies in First Fatal Crash While Using Autopilot Mode," *The Guardian* (July 1, 2016). Accessible at: https://www.theguardian.com/technology/2016/jun/30/tesla-autopilot-death-self-driving-car-elon-musk.

For some, these are the early warning signs that ought to prompt heavier regulation—perhaps the adoption of the precautionary principle. John M. Simpson, for example, a privacy and technology project director with Consumer Watchdog, said the Uber collision demonstrated the dangers of the nascent technology. His advocacy group called for a national moratorium on autonomous car testing as a result of the collision, and Simpson said, "Robot cars cannot accurately predict human behaviour, and the real problem comes in the interaction between humans and the robot vehicles."[78]

Others disagree. The governor of Arizona, Doug Ducey, has so far been an ardent proponent of using his state as a testing ground for corporations that want to experiment with autonomous cars. With his state having one of the highest rates of poverty in the United States, Ducey keenly courted the large technology company in the hopes their presence would boost the local economy. "Arizona welcomes Uber self-driving cars with open arms and wide-open roads," he said. "While California puts the brakes on innovation and change with more bureaucracy and more regulation, Arizona is paving the way for new technology and new businesses."[79] Did he know the bet he was taking when he opened up his state?

The consequence of the Uber collision was tragic: an innocent woman lost her life, and the company had to suspend testing in Tempe, Pittsburgh, San Francisco, and Toronto. Regardless

---

[78] Levin, S. & Wong, J.C. "Self-Driving Uber Kills Arizona Woman in First Fatal Crash Involving Pedestrian," *The Guardian* (March 19, 2018). Accessible at: https://www.theguardian.com/technology/2018/mar/19/uber-self-driving-car-kills-woman-arizona-tempe.

[79] Wong, J.C. "Uber Packs Up Failed Self-Driving Car Trial in California and Moves to Arizona," *The Guardian* (December 22, 2016). Accessible at: https://www.theguardian.com/technology/2016/dec/22/uber-self-driving-car-san-francisco-arizona.

of the likelihood of someone crossing the street, an AI able to risk think would have hedged its bets and decelerated to a speed that would have given it enough time to stop if such an event happened.

Instead, Uber's autonomous car took no action, a deterministic decision in the face of radical uncertainty. We know that regardless of the event, if it is uncertain, the optimal solution for the vehicle would have been to hedge (i.e., slow down). But deep learning (a commonly used algorithm in AI) seeks deterministic answers and, we believe, is not as yet designed to output a hedging strategy. Yet this is exactly what we do well as humans. And that is what the good driver would have done. Good drivers are always anticipating the possibility of unexpected moves by others. Moreover, a good, experienced driver knows that the next possible accident is one that they have not seen before.

Rethinking AI in Autonomous Vehicles

We can take the Uber example above to consider how a future AI might handle such a situation differently. It was nighttime, and the car was travelling in autonomous mode at 40 miles per hour down a city street. The car's sensors were operating as designed and even managed to sense the cyclist on the sidewalk a few lanes over.

At that instant, what was the AI "thinking"? I presume that, in all of its training, it had not encountered a cyclist walking/running across its path where there was no crosswalk. Now, if that were an experienced human driver, even if they had never seen such an event before, had they noticed a cyclist on their left on the sidewalk, they would have done the following analysis. As an example, they would have found three possible scenarios worth considering:

a) The cyclist would stop walking.
b) The cyclist would start walking slowly across the first lane separating them.
c) The cyclist would dart across the road.

In such situations, where there is great uncertainty and the driver had never seen scenarios (b) and (c) before, she would have calculated that if scenario (c) were to occur, for example, there was a chance that she would hit the cyclist and, at the speed she was travelling, could cause grave harm or even death. So, what to do? Brake to a stop? Brake a little, to slow down immediately? Do nothing? Experienced drivers would have hedged by slowing down.

The Uber AI decided to do nothing, and we know what resulted.[80] Braking to a complete stop just in case the cyclist crossed the road would have been too radical and perhaps dangerous. The appropriate action was slowing down to a speed that would hedge the possibility of great harm and also give the driver the time to see if more drastic action was needed. It is the action we take when we see unusual things while driving that could cause great harm but are very rare. This is how we hedge against the black swans. And we do this because the consequences are so extreme that discretion becomes the better part of valor.

How could we train AI to make decisions that involve reasoning and not only rote learning?

The answer is to turn our AIs into good risk thinkers, like our experienced driver. To do so requires enabling AI with risk thinking. Put simply, risk thinking would deal with radical

---

[80] There might have been other factors at play, but since we do not know what they were, if any, we use this to illustrate a point and not to point a finger at Uber or any other autonomous vehicle manufacturer. Unfortunately, or fortunately, they are held to a higher bar than the current drivers on the road. It is my opinion that autonomous vehicles will ultimately lead to safer roads but having them "know" how to risk think could add value.

uncertainty by coming up with a set of scenarios and a resulting hedge. In a deterministic or stationary stochastic situation, the nature of a solution would be a single strategy. The key problem with AI is that it is a predictor rather than a hedger, regardless of the stochastic or deterministic nature of the type of future it faces.

The implications of this for Uber are the following. The AI would have to generate forward-looking scenarios at every decision point (i.e., in real time for autonomous vehicles) and then analyze the scenarios to come up with a hedge. This requires each scenario to be assigned a value and possibly a likelihood and a hedge to be developed with this information, much like our driver did for the three scenarios above.

A major issue with this is that, typically, scenarios are derived by a collection of experts sitting around a table and examining the facts to collectively come up with them (BOGSAT!). Clearly, we need to automate this process since there would not be enough time to generate the scenarios we need for our next decision. How do we set up machines to do this automatically and with great speed? Lives may depend on it.

First, to prepare the AI for a decision, we analyze all the material factors that we need to take into account to measure forward risk in the situation at hand. In this example, some of the material factors might be:

- people on the sidewalk
- an intersection ahead
- an object on the road
- an indeterminate object nearby

Note that in this list we have included "an indeterminate object." This is important since we always need to capture things that we have not encountered before. It would be rare that the next accident we might experience would occur identically to the last one.

For each of these factors, at the decision horizon (which in this case is in the next few fractions of a second), there is a distribution of possible values or outcomes that these factors might assume. For example, one of the people on the sidewalk may suddenly decide to cross the road. The outcomes for this factor might be:

- Someone turns slowly and faces the road and edges toward the edge of the sidewalk.
- Someone turns and leaves the curb moving slowly.
- Someone turns and leaves the curb rapidly, starting towards the middle of the road; and so on.

In another example, the car is getting close to a green traffic light. The factors to consider, for example, might be:

- Is it daytime, dusk, early morning, or nighttime?
- Is there traffic moving ahead of the car nearing the intersection?
- Is anything visible heading towards the intersection in the cross street?
- If so, how fast is it going?

These risk factors have more to do with what is in the minds and the actions of other players, and so they are inherently and radically uncertain. When we drive, experienced drivers are constantly looking for situations that are caused by others and not only by themselves.

In a third example, the car spots an "indeterminate object" close by and has no idea what actions this object might take. This case is important because we always have to deal with things that arise that the AI has not been trained for. Naturally, the AI should "keep a close eye" on this object until it is out of harm's way. For example, if it starts to move, it would change the possible actions that should be considered. As humans, we gather more information on the object over time and determine whether to ignore it or to take its movements into account in our decision-making process. For now, a single factor would suffice, i.e. it could move into the way of the car (and be dangerous).

Just as our headlights only light up a part of our view at night, so the scenarios we generate "light up" the possible futures.

In their book, *Prediction Machines*, Ajay Agrawal, Joshua Gans, and Avi Goldfarb[81] propose a very useful and instructive diagram, shown below in figure 13, describing how AI works as a learning machine.

Figure 13
Anatomy of a Decision
Diagram describing how artificial intelligence works as a learning machine.

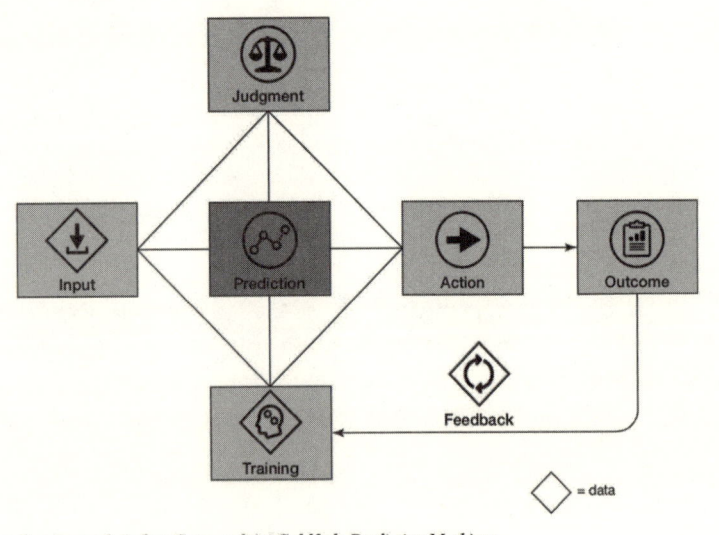

Source: *Ajay Agrawal, Joshua Gans, and Avi Goldfarb, Prediction Machines.*

---

[81] Agrawal, A., Gans, J. & Goldfarb, A. *Prediction Machines: The Simple Economics of Artificial Intelligence* (Harvard Business Review Press, 2018).

In many situations, the *prediction step* must produce a forecast for the next iteration that is made under great uncertainty. Such is the case for climate change for example. In others, such as FX prediction for very short horizons, the problem is far more deterministic. When there is less uncertainty, the above model is appropriate. However, when there is tremendous uncertainty at this step, risk management is called for.

We propose that the prediction step be replaced by a *scenario-generation step* and that the action step that follows, instead of being a definitive action, would be a hedging strategy (figure 14, below). The motivation for this is that at each step of this process, the AI has to deal with a radically uncertain future. The nature of the decision it should adopt should take the form of a hedge and not a deterministic action based on a forecast. One way of calculating a hedge would be to solve a *scenario-optimization problem*[82] that minimizes downside over the scenarios that would be calculated in lieu of the prediction step.

To compute possible risk scenarios, which are various combinations of these risk factors, we will need to have distributions of the possible values that they might assume at the chosen horizon. In an autonomous car, this horizon could be a fraction of a second away. With these distributions and a scenario tree that dictates the actions needed under each possible scenario, we can generate scenarios from which decisions could be made. Then, hedges could be set in place, depending on their likelihood of occurrence and the outcomes that result.

For example, imagine if one of the scenarios, independent of its likelihood, could result in a serious accident leading to the death of a person and therefore very serious consequences. Regardless of its likelihood, we should hedge some of this risk

---

[82] Dembo, R. S., Scenario Optimization, US Patent 5148365A, 1989; Dembo, R.S. "Scenario Optimization," *Annals of Operations Research*, 30 (1991), 63–80. Accessible at: https://doi.org/10.1007/BF02204809.

Figure 14
AI with Risk Thinking
We propose that the Prediction step be replaced by a Scenario Generation step and that the action step that follows, instead of being a definitive action, would be a hedging strategy.

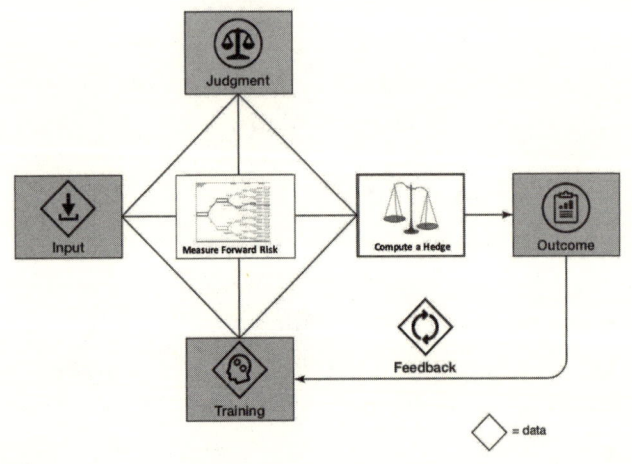

Source: Author

because its consequence would involve huge regret. The decision that needs to be taken is just how much to hedge. An example of a hedge would be to slow the car down to a speed for which the consequence of the accident, were it to occur, would be mitigated.

In the example of the Uber vehicle, the appropriate action might have been to hedge the scenario in which the uncertain object would suddenly dart across the road, possibly leading to a fatal accident at that speed. The hedge would have been calculated as an immediate speed reduction, which would have significantly reduced the possibilities of a fatal accident should the woman have crossed the road and been hit. It would also have bought time at the next decision point (a fraction of a second later) where if the woman was now detected as moving into the road, further action could have been taken (i.e., a further reduction in speed or braking to a stop since the likelihood of a serious accident would have increased).

CAN WE TEACH AI TO RISK THINK?

In many cases, the distributions of the possible values for each risk factor may be computed in real time. But we can imagine, in some cases, some precomputation might be required to be able to compute risk at any instant in real time.

An example could be the lady on the bike turns and starts moving into the road. For different values of how fast she moves, we have different scenarios on whether she will move into the way of the car. This sort of calculation could be done in advance and stored in a table for a lookup. Or, if sufficient parallel computing power were available, it could be calculated on the fly. Either way, the speed with which these results are calculated is key.

The AI that is making decisions for us while driving a car is serving us and not itself. By that, I mean that its risk tolerance, while driven by some high standard of quality, should, at the same time, be driven by the risk tolerance of the occupants for whom it is working. Also, the regret[83] (downside) it uses in its calculations should be influenced by the regret that its occupants, owners, or people affected by the crash will feel in the event of a miscalculation. For example, the mistake committed by the AI in the Uber case caused immense pain to the friends and family of the victim—and cost Herzberg her life. It caused huge embarrassment to Uber and a halting, in part, of its autonomous vehicle program.

The regret of killing someone while driving is so huge as to make us very risk averse if such a possibility exists, regardless of its probability. And rightly so.

We as humans, especially the experienced drivers among us, take this into account when we drive. Passing through a crowded, narrow street in a downtown area, we drive more cautiously than in an empty three-lane boulevard, all other things being equal.

---

[83] Dembo, R. and Freeman, A., *Seeing Tomorrow: Rewriting the Rules of Risk* (New York: Wiley, 1998), chapter 4; Dembo, R. and Stoffman, D. *Upside Downside: Simple Rules of Risk Management for the Smart Investor* (Toronto: Doubleday, 2006).

But we are all different. I often find myself in a taxi on my way to an airport, and the driver is holding the bottom of the steering wheel with one hand, less than a car length away from the car in front and all this at 120 kilometers per hour. I have learned to impose myself on this driver and tell him or her to slow down, keep a safe distance, and hold the wheel properly. Similarly, I expect passengers to impose some of their risk aversion on the AI driving them. In short, we should not be slaves to AI. The reverse is true. I can picture myself in a risk thinking-enabled car in the future that has some dials that let me choose my risk-aversion value. This would allow me to trade off time to the destination with safety, for example.

All of these types of risk considerations need to be accounted for since they will influence the decisions (hedges) that the AI has to produce as a consequence of enabling it with risk thinking.

Adding risk thinking to AI takes it a step forward. The computational process might be daunting if real time is required. But it still feasible, and surely more so as our computing power increases and becomes cheaper at the same time (thank you, Moore). The risk-thinking framework we have presented here provides AI with a way to reason and take account of future uncertainty. It could be a powerful addition to an AI that can account for each and everyone's individual risk aversion. And perhaps it will get us to Jeff Dean's dream of an AI that can "flexibly learn how to solve new problems on its own."

CHAPTER 8

MEASURING THE FINANCIAL RISK OF CLIMATE CHANGE

Climate change is probably the most complex and serious problem we have faced as a species. In the face of such total, irreversible change, getting our hands around the problem and creating a strategy for survival seems impossible. But let us think of it as risk thinkers. What is deterministic (known for sure), and what is stochastic (radically uncertain)?

We know for sure that the carbon dioxide concentration in the atmosphere is higher than it has been for more than 3 million years.[84] This is a scientific fact and can be measured precisely. It is deterministic. By burning fossil fuels, we have emitted nearly 2.5 trillion metric tons of CO_2 into the atmosphere since the Industrial Revolution began, raising concentrations by 67%.[85] This dirty energy is cooking our planet—another verifiable, deterministic fact. Its surface temperature has jumped more than

---

[84] Kunzig, R. "Climate Milestone: Earth's CO_2 Level Passes 400 ppm," *National Geographic News* (May 9, 2013). Accessible at: https://www.nationalgeographic.com/pages/article/130510-earth-co2-milestone-400-ppm.

[85] McKinsey & Company, *McKinsey on Climate Change, September 2020* (2020), 7. Accessible at: https://www.mckinsey.com/business-functions/sustainability/our-insights/mckinsey-on-climate-change.

1.8°F (1.0°C) over the past 115 years, and the average rate of change is accelerating.[86] As self-reinforcing feedback loops push us past more tipping points, like the thawing of permafrost, the Paris Agreement's target of keeping the global temperature below a 2-degree rise from preindustrial levels slips from our grasp. The world, it seems, will continue to burn.

The deterministic reality is that we are destroying the very planet we live on. And, we do not have a plan(et) B. You would think this would shake us up—prompt us to treat climate change with the same urgency we have for wars (or pandemics, for that matter).

But it has not. And worse, what we do not know is how exactly this additional carbon in the atmosphere and the rising average global temperature will play out. That is the stochastic part. Will England become a tropical paradise or be buried under a sheet of ice? Will we still be able to grow crops where we do now? Will our rain forests dry out? Will we get runaway climate change? Will mass migrations cause social havoc? Will we collaborate sufficiently among nations, in a completely unprecedented way, to avoid a climate catastrophe? All of this is radically uncertain.

There is no way to eliminate the stochastic elements even by ceasing carbon emissions. The CO_2 we have already emitted in the atmosphere will be with us for millennia, and the exact effect it will have is radically uncertain.

Yet another problem is "the deeply held belief that a firm's only duty is to maximize shareholder value." As a result, says Harvard professor Rebecca Henderson, firms

---

[86] Updated reports on this constantly changing figure are available via the National Oceanic and Atmospheric Administration's NCDC State of the Climate: Global Analysis. Also useful are Columbia University Reports. See Hansen, J. & Sato, M. "Global Warming Acceleration" (December 14, 2020).

... fish out the oceans, destabilize the climate, fight against anything that might raise labor costs—including public funding of education and health care, and (my personal favorite) attempt to rig the political process in their own favor. In the words of the cartoon [Tom Toro]: "Yes, the planet got destroyed, but for a beautiful moment in time we created a lot of value for shareholders."[87]

But this belief is slowly shifting. Across the world, regulators, governments, and investors have started to recognize the financial dangers of inaction and increasingly require that corporations disclose risks related to climate change. That goes for participants in every facet of the economy, including energy, infrastructure, agriculture, residential and commercial property, as well as human health and labour productivity.

On January 14, 2020, Larry Fink, the founder and CEO of the $6 trillion investment firm BlackRock, provided a stark reminder in a letter to the CEOs of the firms in his portfolio that "climate risk is investment risk":

Climate change has become a defining factor in companies' long-term prospects. Last September, when millions of people took to the streets to demand action on climate change, many of them emphasized the significant and lasting impact that it will have on economic growth and prosperity—a risk that markets to date have been slower to reflect. But awareness is rapidly changing, and

---

[87] Henderson, R. *Reimagining Capitalism in a World on Fire* (PublicAffairs: 2020), chapter 1.

I believe we are on the edge of a fundamental reshaping of finance.[88]

And he is not alone.[89] Regulators, such as the Market Risk Advisory Committee of the US Commodity Futures Trading Commission, have bluntly outlined the "complex risks" that climate change poses to the US financial system, including "disorderly price adjustments in various asset classes with possible spillovers into different parts of the financial system, as well as potential disruption of the proper functioning of financial markets." Even the very process of combating climate change and shifting to a zero-emissions economy poses risks to markets and market participants unable or unwilling to adapt. Their biggest

---

[88] Fink, L. "A Fundamental Reshaping of Finance," *BlackRock* (January 14, 2020). Accessible at: https://www.blackrock.com/uk/individual/larry-fink-ceo-letter.

[89] A recent survey by the Harvard Business Review of 70 senior executives at 43 global institutional investing firms, including the world's three biggest asset managers (BlackRock, Vanguard, and State Street) and giant asset owners such as the California Public Employees' Retirement System (CalPERS), the California State Teachers' Retirement System (CalSTRS), and the government pension funds of Japan, Sweden, and the Netherlands and discovered that Environment, Sustainability, and Governance (ESG) issues were almost universally top of mind for these executives. Eccles, R. & Klimenko S. "The Investor Revolution," *Harvard Business Review* (May 2019). Accessible at: https://hbr.org/2019/05/the-investor-revolution. As Simon Weaver, Co-Head of Climate Risk and Decarbonisation Strategy at KPMG UK, said: "Understanding the impacts on your business from climate change is no longer an 'added extra.' It's a core issue which we all, as corporate leaders, must respond to—not just from a wider purpose perspective, but crucially for the resilience of our own organizations." Published on Continuitycentral.com. Accessible at: https://www.continuitycentral.com/index.php/news/erm-news/5482-future-climate-risks-being-discussed-in-boardrooms-but-few-organizations-have-plans-in-place.

fear, they argue, is how little we know about the uncertainty of this climate-related financial impact. And they demand that financial regulators "move urgently and decisively to measure, understand, and address these risks."[90]

We are making headway in this area. The Task Force on Climate-Related Financial Disclosures (TCFD), established in December 2015 by the former Bank of England governor, Mark Carney, and former mayor of New York, Mike Bloomberg, is an organization that aims to develop a set of voluntary climate-related financial risk disclosures that companies can adopt to inform their investors and the public of the climate risks they face. In 2020, it reached 1,440 supporters throughout the private sector with a market capitalization of more than $12.6 trillion. Thanks to the TCFD, more businesses are being asked to measure and report on their financial risk of climate-related change. And it is for their benefit: we create value when we can translate climate science information into actionable insights for managing risk.[91]

Still, there are problems yet to be solved. To put it in Carney's words:

---

[90] "Managing Climate Risk in the US Financial System," Report of the Climate-Related Market Risk Subcommittee, Market Risk Advisory Committee of the US Commodity Futures Trading Commission (September 2020).

[91] In their survey of 247 firms that participated in the European Union's Emissions Trading Scheme, Cadez et al. found market pressures for reducing GHG emissions had a positive effect on GHG–related performance—not only in terms of reducing GHG emissions, but in reduction of GHG–related costs. They note "that this single relationship explains 27% of the total variance of GHG performance." Cadez, S., Czerny, A., Letmathe, P. "Stakeholder Pressures and Corporate Climate Change Mitigation Strategies," *Business Strategy and the Environment*, 28 (2019), 1–14. Accessible at: https://doi.org/10.1002/bse.2070.

> The financial industry must create conventions for how companies measure and disclose to investors their climate impact, along with a way of judging how badly failure to act will hurt an investment or portfolio, a standard way of measuring the payback from an investment in climate mitigation or adaptation and ways of redirecting capital toward lower climate damage.

Currently, we lack that. Yet that is the goal: a top-down, science-based, data-driven, scalable, and repeatable approach to creating standards and software for measuring and managing climate-related financial risk. Organizations should be able to take nonfinancial scenarios involving physical risks such as drought, flooding, and other manifestations of climate change and convert them into financial variables that affect their businesses. We believe stress testing portfolios in this way will ultimately lead to a massive reduction in environmental impact. And this chapter reveals the risk-thinking method for doing it.

Adopting the Risk-Thinking Lens

As we discussed in chapter 1, imagine that you are the Singaporean government and grappling with the problem of sea level rise and possible extreme weather that could effectively destroy Singapore later this century. You are not alone. The whole southern tip of Manhattan, including Wall Street, could be underwater if no mitigation were to happen. So, what do you do? You do what the Dutch have been doing for centuries. You plan to build a wall around the city-state to keep water out. But how high should that wall be? Where do you even get the data from for the year 2100, your planning horizon?

If you went to the International Panel for Climate Change (IPCC), a UN initiative, you would hear conflicting reports. You would be confronted with a load of *transition scenarios* (descriptions of how carbon concentration in the atmosphere will evolve over the next 80 years) and also a whole host of economic and social change hypotheses and the assumptions that go with them. There would be (radical) uncertainty in the science that predicts what the sea level rise around Singapore would be between now and 2100. To make it worse, in December 2019, scientists had one set of opinions, and just a month later, in January 2020, the predictions had changed, after scientific papers showed that Antarctica and Greenland's ice cover was melting 6 to 10 times faster than we thought.

It is no small task and a huge cost to build such a wall. Most predictions hovered around a one-meter rise in seas around Singapore as a "worst case." However, some scientists, with a proper scientific basis, were talking about possibilities of a six-meter rise. Clearly the cost difference in mitigating a six-meter rise in sea level and a one-meter rise is significant. So, to whom do you listen? Whose opinions should you choose? You cannot just wait and see; you need to do something now to mitigate the effects of an inundated Singapore or Wall Street underwater. The costs of not doing something are also huge.

It starts with what is deterministic here and what is stochastic. The fact that inundation will occur is almost certain (deterministic). Hurricane Sandy, on October 9, 2012, was likely a foretaste of things to come. It killed 232 people in the Caribbean and North America and inflicted more than $70 billion in damage. In Manhattan, it breached an 8-foot wall designed to protect the city from extreme storms.

The stochastic part is exactly how high a wall will protect Manhattan or Singapore in the future?

The cost of getting it wrong is hard to imagine. So, by now, we know that the form of any "solution" that is proposed to such a problem should be a hedge and not a plan based on a forecast. This is where risk thinking could help the average decision-making in government. If you heard a proposal based on deterministic reasoning you would immediately question it, even if you knew nothing about hydrology. It must be a hedge.

So, in this case, a hedge would be to build a wall that could be extended rather than a one-off wall that would have to be replaced when you found out in the future that you were wrong and bore the brunt of some huge disruption. An extendable wall is surely more costly than a one-off wall. Still, the upside that an extendable wall brings surely outweighs the downside costs of a wall that is too low.

As I write this chapter (February 2021), Texas is without power. A winter storm has brought the Texan economy to its knees and is resulting in massive costs to the state in both human suffering and its economy. This is another foretaste of things to come as climate change causes the polar vortex[92] to weaken. We know from science that the Northern Hemisphere will heat up more as the world average temperature rises due to a rising carbon dioxide concentration in the atmosphere, in turn due to our reliance on fossil fuels (essentially deterministic). It will affect the polar vortex but exactly how and when is radically uncertain (stochastic). Texas (and many other jurisdictions) will need to come up with a hedge to mitigate the potentially significant future costs of not having enough backup electricity. It is time they adopted a risk-thinking approach to looking at the problem and not a forecasting one.

---

[92] A polar vortex is a low-pressure area, a wide expanse of swirling cold air, located in polar regions. The polar vortex at the North Pole expands during winter, sending cold air southward. It happens somewhat regularly.

Measuring the Physical Risk to an Asset

The first thing to recognize is that the financial impact of climate change is a problem in radical uncertainty. This implies that much of the economic and typical scenario modelling does not fit. Correlations are practically useless in deriving future climate scenarios. The past is not of much use, and probabilities do not mean much at all. Historical data is sparse and of little use as well.

A recent McKinsey report looked at several case studies based on the Representative Concentration Pathway (RCP) 8.5 scenario.[93] By 2030, it suggested, up to 200 million outdoor workers in India would be at risk of lethal heat waves, reducing GDP by at least 2.5%. In Florida, rising sea levels, tidal flooding, and severe storms would sink property-tax revenue by 15–30% as millions of homes become threatened. A once-in-100-years hurricane in the Western Pacific would be more than four times more likely by 2040 and could shut down the semiconductor supply chain completely; unprepared downstream players might see revenue dip 35% in a single year if that happens.[94]

Will these scenarios happen exactly? Perhaps, perhaps not. We simply do not know precisely what the climate impact will be over the next generation—in which particular ways it will hit our industries, cities, and societies. So, we need an approach that can accommodate radical uncertainty.

This all starts with comprehensive, reliable data. This is data on the climate, on transition scenarios, machine-learning-derived uncertainty data, and sentiment data.

---

[93] RCPs are greenhouse gas concentration (not emissions) trajectories (possible climate futures) adopted by the Intergovernmental Panel on Climate Change (IPCC), which is the United Nations body for assessing the science related to climate change.
[94] McKinsey & Co. "McKinsey on Climate Change" (September 2020).

When computing climate-related financial risks, there are really two cases to consider. They are a transition regime that leads to investment risks, and the same transition regime that leads to physical risks. For a single firm, conditioning on the same transition scenario for each type of risk leads to consistency in the calculation of physical and investment risk.

Here, we will provide a top-level overview of both processes before examining a case study in detail.

The calculation of physical risk involves modelling the causal effects of climate change. Yet many climate drivers can affect the risk factors of climate change. Fortunately, climate science gives us the causation. It informs us of the climate modulators that affect each climate region and how the weather in each region is linked to other regions.

Based on this science, the IPCC has categorized the world's homogeneous climate regions—the regions in which a homogeneous set of climate drivers and risk factors are present.

Associated with each region are the climate macro factors that affect that region: world average factors such as world average temperature rise, world average sea level rise, and so on. Within each climate region are economic regions with associated economic macro factors, which are impacted by the climate-related risk factors. These climate factors combine to generate corresponding multifactor macroeconomic shocks, which cause portfolio shocks.

So, we have all the pieces of the puzzle to translate physical risk into financial risk. We just need a way of combining them to create potential scenarios for an organization (figure 15).

MEASURING THE FINANCIAL RISK OF CLIMATE CHANGE 143

Figure 15
Workflow, Physical Risk
Assessing the impact of a possible transition scenario on the physical assets (e.g., buildings) of a company, at some future horizon, requires an understanding of climate science.

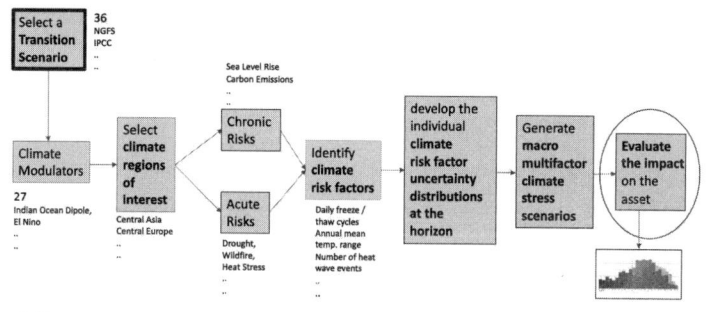

Source: Author

The 27 climate modulators affect all regions in the world. They are, for example, El Nino, the Indian Ocean Dipole, the North Atlantic Current, and so on. For the particular problem we are considering, we select the regions where the physical assets (and their supply chains) are located. From this, the nature of the physical asset and the climate modulators, we can ascertain which chronic risks and acute risks will be relevant, and we can then identify the climate risk factors.

The next step in this process uses structured expert judgment to develop the individual risk factor uncertainty distributions at the chosen horizon—this uses the same methodology that we explored in chapter 2.

From the distributions, we generate the multifactor climate scenarios using our risk-thinking algorithm for scenario generation, which chapter 6 detailed with the scenario tree. These scenarios combine multiple risk factors, and they are critical to measuring possible physical events that cause stress, such as heat, drought, and high winds that combine to result in events like forest fires.

Finally, it is often necessary to bring in the owner of the

physical asset to determine the impact that each of these multifactor scenarios might have on their asset. Without them, we would require a very detailed audit of every contract they have written, their supply chain, and the details of their physical assets that are not public.

By following this process, we have translated physical risk into financial impact.

How Does This Work for Investment Risk?

For investment risk, we follow a similar route. We start by identifying the key material macroeconomic factors that might affect a portfolio or group of portfolios (figure 16).

Figure 16
Workflow, Investment Risk
To assess for investment risk, the key challenge is ascertaining the effect of a climate transition scenario on the macroeconomic factors affecting the portfolio's value.

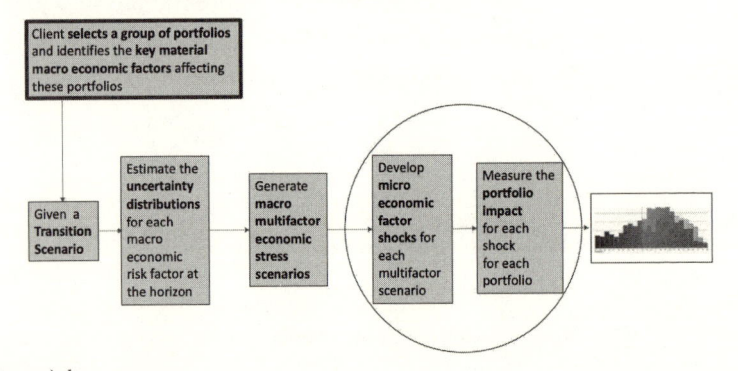

Client selects a group of portfolios and identifies the key material macro economic factors affecting these portfolios

Given a Transition Scenario → Estimate the uncertainty distributions for each macro economic risk factor at the horizon → Generate macro multifactor economic stress scenarios → Develop micro economic factor shocks for each multifactor scenario → Measure the portfolio impact for each shock for each portfolio

Source: Author

Given a transition regime describing a possible future, we estimate the future uncertainty for each macroeconomic risk factor, at a chosen horizon, individually. This takes the form of a distribution of values, reflecting the uncertainty of science and economics regarding the future values of this factor. We do this using machine learning algorithms or polling, in a structured expert judgment framework.

With this, we can now generate multifactor economic stress scenarios using a patented algorithm. We compute corresponding microeconomic shocks consistent with the macro factor shocks using standard financial engineering methods. This allows us to value the portfolio shocks. The end result is a distribution of gains and losses for the portfolios under the set of scenarios that were generated.

Just as the Federal Reserve Bank's Comprehensive Capital Analysis and Review (CCAR)[95] helped banks manage their business better, this will lead to a mitigation of climate risks, better capital reallocation, different liquidity policies, and so on. But a key to this is being able to generate the gains and losses consistently across all bank functions in all geographies under future climate stress.

The distribution of gains and losses is obtained by generating a set of climate financial stress scenarios, for some horizon, and then valuing their effect on each and every business unit (figure 17).

Figure 17
Distributions of Gains and Losses Under Stress
We obtain the distribution of gains and losses by generating a set of climate financial stress scenarios, for some horizon, and then valuing their effect on each and every business unit.

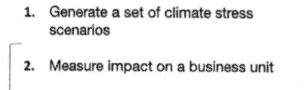

1. Generate a set of climate stress scenarios
2. Measure impact on a business unit
3. Aggregate like gains and losses
4. Form the distribution of gains and losses
5. Repeat for all business units

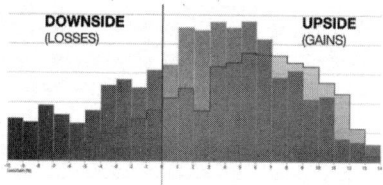

Source: Author, Riskthinking.AI

---

[95] https://www.federalreserve.gov/supervisionreg/ccar.htm.

For each single business unit, we form this distribution by aggregating the gains and losses due to different stress scenarios into ranges and then plotting the weighted sum to form each bar in the graph.

In this depiction, we show the gains as solid light grey and the losses as solid dark grey. The transparent distribution is obtained from the same stresses applied to some benchmark portfolio.

Now let us define the rating metric as CaR, the *climate-risk adjusted return*. CaR is computed by dividing the upside by the downside as a measure of the risk-adjusted upside. The upside is given by the area covered by the light grey bars and the downside is the area covered by the dark grey bars.

A CaR of less than one implies a likely financial impact on profitability under these stresses. A CaR of greater than one implies a likely benefit in the future from these stresses.

This gauge shown in figure 18 could represent the spectrum of possible gains or losses to climate stress: light grey for material positive impact, medium grey for nonmaterial impact, and dark grey for negative material impact.

Figure 18
CaR Profitability Impact
A grey-shaded or colour-coded gauge could represent the spectrum of possible material and nonmaterial impacts of climate stress.

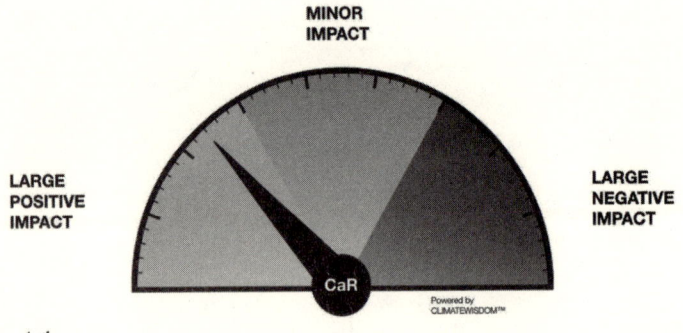

Source: Author

Now consider a bank that operates in two geographies, Canada and the United States. A simple dashboard could depict where climate impact is material and negative (figure 19) and similarly where it is material and positive. The degree of impact would be the CaR number.

The same rating idea could be applied to the asset-management side of the bank, thereby obtaining a consistent way of comparing climate risk across the entire corporate structure.

An Example of the Process in Action

Let us assume we are a Tier 1 Bank in Australia. We are interested in how climate change might affect our earnings. To do this, we must identify the most relevant climate modulators; we need to know what transition scenario we will consider; and we need to identify the climate risk factors.

Figure 19
Climate Impact on a Bank
A simple dashboard could depict where climate impact is material and negative, and the degree of impact would be the CaR number. Black is negatively affected by climate and light grey positively affected by climate. Medium grey levels are units essentially unaffected.

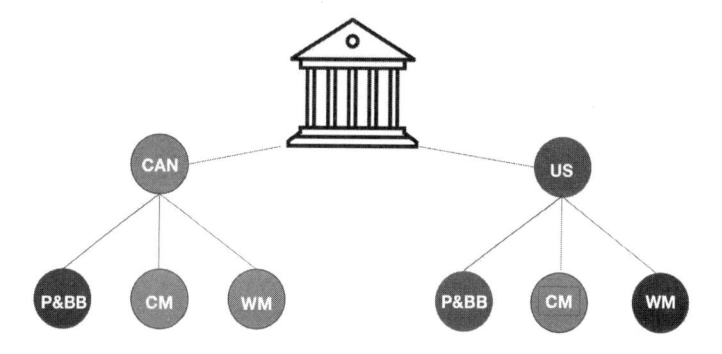

Source: Author, Riskthinking.AI

Figure 20
Climate Modulators
Scientists have collated many different climate modulators that can affect weather patterns.

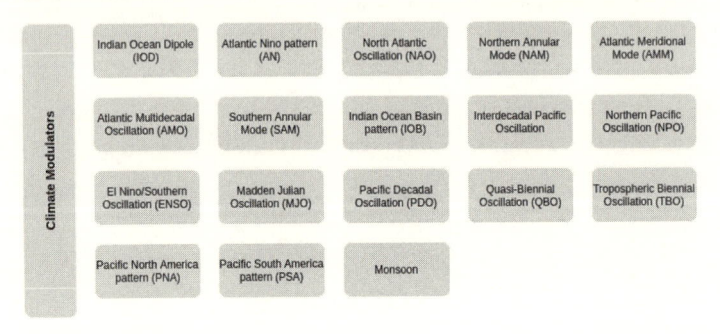

Climate Modulators				
Indian Ocean Dipole (IOD)	Atlantic Nino pattern (AN)	North Atlantic Oscillation (NAO)	Northern Annular Mode (NAM)	Atlantic Meridional Mode (AMM)
Atlantic Multidecadal Oscillation (AMO)	Southern Annular Mode (SAM)	Indian Ocean Basin pattern (IOB)	Interdecadal Pacific Oscillation	Northern Pacific Oscillation (NPO)
El Nino/Southern Oscillation (ENSO)	Madden Julian Oscillation (MJO)	Pacific Decadal Oscillation (PDO)	Quasi-Biennial Oscillation (QBO)	Tropospheric Biennial Oscillation (TBO)
Pacific North America pattern (PNA)	Pacific South America pattern (PSA)	Monsoon		

Source: Riskthinking.AI

For a bank in Australia, one climate modulator would be the Indian Ocean Dipole (figure 21).

The dipole is the difference in temperatures between the eastern and western areas of the Indian Ocean.

Figure 21
The Indian Ocean Dipole
As the world average temperature rises, the dipole may become more pronounced, affecting the climate both over eastern Africa and western Australia.

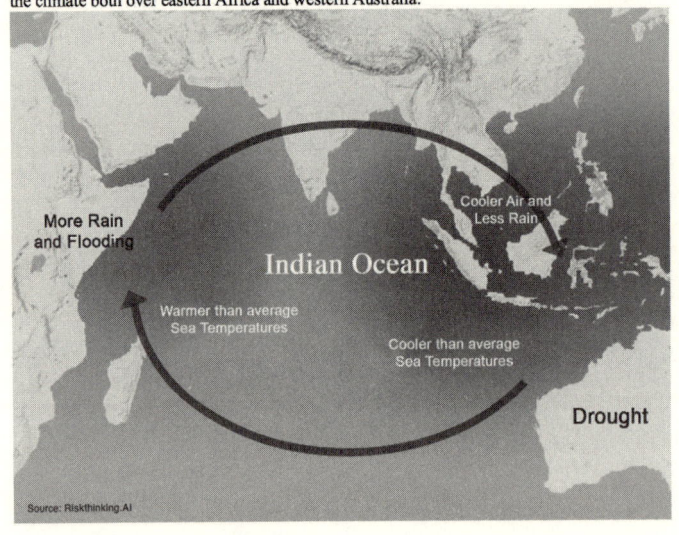

Source: Author

As the world average temperature rises, the dipole may become more pronounced. As the sea heats up in the east, more evaporation occurs, making the air above East Africa more prone to precipitation and extreme weather. In contrast, as the water cools in the ocean bordering Northern Australia, the precipitation over Australia drops, causing drought conditions coupled with high temperatures.

In the late spring and summer of 2019–2020, Australia experienced one of its most devastating bushfire seasons on record—the burning of more than 18 million hectares caused billions of dollars in economic damage.

Conditioned on a transition pathway for carbon (for example the high carbon emissions scenario SSP5-8.5[96]) climate science shows how carbon emissions will affect the concentration of greenhouse gases in the atmosphere, which will affect the world average temperature rise in the future, which may exaggerate the Indian Ocean Dipole. As the dipole grows, so might the precipitation in East Africa and drought in Australia. The risk factors are:

- the future transition pathway for carbon emissions
- the resulting greenhouse gas concentration in the atmosphere
- the world average temperature
- the Indian Ocean Dipole

This process may be represented by a causal graph, based on science (figure 22).

---

[96] https://www.carbonbrief.org/explainer-the-high-emissions-rcp8-5-global-warming-scenario.

Figure 22
Example of Causal Relationships in the Indian Ocean
How climate factors in the Indian Ocean could affect Australian interest rates and the Australian dollar.

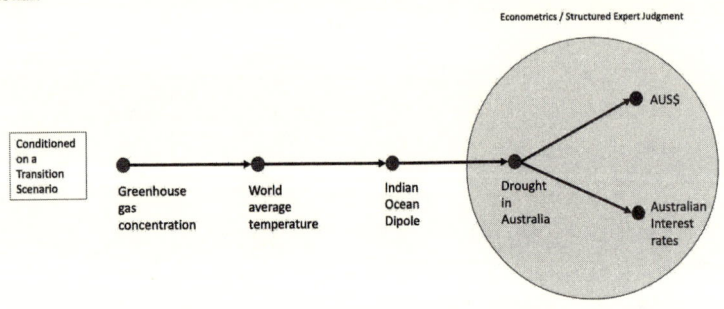

Source: Author

As we know from the previous chapter on scenario generation, we can use the causal graph to develop a multifactor scenario tree (figure 23). Each path is a scenario made up of three risk factors: carbon concentration, world average temperature, and Indian Ocean Dipole. The bold path is the following scenario:

> Carbon concentration in the atmosphere grows less than scientists believe, and the world average temperature rise is lower than scientists imagine, however, the Indian Ocean Dipole is larger than was anticipated.

Figure 23
Corresponding Scenario Tree
This shows the Scenario Tree corresponding to the Causal Graph shown in Figure 22.

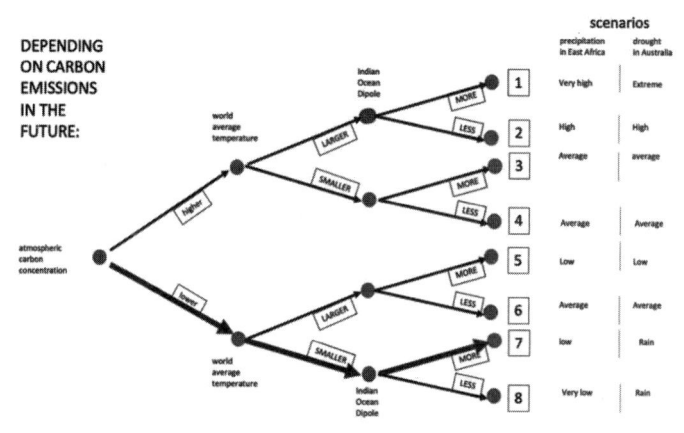

Source: Author, Riskthinking.AI

We use structured expert judgment and machine learning to obtain the uncertainty distributions for each risk factor—that is, frequency distributions of the different values that a population of trusted scientists might ascribe to a particular risk factor at some particular point in time (figure 24).

Figure 24
Expert Forward Sentiment
We generate the uncertainty distributions for each risk factor, using structured expert judgment and machine learning.

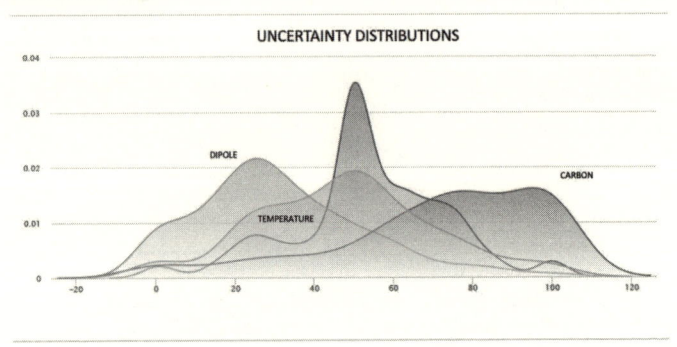

UNCERTAINTY DISTRIBUTIONS

[Chart showing uncertainty distributions for DIPOLE, TEMPERATURE, and CARBON across a range from -20 to 120, with y-axis from 0 to 0.04]

The key is eliciting the uncertainty at the nodes

Source: Author, Riskthinking.AI

This represents the possible range of values and their frequencies as seen by the latest science, which itself is uncertain.

By focusing on the extremes of these distributions and the weight of the distribution above and below the commonly accepted values, we can fill in all the numbers missing in the tree and generate quantitative values and likelihoods for these scenarios.[97]

But if we want to link climate scenarios to the financial effects on institutions or portfolios, there is a piece missing (figure 25).

---

[97] This is presented formally and mathematically in the appendix.

MEASURING THE FINANCIAL RISK OF CLIMATE CHANGE

Figure 25
How to Link Climate Causality to Financial Impact?
We have so far struggled to link climate scenarios to the financial effects on institutions or portfolios. Here we show the full process of linking a Transition Scenario to its ultimate effect on a portfolio.

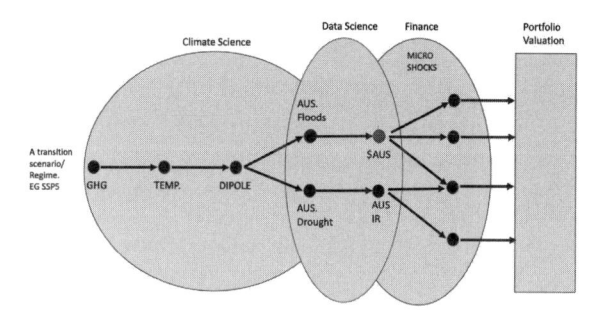

Source: Author, Copyright Riskthinking.AI

To link these climate-related variables to financial effects on institutions or portfolios, we must first understand the relationship between climate shocks, such as drought and temperature, and their corresponding macro-financial impacts such as the Australian dollar and Australian interest rates.

Where can we get such information? Again, this is where structured expert judgment plays a central role. As an example, we could ask Australian traders, economists, and policy-makers for their views on how a drought might affect macro-financial factors in Australia, such as Aussie GDP, the Aussie dollar, and interest rates. This will give us the uncertainty distributions we need.

We now use standard financial tools to generate shocks on micro-financial variables so we can evaluate their effects on the contents of investment portfolios. The translation of the macro-financial factors to micro shocks is a common, well-studied problem in finance, and therefore not an issue. Of course, this step could also be improved but is well accepted at present as a necessary evil that is used in every bank, daily.

We now have the full causal map between carbon emission regimes and their impact on specific portfolios. From this causal map, we can generate a scenario tree (graph) and uncertainty distributions on all the risk factors involved.

This is how we generate multifactor scenarios for the future that link climate and financial impacts in a consistent manner, something the TCFD has been seeking. And now we have all the ingredients to measure the impact of climate risk transition scenarios on investment portfolios.

Consider a large multinational fund manager. We apply the micro shocks to all the portfolios managed by the fund. Different subsets of micro shocks might apply to each portfolio. Valuation is done for every scenario on every portfolio. One set of micro stress shocks is valid for all portfolios.

This high level of consistency allows for the creation of benchmarks hitherto unavailable to clients.

An example is a client being able to see how each portfolio will compare to the average of their peers' exposure—a highly desirable piece of information that, in the past, has never been available.

To give you an idea of the scale that is possible, we at Riskthinking.AI are currently working with a firm with one-third of the world's managed portfolios under custody! A single analysis may be applied to all of these portfolios, which creates huge economies of scale and consistency. Consequently, this methodology together with investor activism could have a significant effect on reducing environmental impact.

CHAPTER 9

ANALYZING POLITICAL DECISIONS AROUND ENERGY AND CLIMATE

Having explored the mechanics of scenario generation in a complex issue such as the financial risks of climate change, we must now turn to strategizing and see how from a policy-oriented, decision-making level, we might chart a course by using the risk-thinking methodology to create regimes, assess our risks, and hedge our bets. We begin with an imagined example of how a risk-thinking consultant might approach a political decision involving considerable uncertainty, basing our summary of the nuclear energy problem in Germany in 2011.

Merkel's Nuclear Energy Dilemma

Japan's March 2011 earthquake and the resulting tsunami, while causing major supply line disruptions around the world, also caused a nuclear emergency. As the tsunami swept inland and disabled the region's power supply, three of the Fukushima Daiichi nuclear power plants were damaged and unable to cool their reactors. Within the first three days of the incident, these cores had melted entirely, and radioactivity was released into the surrounding area. Despite 100,000 people being evacuated from their homes as a precaution, there have been no fatalities directly attributable to the nuclear accident.

That, of course, did not prevent a worldwide panic and rapid reassessment of nuclear power. The Italian government—new to nuclear energy at the time—immediately imposed a one-year moratorium on its use and development and held a referendum on June 13 in which 94.05% of the participants voted against nuclear power.[98] Switzerland and Spain both banned the construction of new reactors, and a band of other countries that had always been opposed to nuclear energy, such as Luxembourg, Australia, and Denmark, reaffirmed their opposition. Others such as Taiwan pledged to reduce their reliance on nuclear energy, while Mexico shuttered construction of 10 reactors and instead looked to developing natural gas plants.[99] Countries such as Belgium and Switzerland planned phaseouts by 2030—leaving themselves enough time to find a suitable, green alternative and see out the end of their current reactors' life spans.[100]

No one's reaction was starker, however, than that of German Chancellor Angela Merkel. In the face of country-wide protests—including a human chain of 50,000 people that stretched 45 kilometers from Stuttgart to a nearby power plant in Neckarwestheim—she held an emergency meeting with five state

---

[98] Department for Internal and Territorial Affairs. "Referendum of 12 and 13 June 2011." Accessible at: https://web.archive.org/web/20120325171121/http://referendum.interno.it/referendum/refe110612/RFT0003.htm.

[99] Sokolski, H. "Nuclear Power Goes Rogue," *The Daily Beast* (November 28, 2011). Accessible at: https://web.archive.org/web/20121218012428/http://www.thedailybeast.com/newsweek/2011/11/27/post-fukushima-nuclear-power-changes-latitudes.html.

[100] Kanter, J. Switzerland Decides on Nuclear Phase-Out," *New York Times* (May 25, 2011). Accessible at: https://www.nytimes.com/2011/05/26/business/global/26nuclear.html.

premiers.[101] Their decision was momentous: 7 of Germany's 17 nuclear power stations would be shut down during a three-year minimum moratorium and a nuclear phaseout, previously scheduled for 2036, would be brought forward to 2022.

This decision was all the more surprising in light of Merkel's previous support for nuclear power and her decision just a year earlier to overturn a decade-old plan to close nuclear plants by 2022; 71% of the population believed it to be a political manoeuvre designed to gain her favour with the Green Party for the upcoming state elections.[102] In acting as she did, Merkel was likely hoping to minimize regret. She was rapidly losing political support, with her Christian Democrats (CDU) and their Free Democrat (FDP) allies suffering a string of disastrous election results. By abandoning nuclear, she hoped to take votes from the Greens and, failing that, perhaps pave the way for a coalition with them—the atomic issue was the only obstacle to that. Inaction, or a slower course of action, towards nuclear phaseout, would have risked her losing her power, a strong motivator.

Merkel's aim, she said, was to preserve Germany from the "helplessness" of Japan, which still suffered disaster despite being an industrialized and technologically advanced nation.

> As the first big industrialized nation, we can achieve such a transformation toward efficient and renewable energies, with all the opportunities that brings for exports, developing new technologies and jobs. We don't only want to renounce nuclear

---

[101] McVeigh, T. "Nuclear Safety Worries Spread to Europe," *The Guardian* (March 12, 2011). Accessible at: https://www.theguardian.com/environment/2011/mar/12/nuclear-safety-worries-spread-europe.

[102] "Wähler strafen Union für Atomkurs ab," *Spiegel Politik* (March 23, 2011). Accessible at: https://www.spiegel.de/politik/deutschland/umfrage-waehler-strafen-union-fuer-atomkurs-ab-a-752631.html.

energy [a renewable energy source] by 2022, we also want to reduce our CO_2 emissions by 40% and double our share of renewable energies, from about 17% today to then 35%.[103]

It was an ambitious plan, and no political party opposed her. But was it the right decision?

According to an article published in the *New York Times*, Merkel, a trained scientist with a PhD in physics, came to the decision after a long night of soul-searching—over a glass of red wine in their Berlin apartment with her husband, Joachim Saur, another physicist and university professor. The opportunity was to lead Germany into a new era of more efficient wind and solar energy production, while shutting down nuclear ensured the population's safety in the face of "risks ... too enormous to be controlled by humans."[104] As she said again later on, "The residual risk of nuclear energy can be accepted only if one is convinced that—as far as it is humanly possible to judge—it won't come to pass."[105] She was unconvinced. Safety and security were paramount, and so, in essence, Merkel adopted the precautionary principle: we are uncertain of our ability to limit the dangers of this technology; therefore, its use must cease.

But switching off nuclear power, which at the time accounted for about a quarter of Germany's energy supply, in a country heavily dependent on energy-intensive industry such as chemicals

---

[103] Baetz, J. "Germany Decides to Abandon Nuclear Power by 2022," *The Associated Press | Massive Live* (May 30, 2011). Accessible at: https://www.masslive.com/news/2011/05/germany_decides_to_abandon_nuc.html.

[104] Dempsey, J. "How Merkel Decided to End Nuclear Power," *New York Times* (August 13, 2011). Accessible at: https://www.nytimes.com/2011/08/13/world/europe/13iht-germany.html.

[105] Bittner, J. "The Tragedy of Germany's Energy Experiment," *New York Times* (January 8, 2020). Accessible at: https://www.nytimes.com/2020/01/08/opinion/nuclear-power-germany.html.

production, had significant repercussions. While there were not the predicted blackouts, there were increases in massive voltage fluctuations that damaged industrial facilities. The German government faced multiple (6 as of 2016) lawsuits from nuclear plant operators seeking damages of up to €19 billion for lost investments made in "good faith,"[106] while the cost to dismantle the existing plants was around €18 billion.[107]

Meanwhile, the transition to clean energy stumbled over one hurdle after another. Nuclear energy had saved 170 million tonnes of CO_2 from being dumped into the atmosphere as it was, essentially, carbon neutral. Absent it, and with renewables not currently developed enough to take the load, Germany had to resort to fossil fuels.

One NBER Working Paper found that "the social cost of this shift from nuclear to coal is approximately $12 billion per year. Over 70% of this cost comes from the increased mortality risk associated with exposure to the local air pollution emitted when burning fossil fuels."[108]

As of 2019, Germany still extracted lignite (or brown coal) from mines to produce power on a large scale. Germany was the world's biggest producer of this dirty energy—166.3 million tonnes in 2018—which emits some of the highest levels of CO_2 of all fossil fuels (about double that of coal). This is because lignite contains much more water, mercury, sulphur, and other impurities

---

[106] "German utilities eligible for "adequate" nuclear exit compensation," *Clean Energy Wire* (December 6, 2016). Accessible at: https://www.cleanenergywire.org/news/nuclear-exit-compensation-utilities-energy-spin-offs-enter-mdax/german-utilities-eligible-adequate-nuclear-exit-compensation.

[107] Zimmermann, N. "Nuclear reactor sites: Dismantle or fence off?," *Deutsche Welle* (April 26, 2016).

[108] Jarvis, S., Deschenes, O. & Jha, A. "The Private and External Costs of Germany's Nuclear Phase-Out," *NBR Working Papers*, 26598 (December 2019). Accessible at: https://www.nber.org/papers/w26598.

than traditional coal, meaning much more of it has to be mined, transported, and burned for the same energy output.[109] Also, gases such as mercury and sulphur are highly dangerous; a European lignite power station emits up to a half-tonne of toxic mercury per year, which ends up in the water supply and consequently in humans, causing kidney damage. Sulphur dioxide emissions, on the other hand, are responsible for acid rain. Although it has plans to shut down all coal power by 2040 to meet the Paris Climate Agreement, Germany as yet has the largest fleet of coal-fired plants in Europe.[110]

Why has green not filled the gap? The problem with wind energy, like other renewables, is that it is unreliable. "You cannot

---

[109] Wettengel, J. "Germany's dependence on imported fossil fuels" *Clean Energy Wire* (June 19, 2020). Accessible at: https://www.cleanenergywire.org/factsheets/germanys-dependence-imported-fossil-fuels. Lignite contains about 40–60% water, making it difficult to burn. Per mass unit, lignite has about half the energetic value compared with coal. A recent study of energy emissions in New Zealand found that the emissions intensity of synthetic diesel made from lignite using the Fischer-Tropsch process was about 5.8kg CO_2 eq per liter of diesel, including upstream and tailpipe emissions. This was compared with 3.1kg CO_2 eq of typical petroleum diesel—almost half the emissions intensity. Wright, J., *Lignite and Climate Change: The High Cost of Low Grade Coal*. Report of the Parliamentary Commissioner for the Environment (November 2010). Accessible at https://www.pce.parliament.nz/media/pdfs/PCE-Lignite.pdf. According to one report, Jänschwalde, the largest lignite plant in Germany, is responsible for 470 premature deaths per year and up to €1,290 million in health costs. Health and Environment Alliance, "Lignite Coal: Health Effects and Recommendations from the Health Sector," *Heal Briefing* (December 2018). Accessible at: https://www.env-health.org/wp-content/uploads/2018/12/HEAL-Lignite-Briefing-en_web.pdf.
[110] "Germany ditches fossil fuels and looks to renewable energy," *Power Technology* (February 25, 2019). Accessible at: https://www.power-technology.com/comment/germany-ditches-fossil-fuels-and-looks-to-renewable-energy/.

always have the wind when you need the energy," says Professor Wolfgang Pfaffenberger of the Bremen Energy Institute, "so we have to build up an enormous overcapacity, which adds to our cost."[111] And then there is the price: at the time of Merkel's decision, an average kilowatt from wind cost 10 cents, whereas the average cost of the energy on the market was about a third of this. Since then, renewable energy has become much cheaper, and with the right advancements, it will be made stable enough to replace traditional means of power generation; in the meantime, Germany has suffered thanks to Merkel's rather hasty decision.[112]

One wonders if the German chancellor had thought through these scenarios properly and applied a risk-thinking mentality. For example, if Merkel had decided to keep the nuclear plants on their longer phaseout plan, she could have planned out a scenario in which a meltdown did occur, assessed its likelihood, and decided whether or not the risk was worth taking.

For a start, nuclear power kills far fewer people than other energy sources even with disasters included, according to a 2002 review by the International Energy Agency (IAE).[113] In fact, on their list, it caused the lowest number of fatalities of all types of energy generation.

On the other hand, fine particles from coal plants kill approximately 13,200 people each year in the United States, according

---

[111] "Germany Split over Green Energy," *BBC News* (February 25, 2005). Accessible at: http://news.bbc.co.uk/1/hi/world/europe/4295389.stm.

[112] A recent report found that "Solar PV and onshore wind are now the cheapest sources of new-build generation for at least two-thirds of the global population." See "Scale-up of Solar and Wind Puts Existing Coal, Gas at Risk," *Bloomberg NEF* (April 28, 2020). Accessible at: https://about.bnef.com/blog/scale-up-of-solar-and-wind-puts-existing-coal-gas-at-risk/.

[113] "Environmental and Health Impacts of Electricity Generation. A Comparison of Environmental Impacts of Hydropower with Those of Other Generation Technologies," *The International Energy Agency* (2002). Accessible at: https://www.ieahydro.org/reports/ST3-020613b.pdf.

to the Clean Air Task Force's 2020 *Toll from Coal* report.[114] A recent study of 257 of 280 coal-fired power plants in the EU found that emissions in 2013 caused more than 22,900 deaths, tens of thousands of illnesses from heart disease to bronchitis, and up to €62.3 billion in health costs.[115] In Germany, 3,630 people died from coal-related illnesses in 2013. And mining itself is dangerous. In China in 2002 alone, 6,995 people died from accidents while working in coal mines.[116]

Even if there was a nuclear disaster, what would the downside be? The worst meltdown so far, Chernobyl in 1986, caused the deaths of 9,000 people from cancer. That is a tragedy, but it is also a far lower impact than coal, and there is a very low chance of it happening. From a risk-thinking perspective, it could be a risk worth considering in light of alternatives. The reason we do not take that risk is likely due to the fear factor associated with nuclear disasters. This is in large part due to the abundance of postapocalyptic narratives based around nuclear fallout. But it is also, according to James Hammitt of the Harvard Center for Risk Analysis in Boston, because large-scale nuclear releases are considered catastrophic events,

---

[114] Mckenna, P. "Fossil fuels are far deadlier than nuclear power," *New Scientist* (March 23, 2011). Accessible at: https://www.newscientist.com/article/mg20928053-600-fossil-fuels-are-far-deadlier-than-nuclear-power/.

[115] Crisp. J. "Germany Suffers More Coal-Linked Deaths Than Rest of EU," *EURACTIV* (July 5, 2016). Accessible at: https://www.euractiv.com/section/health-consumers/news/report-germany-suffers-more-coal-linked-deaths-than-rest-of-eu/.

[116] By 2017, that had fallen to 375, according to the official Xinhua News Agency. MacDonald, A. "As Global Mining Fatalities Fall, Brazil Deaths Show Problems Remain," *The Wall Street Journal* (January 28, 2019). Accessible at: https://www.wsj.com/articles/as-global-mining-fatalities-fall-brazil-deaths-show-problems-remain-11548709388.

whereas deaths by coal emissions are slow and invisible to us without careful observation.[117]

By shutting down nuclear in such a way, Merkel also eliminated the possibility for the emergence of future mitigation strategies that would have allowed for the use of nuclear even more safely and efficiently, which would have enabled her to capture a greater upside: a quicker transition to an emission-free energy sector and full energy independence from Germany's neighbours. For example, Germany's strict antinuclear stance has left it unable to capitalize on advances in the technology. Scientists in Russia, America, and China now believe that it is possible to reuse radioactive waste to run nuclear plants, eliminating the current problem of storing waste fuel elements. As one analyst succinctly put it: "By shutting down its entire nuclear sector in a rush, Germany loses more opportunities than dangers. It forfeits the capacity to connect to a technology that might prove the safest and most climate-friendly mankind has yet seen."[118]

Looking for a Different Solution

It is easy to criticize Merkel, but what would we have done differently? How could Merkel have applied risk thinking to her decision in a structured manner, especially under such a short time constraint with public opposition mounting against her inaction?

Let us imagine that we are brought in as consultants on the

---

[117] Mckenna, P. "Fossil fuels are far deadlier than nuclear power," *New Scientist* (March 23, 2011). Accessible at: https://www.newscientist.com/article/mg20928053-600-fossil-fuels-are-far-deadlier-than-nuclear-power/.

[118] Bittner, J. "The Tragedy of Germany's Energy Experiment," *New York Times* (January 8, 2020). Accessible at: https://www.nytimes.com/2020/01/08/opinion/nuclear-power-germany.html.

issue following the Fukushima disaster, just as the protests are reaching their peak. Merkel admits she is under pressure, but what *Time* magazine said about her was right—she is "no flair, no flourishes, no charisma, just a survivor's sharp sense of power and a scientist's devotion to data."[119] She wants a structured methodology to make her decision, and that is what has got us a seat at her table.

We discuss options:

- Regime 1: Do nothing. We sit tight, ignore the protests, and carry on the operation of the nuclear plants.
- Regime 2: Slow, managed phaseout of nuclear energy to allow renewables to take up the load gradually. We could time the implementation by the development of alternative sources of energy.
- Regime 3: Quick phaseout designed to rapidly transition to renewable energy and safely shut down nuclear operations.
- Regime 4: End it. We announce a moratorium on nuclear energy and establish an aggressive shutdown plan on a short time frame.

Each of these regimes (transition scenarios) has risks and benefits over the short and long term. How could we (and how quickly could we) replace the base power provided by the nuclear plants? What mix of energy sources should we plan to use to replace the nuclear at shutoff? What would it cost? Could it be sold to the Greens? Exposing these risks and benefits, for each regime, is the key to risk thinking.

Together, we rattle through them. They are easy enough to

---

[119] Gibbs, N. "Time Person of the Year: Angela Merkel," *Time* (2015). Accessible at: https://time.com/time-person-of-the-year-2015-angela-merkel-choice/.

identify—Merkel already has them in her head—so we run the regimes between us.

Immediately, we see that regime 1 is untenable—there is too much political opposition. So, we strike it off. This leaves us with regimes 2, 3, and 4.

What about regime 4, end it? "I like this," she says. "I know I can sell it to the Greens."

This is the one Merkel chose in real life. But it is a deterministic approach to a fundamentally stochastic (risky) problem. It tries to box the future into a single outcome, and so it is the wrong form for a solution.[120]

Look at pollution, for example. There would be a very high likelihood of increased pollution because the only alternative in the short term would be to turn to fossil-fuel energy. How would this be done? Who would we have to strike deals with to get this going? When could green energy step in? And what are the dangers of rapidly switching off nuclear power plants? All this is wildly uncertain—and "end it" does not have an answer.

And what about costs? Contracts would have to be terminated, alternatives hastily agreed upon, and compensation paid out. There would also be huge costs associated with shuttering nuclear plants and rapidly upscaling alternative energy provision. Already it is obvious the downsides are too big for this regime. As we role-play a risk analysis—generate a few mental scenarios—we quickly find that regime 4 incurs too many high-likelihood, high-impact risks across most of its factors. So, we scrap it.

That leaves us with regimes 2 and 3, a slow or fast phaseout of nuclear. These have potential—a greater risk-adjusted upside based on the scenarios we discuss. She asks for a detailed analysis to be delivered within a week.

As consultants on the project, we would then go away and

---

[120] Ron Dembo, "Risk Thinking," TED Global University 2010. Accessible at: https://youtu.be/KQ_I0KEeeFY.

generate a multifactor, forward-looking scenario tree for these risk factors and assess their uncertainty by soliciting expert judgment from the widest possible range of nuclear energy experts, renewables experts, political analysts, etc. This would allow us to get our hands on the many different futures that could occur if a particular regime is chosen.

By turning to the experts and quantifying the uncertainty in distributions, we would capture the highest potential upsides for each factor, such as the possibility for advances in nuclear waste disposal that might significantly reduce the safety concerns and costs of nuclear energy. We would also capture the worst-case downsides, such as the possibility of a meltdown at one of the reactors. Our spanning sets of scenarios, one for each regime, would allow us to capture the best- and worst-case outcomes for each regime, which would be extremely useful for Merkel when she came to make the decision.

The political risk is whether or not Merkel can explain the shutdown plan in a way that would satisfy protesters. The risk might be highest for regime 2, a slow phaseout, since it would be more difficult to convince voters that decisive action was being taken. It might be moderately low by comparison with regime 3, a fast phaseout, but it could also be the case that there is little difference in political risk between the two regimes—a survey of voters might reveal little distinction between a slow versus fast plan. This in itself would be a useful piece of information because we could discount the political response from our decision-making process.

Then we could look at the other factors. Consider pollution. Under regime 3, a fast phaseout, it will be harder to replace the lost nuclear energy, and so the dependency on dirty fossil fuels might be higher until green solutions become available. This pollution would bring with it higher health risks to the general population. In regime 2, there would be fewer risks of pollution because nuclear energy could be depended upon until renewable alternatives become available.

In addition to comparing the risk of downsides for each factor, we would also compare the possibility of upsides. For example, under regime 2, by keeping some nuclear plants running for longer, you expose yourself to a higher possibility to benefit from advances in nuclear technology and lower costs in the renewable alternatives. This could improve the safety risks over the long term.

To help us decide between the regimes, we would examine each of our worst-case scenarios and see if there were any potential hedges to reduce the downside risk. One hedge, for example, against the worst-case outcome of a nuclear meltdown would be to put much more money into safety precautions at the power plants, carry out more maintenance, and up the level of stress testing performed at the facilities. This costs a reasonable amount, but it mitigates the worst of the downside not to mention that shutting down precipitously would be very costly. Enacting this hedge might lower the short-term safety risks across both regimes. We could also hedge against some of the political risks by committing to a public education campaign that explains the strategy to the general population. Or we might try to hedge for an upside: commit to subsidies for green energy that would stimulate faster development.

Having performed this analysis and calculated the potential hedges, we would present these options to Merkel and assist with creating a strategy that minimized the worst downside risks and captured the upsides. This strategy should also allow room for adaptation. For example, the nuclear phaseout target date could be flexible, able to be advanced or delayed depending on the development of renewables. This would allow her to adjust her course to capitalize upon the best opportunities as they present themselves.

At the very least, this approach to the problem would expose the risks and highlight the benefits and would almost certainly have been less risky than the decision that was taken.

A day after we deliver the report, Merkel announces her plan in the Bundestag, and at the same time, she releases a detailed risk thinking-based report with a justification for the decision and an analysis of the risks and benefits showing why it is the best way forward given all the uncertainties involved. She also promises an annual review with the future scenarios updated each year and updated risk estimates. This allows her to manage expectations well in advance of any adverse events.

CHAPTER 10

MEASURING FINANCIAL RISKS DURING THE COVID-19 PANDEMIC

Most governments acted swiftly but often rashly to combat the Covid-19 outbreak of 2020. Between the "hammer" and the "dance" approach first outlined by engineer and columnist Tomás Pueyo[121] on March 19, it was the hammer that won out. Borders were closed, schools and businesses were shut, public events were banned, masks became mandatory, and shelter-at-home orders came into force.

One of the key decisions facing policy-makers concerned the restriction of movement, both domestically and internationally. Here, we observe a variety of approaches. The US did nothing and then suddenly implemented blanket travel bans early on. Then, in September, it began relaxing border controls too early despite rises in infections. Meanwhile, European countries lifted, and then quickly reimposed travel bans, leaving holidaymakers abroad and travellers stranded from their loved ones. Within

---

[121] Pueyo, T. "Coronavirus: The Hammer and the Dance," *Medium* (March 19, 2020). Accessible at: https://medium.com/@tomaspueyo/coronavirus-the-hammer-and-the-dance-be9337092b56.

their borders, governments also imposed severe restrictions on activity to varying effects. The Oxford University's Stringency Index showed Japan, Taiwan, and South Korea had some of the loosest policies, whereas Brazil, Russia, and the United States had some of the toughest. Surprisingly, it was the latter group that had among the worst outbreaks in the world.

One of the reasons for the ineffectiveness of the restrictions was how they were applied. Those countries that were able to take decisive, uniform, and coordinated action early were able to effectively apply the hammer and shut down the spread. Those who were initially lax and disorganized in their approach, such as the United States and Russia, and who left it to individual states to determine and impose lockdowns suffered the worst.

For example, in Brazil, President Bolsonaro ridiculed social distancing measures, suggesting that the coronavirus was akin to a common cold, and called for his economy to reopen its doors. With the individual states left to decide their own level of risk tolerance, some adopted strict measures such as "shelter-in-place" orders, limited public transport, and the closure of businesses. But others did not, and almost none of the states closed borders with each other. As a result, the pandemic spread massively in Brazil, with no observable hammer effect to quash the initial surge. By June 19, when many other countries were experiencing their lows, Brazil's new daily cases hit 54,771. In total, as of February 24, 2021, it had suffered 10.3 million cases (a figure that only the United States at 28.3 million and India at 11 million exceeded).[122]

But for many countries, the hammer tactic initially proved effective. The UK, Canada, France, Germany, Spain, and even Italy, where the early outbreak had been so virulent, were able to bring new cases down significantly toward the end of April.

The problem with the hammer phase was the effect it had on

---

[122] Figures are taken from the Wikipedia and *New York Times* mapping projects.

the economy. Up to 80% of countries faced workplace closures due to lockdown measures. In the week of April 25 alone, 3.8 million Americans made unemployment claims.[123] In Canada, a million people lost their jobs in March, then another two in April.[124] Over August 2020, the UK witnessed its first recession and largest quarterly decrease in employment since 2009, with 140,000 redundancies announced in June alone and 2.7 million people claiming universal credit in July (up 117% on March).[125]

Emerging and developing countries were even worse off. This was due to their heavy reliance on global trade, tourism, commodity exports, and external financing—all of which were effectively slashed. The World Bank predicted that in the developing world, 100 million people would suffer extreme poverty as a result of a projected 2.5% contraction of GDP in emerging markets.[126] In other words, these markets would simply cease to emerge, if only temporarily.[127]

To balance the damage to the economy with the need for lockdown measures, governments were supposed to implement

---

[123] Department of Labor. "Unemployment Insurance Weekly Claims," *DoL News Release* (April 30, 2020). Accessible at: https://www.dol.gov/sites/dolgov/files/OPA/newsreleases/ui-claims/20200774.pdf.

[124] Statistics Canada. "Labour Force Survey, April 2020" (May 8, 2020). Accessible at: https://www150.statcan.gc.ca/n1/en/daily-quotidien/200508/dq200508a-eng.pdf?st=LJUMeu9w.

[125] "Boris Johnson Warns 'Long, Long Way to Go' for UK economy," *BBC News* (August 11, 2020). Accessible at: https://www.bbc.co.uk/news/business-53733440.

[126] Politi, J. "Emerging economies forecast to shrink for first time in 60 years," *The Financial Times* (June 8, 2020). Accessible at: https://www.ft.com/content/47998ee3-b2d3-4066-a914-edbf60b797b5.

[127] Meanwhile, the world's richest grew in wealth by 27.5% to $10.2tn between April and July, according to Swiss bank UBS. "Extreme Poverty Set for First Rise Since 1998, World Bank warns," *BBC News* (October 7, 2020). Accessible at: https://www.bbc.co.uk/news/business-54448589.

the "dance" phase, where lighter but more intelligent measures prevented the pandemic from returning while keeping the countries afloat financially.

A great many failed at this stage. By September 18, for example, Spain's daily new case count had gone from a low of 181 on June 15 to a whopping 14,389. Meanwhile, Canada, which had a low of 172 in June, shot up to 2,176 in September. The UK hit 352 on July 6, then 22,961 by October 4 after a glitch in an IT system revealed an additional 16,000 cases had been overlooked.[128]

Much of this failure boiled down to decisions over the level of restriction to impose on citizens and persons already within borders, and to what extent they were followed. For example, Alaska applied a hammer early on when it had about 100 cases. It required at the end of March that all persons entering the state should self-quarantine, and it also banned internal travel for everyone except essential workers or critical personal needs. Cases dropped from 150 to less than 50 in a couple of weeks.

In May, the state fully reopened. It threatened quarantine violators with $25,000 fines and prison time, but the rule went unenforced, and it was flagrantly ignored. Cases grew rapidly, with infections arriving on seafood boats and emerging from food-processing plants before subsequently entering communities. Cases went from a low of four per 100,000 in May 2020 to more than 200 in July, a fiftyfold increase.[129] A similar thing happened in Hawaii, where only an estimated 40% of visitors followed quarantine rules.

---

[128] "Covid: 16,000 Coronavirus Cases Missed in Daily Figures After IT Error," *BBC News* (October 5, 2020). Accessible at: https://www.bbc.co.uk/news/uk-54412581.

[129] Pueyo, T. "To Beat the Coronavirus, Build a Better Fence," *New York Times* (September 14, 2020). Accessible at:
https://www.nytimes.com/interactive/2020/09/14/opinion/politics/coronavirus-close-borders-travel-quarantine.html.

The radical uncertainty in Covid clearly required a risk-thinking approach to government strategy. That is, it required an understanding of the risk factors that affect a strategy, data-driven, forward-looking scenarios, and decisions on how to mitigate the risks (hedge) under some extreme scenarios. It also required regular review of these scenarios driven by data and science as the world and developments unfolded, feeding into updates to the strategy.

The right approach required assessing and balancing our risk. On the one hand, we wanted to reduce the rate of infection, minimize its impact on vulnerable communities, and ensure the availability of medical resources for those who needed them. On the other hand, we wanted to enable people to participate in their communities and contribute to their economy by returning to work and spending on local goods and services. There is a cost/benefit trade-off, and it was up to local governments to decide on how and when to act. Like all important decisions under extreme uncertainty, the best we can do is to work with several scenarios that allow us to understand the risks and benefits we might experience. That means we need to apply risk thinking to manage our strategy as the future unfolds.

Mapping a Pandemic Strategy

How would this approach be applied, using Ontario, Canada as an example? We know that we could almost certainly reduce transmission of the disease by as much as 85% by properly wearing appropriate masks, washing hands after every encounter or interaction, and maintaining social distancing. So, it seems obvious that these actions should become the cornerstone of any strategy—the efficient solution to the deterministic part of the problem.

The stochastic part is the compliance with this strategy. It is well known that compliance with masks, etc., differs widely across locations.

We imagine this is when we, as risk thinkers, could be brought in for a consultation. Our role would be to help policy-makers determine how quickly lockdown measures could be released while keeping the daily case numbers below 100.

To begin with, we would set out our regimes—our possible courses of action. These are the different stages of lockdowns proposed within Ontario's *Framework for Reopening our Province*.

- Regime A: Full Lockdown. This is the default, current regime imposed following the failure of the reopening. All non-essential services are closed. People must stay home and self-isolate except for emergency and essential travel. Other measures include closing outdoor amenities in parks, recreational areas and public spaces, as well as bars and restaurants, and restricting social gatherings. Social distancing is in place, as is handwashing and respiratory hygiene (i.e., mask wearing).
- Regime B: Stage 1, very limited reopening. Select workplaces that can immediately meet or modify operations to meet public health guidance and occupational health and safety requirements will be allowed to open. Some outdoor parks will be allowed to open. Continued practice of physical distancing, handwashing, and respiratory hygiene is mandatory.
- Regime C: Stage 2, moderate reopening. This entails opening more workplaces, based on risk assessments, which includes some service industries and additional office and retail workplaces. Authorities will open even more outdoor spaces and allow larger public gatherings. Continued physical distancing, handwashing, and mask wearing are in place.

- Regime D: Stage 3, total reopening. All workplaces are open, all but the largest of gatherings are permitted (i.e., not outdoor concerts and sporting events), and physical distancing, handwashing, and respiratory hygiene are encouraged.

Having created our possible courses of action, we must determine the risk factors that will influence the outcome of our regimes and the impact on the variables we care about: the spread of the pandemic and the health of the economy. Currently, we are uncertain about the number of people who will adhere to the recommendations, the required percentage of people following the recommendations for them to be effective, and the impact of the different regimes on the economy.

As such, our risk factors (in this simplified example) will be the following: adherence to lockdown measures, including gathering size, mask usage, physical distancing, and personal hygiene; the number of new cases; and an economic benchmark—let us say one of the market indices like the TSX Composite. Thanks to our scenario tree, we can combine these risk factors, both financial and nonfinancial, to see how they might influence a scenario. This ability is particularly important to note because many current risk models encounter great difficulty in trying to weigh seemingly incommensurate risk factors against one another.

Having determined our risk factors, we would then set a horizon for which we wish to strategize. In the case of a fast-moving pandemic, this would likely be short—two to four weeks, at the most. It is this horizon that was sketched out as the length of each stage by the Ontario framework. However, as risk thinkers, we would not stick rigidly to this plan. In fact, we would anticipate that we would need to extend or shorten the stages as more information becomes available. However, for now, it is a useful time frame with which to work.

Then, for each of our risk factors we would go out and solicit expert judgment from as many experts as we can across a wide variety of disciplines. For example, for the lockdown-adherence factor, we might solicit judgment from social psychologists, behaviour analysts, law enforcement experts, and even community support officers who have been on the ground and witnessing current adherence in the locality (this is our *structured expert judgment*, as covered in chapter 2). Or we could use machine learning algorithms, natural language-processing models, and big data analytics to acquire localized data from the real world for the region under consideration—targeted surveys of the local population, for example. The surveys would then quantify the behavioral intent of the population in relation to the risk factors.

As always, it is essential to canvas a broad array of opinions even from non-traditional experts. This allows us to avoid the pitfalls of groupthink and other cognitive biases and will enable us to capture the most extreme opinions. As we know, it is in the extreme values that radical uncertainty lies, and so it is those that we must prioritize when we compile our uncertainty distributions for the variables. This will allow us to get our hands on the best- and worst-case possible outcomes from our factors. And when we string them together in our scenario tree, we will get a spanning set that includes the total range of possible multifactor scenarios. That is one of the key results of the risk-thinking process.

By codifying how we conceptualize possible futures, we can map the totality—as best as our experts can capture it—of potential scenarios that could develop from our chosen regime. This is particularly useful because it means we can meet the uncertainty ahead of us with as much foreknowledge as possible—even if we cannot predict exactly what will happen. We do this frequently to modify our scenarios and strategy as new data unfolds.[130]

Having created spanning sets of scenarios for each regime, we would look at the two regimes that are relevant to our current situation and compare the risks for each.

This will be regime A, the total lockdown, and regime B, the first stage of easing up the lockdown. We do not need to begin weighing up the risks of the later regimes yet because our

---

[130] In this example, we have kept things fairly simple. But it would be possible to support this process with advanced technology. For example, we could feed the survey responses relating to adherence into economic models such as those created by Limestone Analytics to understand the economic impact (positive or negative) of a scenario. We could also feed them into an epidemiological model like that created by Queen's University to understand the potential for spikes or drops in Covid-19 cases under that scenario. The epidemiological model outputs infection rates, hospitalization rates, and other health-related data points, while the economic model outputs employment rates, income, GDP, and other indices. We could also enhance our surveillance of the public: we may also opt in to using aiSight's physical distancing computer vision technology, which allows us to measure the average distance between individuals in public spaces in real time. Enabling this feature will benefit the project immensely as it will provide ground truth to the survey results, update the scenarios with new data, and provide real-time analytics on the effectiveness of mitigation measures undertaken to promote physical distancing within a community. Riskthinking.AI has integrated all of these data points, models, and pathways into a risk-scenario generator that leverages the compute capabilities of Kings Distributed Systems Distributed Compute Protocol (DCP). The DCP is Canada's first and only distributed supercomputer and provides vital infrastructure and resources to the project. In Project Looking Glass, Riskthinking.AI, Queen's University, Limestone Analytics, aiSight, and Kings Distributed Systems have come together to examine and display these tradeoffs via an evidence-based decision support tool to help prepare municipalities and governments for the eventualities they may face in a highly uncertain world. https://riskthinking.AI/wp-content/uploads/2020/06/LookingGlassProject-CaseStudy.pdf.

immediate decision is when we move to regime B and what the effects will be. Only after that will we compare the risk between regimes B and C, and then regimes C and D.

Regime A, total lockdown, is the current regime. We know from experience that it is most effective at shutting down the spread of the virus. Here, we would expect to see high chances of significant damage to the economy, as nearly all businesses are shut. Due to the heavy enforcement of this regime, we might anticipate a high adherence to measures intended to reduce the spread of the virus, and consequently the high likelihood for low case numbers. But keeping the population in this strict lockdown for longer than necessary, especially for a second time, could bring novel downside risk—what if a couple of behaviour analysts predict widespread unrest due to the lockdown measures? Perhaps, as happened in April 2020 with the protests in Michigan, in the United States, the idea of another full lockdown dragging on for four weeks is rejected by armed militia and thousands of people who gather in the street demanding "liberty" from government "tyranny," spreading the virus further and causing case numbers to rise. We would have to know that, if we stayed with regime 1 until the horizon, we would be betting on the population putting up with it.

We would then look at regime B, the first stage of lockdown easing: only the smallest gatherings are permitted, masks and social distancing are required, and a select few businesses can operate but at reduced capacity. Under this regime, the adherence risk factor would play a significant role—perhaps it is predicted that only 60% of gatherings are below the limit, and only 30% of people wear their masks. Under this regime, there could be a high likelihood of case numbers escalating to the same heights as before while the economy still takes a significant hit because most businesses are closed. There would, of course, be potential upside to this regime: perhaps people follow the recommendations much more readily than anticipated due to witnessing firsthand how devastating the pandemic can be if numbers are allowed to rise again. Another potential upside of this regime could be that herd immunity will quickly come into effect as people start mixing again, which is worth bearing in mind. There is also potential downside, perhaps the low likelihood of total disregard for the recommendations and an economy that nonetheless freezes up due to reduced confidence—no one pays attention to the social distancing, but they show a higher propensity to save rather than spend due to uncertainty over their financial futures. Or they break hygiene rules but still refuse to go to work.

Finding Ways to Hedge

When we have created and assessed our regimes and the possible scenarios that could emerge under them, the next step would be to consider possible hedges to mitigate the risks of downsides or capture the possibility for upsides.

For example, to mitigate against the risk of people not complying with social distancing, mask wearing, and personal hygiene, it would be possible to spend money on public outreach programs that educate the public about adhering to government guidelines. Some countries experienced significant resistance to requested behaviour changes, in part due to mistrust of the government, information overload, and inconsistent messaging. Effective communication techniques must combine a variety of channels such as physical signposting, multimedia advertising, and even the use of influencers. For example, in the United States, basketball star Steven Curry held a live Instagram with infectious-disease expert Anthony Fauci in which he asked questions about Covid, and Fauci provided valuable information to an audience of 50,000 people about how important it was for young people to practice social distancing even if they felt healthy.

Investing in activities like this might reduce the likelihood of high levels of disobedience and subsequently lower the risk of transitioning to regime B early.

Another possible hedge, explored by the University of Waterloo, was to develop a model that could determine who should get Covid-19 vaccines first. Planning for a vaccine, when it became available, was an essential step to increase the probability of a successful rollout. Jurisdictions were likely to face vaccination supply constraints in the short term. Designing complete, end-to-end systems to cover supply and delivery, as well as vaccination tracking and efficacy testing, would improve the possibility of capturing the greatest benefits from the discovery of a vaccine, and so put the province in a better position to bear the risk of transitioning to regime B. It might be possible, for example, to invest in training and temporarily expand the roles of lower-qualified medical practitioners to be able to administer vaccines in cases where complication levels are minimal.

There were also potential mitigation strategies for the financial risk factor. The furlough scheme implemented by the UK government was a classic example. It allowed businesses to send their employees home without firing them because the government paid 80% of their wages. This increased the likelihood that the population observed lockdown measures because they were not forced to work to survive, and it also kept the economy afloat because people still had an income to spend on things like rent and food. During the reopening, a short-term stimulus could be provided from local authorities to encourage people to stay at home rather than go into work. This stimulus could also target businesses with strong economic spillovers and weak infection risk, such as banking and pharmaceuticals.

Perhaps another mitigation strategy would be to implement more targeted restrictions on activities. For example, it would be possible to limit operations within businesses that generate strong infection risk externalities, but that generate weak economic ones—such as restaurants and cinemas.

It would also be possible to limit the fallout from a rise in infections. For example, if the decision is made to transition to regime B early, then we could mitigate the risk of more infections by provisioning for increased hospital and critical-care capacity, and we could increase maintenance of routine health services and boost testing. Ensuring that high levels of contact tracing and testing were implemented would help reduce the spread and allow for targeted isolation measures.

It would also be possible to boost investment in technological solutions such as anonymized mobility tracking or even cluster analysis to determine locations that are hotspots and shut them down. For example, handheld checkpoints, which have been the standard so far at airports and other public gathering spots, create bottlenecks, are inefficient, and prevent the return to "normal." So, companies like Patriot One Technologies are creating software modules that integrate with thermal cameras connected to existing monitoring systems. They use machine learning to identify temperature anomalies, and when one is detected, it alerts onsite security for further action. Artificial intelligence enables them to detect other variables as well, like mask-wearing compliance. This multi-sensor approach, when networked, could empower multi-location monitoring and enable the prediction and mitigation of outbreak hotspots.[131]

Another option might be to invest in high-quality airflow filters in particularly dangerous public spaces, such as buses or hospital waiting rooms. Or it would be possible to invest in emergency

---

[131] "Innovative Tech Stocks Using AI to Protect Americans as States Move Forward With Reopening Efforts," *PRNewswire* (July 9, 2020). Accessible at: https://www.prnewswire.co.uk/news-releases/innovative-tech-stocks-using-ai-to-protect-americans-as-states-move-forward-with-reopening-efforts-885088964.html.

food distribution networks, which would mitigate the risk of noncompliance if people can easily and safely get food delivered.

After performing this analysis and calculating the potential hedges, it would be time to form a strategy that minimized the worst of the downside risks and positioned us to capture as many of the upsides as possible. Certainly, it would be impossible to take every mitigation measure onboard, and so the policy-maker would be required to make decisions about which would have the greatest probability of limiting the worst and most likely downsides. And although it would be impossible to hedge against every downside, by performing this structured risk-thinking process, the decision maker would at least be more aware of the bets they were taking. In a situation as radically uncertain as the spread of a virus, getting our hands around the possible futures is a powerful ability to increase our resilience.

Addressing Future Pandemic Risks

As we move forward into a world where pandemics are increasingly likely, developing robustness across our economies, health systems, and societies is essential if we are to survive. Restrictions like physical distancing, closures of schools and businesses, and self-isolation have been key tools in flattening the Covid-19 curve—and they are relatively easy solutions to deterministic processes.

But these restrictions come with huge economic, social, and mental costs for individuals, communities, and businesses. Implementing them has serious ethical consequences. As jurisdictions the world over moved in early 2021 to reopen education facilities, businesses, and public spaces, they had to grapple with the outcomes of their decisions and answer some tough questions. What is an "acceptable cost" when weighed in human lives? Does enforcing mask wearing impinge on personal freedoms—or is it more akin to requiring seat belts by law? And what are the economic and ethical implications of allowing a country to limp on with half-enforced lockdowns, rather than enacting swift, hardcore measures such as in China, which is now open again and fully recovered?

Risk thinking will never be able to answer these ethical dilemmas. But it can provide the forward-looking data to enable decision makers to create informed strategies.

Currently, there are no comprehensive sources for data-driven insight that municipalities, provincial health authorities, or businesses can use to forecast safe levels of interaction. While these sources exist in isolation, integration is missing and is either in short supply or even contradictory, and this erodes the confidence of decision makers and leads to blunders with terrible costs on human life. Moreover, current measures have no built-in feedback on their effectiveness. Given all of the unknowns about the virus, it is tough to understand which measures will successfully keep the Covid-19 curve flattened and which may prove counterproductive. As the world works to navigate what is quickly becoming a new reality, valid, reliable, comprehensive, and dynamic data is sorely needed.

A risk-thinking process acts as a decision-support mechanism, providing policy-makers with the ability to predict what the impact of potential policies will be on public health and economic variables. And it can assist in discovering strategies that maximize positive impacts while minimising health risks. Ensuring we have such a process in place by the time the next pandemic hits could be the difference between a few weeks of hardship and a generation-defining crisis.

CHAPTER 11

STRATEGY: EMBEDDING RISK THINKING IN DECISION-MAKING

It is one thing to know and measure the risks that you might be taking (and we are always taking risks when operating in radical uncertainty), but it is another to understand the bets we are routinely making in an uncertain world. We have seen how risk may be calculated using scenarios, but equally important when heading into the future is knowing the odds for or against you. Good strategy rests on understanding the future trade-offs between risk and return. We are always betting at some level, but most often, the bets are implicit. Knowing the bets you are taking is just as important as knowing the risks.

Know Your Bets

I used to freedive a lot. That is underwater diving where you hold your breath until resurfacing rather than relying on a breathing apparatus such as scuba gear. One day, when I was on holiday in Mexico, I asked a local fisherman where a good place to dive would be. He was taking some regular divers out for the day, and he told me to come along. We headed out into the ocean, and he dropped me off about three kilometers from the shore, telling me he would be back in forty minutes. Then he scooted off with the rest of the divers to another location.

All of a sudden, I had the realisation that I had unwittingly taken some huge bets. First, I was on my own, so if there was an emergency, there would be no one to help me. Second, I had no idea where I was exactly and whether I was drifting with the current. Third, I had no real idea whether the fisherman really intended on coming back. And if he did, would he be able to find me?

A wave of panic swept over me. I suddenly found myself in a very dangerous situation. But, of course, there was little I could do about it. I played through some scenarios in my head—perhaps I should try to swim for shore (which way?—I could not see it); perhaps I could signal for assistance somehow; or maybe I should just try to remain where I was. Ultimately, I decided that the best thing to do was mitigate against the risk of drifting off and hope that he returned. So, I spent the forty minutes going up and down vertically to the same spot on the ocean floor, which was marked clearly by some distinctive coral. What I did not know at the time, and only later found out, was that sharks were known to inhabit the area.

Fortunately, the fisherman came back. But my actions had been stupid. I had put myself in a very dangerous situation without considering the huge bet I was taking—all for the relatively small upside of seeing a few fish.

That exact thing can happen in a business environment. Think of it: How many CEOs and their boards know the bets they are taking at any point in time? Go to any bank and ask the board: "What bets is this bank making?" Do you think they would know? Do you think they should know? I would think it is one of the most important pieces of information they should have. To go further, I think it should be one of the key points of discussion between management and the board. It should also be the key point in any decision we must take under uncertainty.

After all, in a radically uncertain world, we are always taking bets, by definition. There is no way we can account for all risks. There is no decision we can take that is entirely risk-free.

We see this lack of awareness commonly in big businesses; there is a hubris that blinds business leaders from seeing the landscape in which the company is actually operating. Malcolm Gladwell provides a metaphor for this point in his recent retelling of the biblical story of David and Goliath.[132] Commonly, we think of David's victory over Goliath as a moral story about overcoming insurmountable odds—that classic struggle of the underdog. But we have got it wrong, according to Gladwell.

To the millions who have read the story before, David is the underdog—a young, inexperienced warrior poorly equipped for battle who conquers a superior enemy thanks to divine intervention. But Gladwell thinks we have gotten it wrong all these years.

Let us consider David and his slingshot, for it is not quite the child's toy that many imagine. Slingers were a common form of artillery in ancient warfare and were frequently deployed to defeat heavy infantry. An experienced hand—which David's was—could rotate the stone in its pouch at between six and seven revolutions per second, release the stone forward at a speed of 35 meters per second, and strike a foe more than 150 meters away. The force, when you do the maths, is equivalent to that of a .45 calibre handgun, and slingers were so accurate they could smash birds out of the air.

Suddenly, David does not look like such an underdog—rather, when he releases that stone, he has every intention and expectation of a clean strike.

And then there is Goliath. The giant from Gath expects that the duel will be against another heavy infantryman in close quarters. He expects hand-to-hand combat in which his superior strength will grant him an easy victory. So, he is caught

---

[132] Gladwell, M. *David and Goliath* (Little, Brown and Company, 2013).

completely unawares when a long-range missile comes hurtling his way. Furthermore, Gladwell says, Goliath is weighed down by heavy armour, and he is described as slow and lumbering in the scripture—practically a sitting duck.

Then there is another detail. According to Gladwell, there are clues in the narrative that point to Goliath being blind or having difficulties seeing clearly. When David approaches, Goliath asks why he comes with "sticks," plural, but the shepherd carried only his staff. Also, Gladwell points to the fact that an attendant escorts Goliath onto the field of battle, as though he required aid. And finally, Gladwell argues that Goliath's massive form was the likely result of acromegaly—a benign tumour on the pituitary gland that causes an overproduction of human growth hormone, but which can also cause blurred vision as the gland compresses visual nerves. Goliath, says Gladwell, may actually have been much weaker than everybody assumed. And his blindness prevented him from seeing David as a threat.

Gladwell leaves a few stones unturned.[133] But setting aside the

---

[133] One might wonder, for example, why the Philistines would send out a clumsy half-blind oaf as their champion. Also, making medical diagnoses based on historical or biblical accounts is widely discredited. And, further, no matter what translation you look at, Goliath was brought to the field by a *shieldbearer*, not an attendant caregiver—two very different roles. If Goliath were so blind, we might also ask why he carried javelins, ranged weaponry that required keen eyesight to use. Finally, Gladwell does seem to overlook the fundamental morality element of the story, which was the role of divine intervention. For the problems with retrospective medical diagnosis, see Kean, S. "Retrodiagnoses: Investigating the Ills of Long-Dead Celebrities" *Science*, 337 (2012), 30–31. https://doi.org/10.1126/science.337.6090.30; Byard, R., Jensen, L. "Retrospective diagnoses of conditions affecting historical individuals," *Forensic Sci Med Pathol*, 4:1 (2008), 70. Accessible at: https://doi.org/10.1007/s12024-007-9002-z; Karenberg, A. "Retrospective Diagnosis: Use and Abuse in Medical Historiography," *Prague Med Rep.*, 110 (2009), 140–145; Karenberg, A., Moog, F.P. "Next Emperor, Please! No end to retrospective diagnostics," *J Hist Neurosci*, 13 (2004), 143–149. Accessible at: https://doi.org/10.1080/0964704049052158.

rather shaky exegesis, Gladwell's *David and Goliath* does highlight the kind of weakness that many a corporate giant has fallen afoul of in the past: a failure to see possible futures in which they might suffer defeat—an ignorance of the bets they are taking when they proceed with a course of action.

In 2007, Nokia commanded more than 50% of all the profits in the mobile phone industry. But its very success blinded the company to the disruptive power of a new type of technology, the smartphone—in this case, Apple's iPhone. Nokia had built its success on hardware expertise and was acclaimed for turning mobile phones into fashion accessories. But it fell short in the software department, marginalising developers and refusing to imagine how important software and apps could be to the user experience. When the iPhone exploded onto the scene and began stealing its share of the market, Nokia remained blind to the threat. Nokia failed to envision a scenario in which this high-end, low-volume phone could become more than just a fad. And its management was unable to recognize just how fast consumers would punish them for failing to innovate.[134] Blackberry suffered the same fate, clinging to a keyboard-based model and their exclusive BBM messaging service, unwilling to envision a world in which touch screens and cross-platform messaging services (like WhatsApp) would dominate.[135]

We see the same blindness in other industries. Traditional high-street retailers such as Macy's, Nordstrom, JC Penney, and Kohl's have faced rapidly plummeting shares and, in all likelihood, eventual demise or restructuring due to their inability to envision

---

[134] Surowiecki, J. "Where Nokia Went Wrong," *The New Yorker* (September 3, 2013). Accessible at: https://www.newyorker.com/business/currency/where-nokia-went-wrong.

[135] "How Apple Killed BlackBerry," *TechTelegraph* (February 7, 2020). Accessible at: https://www.techtelegraph.co.uk/how-apple-killed-blackberry-imore/.

and hedge against a scenario in which direct-to-customer online retailers such as Amazon would swoop up their market and condemn to the gallows the very requirement for a physical store.

In the automobile industry, combustion engine giants such as General Motors, Ford, Renault, Fiat Chrysler, Rolls-Royce, BMW, and Volkswagen have in the past failed to imagine a world where car ownership was a luxury rather than a necessity, where ride services like Uber and Lyft provided an affordable alternative to taxis, where carbon dioxide emissions were increasingly punished, and where companies like Tesla (which focused almost solely on innovation, at the expense of profitability) would set the new standard for the future: self-driving electric vehicles.[136]

So how do we expose the bets we are taking so that boards and management can have meaningful discussions as to how the company should operate?

To put it simply, we generate scenarios. By creating the spanning set of possible outcomes, we uncover the bets we are unwittingly taking, and we can then choose how to proceed. The bets we take should not be a result of scenarios we are ignorant of—a common consequence of using basic forecasting methods—but those which we have modeled, analyzed, and chosen to ignore, either for upside or downside potential. They should be the new technologies known about but left unexplored or the risks of disruption deemed too unlikely or unthreatening to require action. In short, the bets we are taking are the scenarios we have explicitly chosen to ignore. In one scenario, the fisherman could have failed to return. I ignored this possibility. That was one of the most dangerous bets I have ever taken.

General Motors and the world's carmakers saw Tesla

---

[136] Ewing, J. "The Car Industry Is Under Siege," *New York Times* (June 6, 2019). Accessible at: https://www.nytimes.com/2019/06/06/business/auto-industry-fiat-renault.html.

emerging—the scenario that Tesla would do well was a real possibility—but they ignored it. They took the bet that the electric car would not be so important so swiftly—and they lost!

Liquidity Is Often a Deadly Radical Risk

When I started my former company, Algorithmics, I remember people introducing me as a serious risk taker. I could see why. I had no experience managing a company, and I had never been out of academia. But I never thought of myself as such. To manage uncertainty, I only ever hired a new employee if we had six months of cash in the bank to cover expenses post hiring.

That is risk thinking, though I never expressed it as such. I could have put that money to use elsewhere—either reinvesting it in new equipment for the company or taking on more than one employee. That could have made us more profit in the long run. But it could also have sunk us if, say, a global pandemic struck, and all our revenue evaporated. How would we have paid our employees? But the nest egg bought us time to pivot if we discovered we were on the wrong track or if some radical uncertainty were to strike. I realized then there is a clear difference between risk taking and managing the risks you take. Keeping six months' cash flow in the bank before hiring my next employee was a hedge to manage liquidity risk.

At a fundamental level, managing risk in business is about having enough liquidity—cash on hand, essentially, or a readily accessible store of wealth—that you can easily and cheaply convert into cash. This enables you to hedge bets on things that have not been anticipated. Houses, vintage sports cars, and collections of fine wines, for example, are about the least liquid assets you can get, whereas holding large cash reserves in a global bank is highly liquid.

Finding yourself illiquid is a huge problem if someone calls you on your debts. You can hold astonishing wealth, but if you are unable to use it to meet your obligations, you can go bankrupt in an instant. While this is easy to keep track of on an individual scale simply by holding some reserves in the bank, illiquidity can creep up on larger corporations and financial institutions as they package up and deploy their assets in various locations, leaving them blind to the bets they are taking with their money. And it is a pitfall into which companies of any size and persons of any value can fall.

One of the biggest was Lehman Brothers, a 158-year-old investment firm named after a set of brothers from the US Deep South: Henry, Emanuel, and Mayer Lehman.

By the time its end came on September 15, 2008, Lehman Brothers Holdings, Inc., was the fourth-largest investment bank in the United States and had more than 25,000 employees around the world. Its bankruptcy, in which it listed $639 billion in assets and $619 billion in debt, was the largest in modern economic history and the poster child of the 2008 global financial crisis that began in the US subprime mortgage industry just a year before, spread to the credit markets, and then set fire to the whole world's financial markets. The Lehman estate's creditors ultimately filed $1.2 trillion of claims against it alone, while overall, the crisis that ensued wiped out, by some estimations, more than $10 trillion from the US economy, 6 million jobs, and caused the Dow Jones Industrial Average to drop an astonishing 5,000 points.[137]

---

[137] Rosalind Z. Wiggins, R. Z., Piontek, T. & Metrick, A. *"The Lehman Brothers Bankruptcy A,"* Yale Program on Financial Stability Case Study 2014-3a-v1 (October 1, 2014). Accessible at:
http://som.yale.edu/sites/default/files/files/001-2014-3A-V1-Lehman-Brothers-A-REVA.pdf; Chadha, P. "What Caused the Failure of Lehman Brothers? Could it have been Prevented? How? Recommendations for Going Forward," International Journal of Accounting Research, S1 002 (2016), 1–5. Accessible at: https://www.longdom.org/open-access/what-caused-the-failure-of-lehman-brothers-could-it-have-beenprevented-how-recommendations-for-going-forward-2472-114X-S1-002.pdf.

How did it happen?

The mid-2000s saw a boom in the US housing market, and a simultaneous glut of available funds resulted in a rapidly expanding market for subprime mortgages and the securitization of mortgage-backed securities (MBS), wherein the contractual debt would be packaged up into marketable securities and sold to investors. Lehman began by buying mortgages to incorporate into their MBS, but they soon saw how profitable securitization was becoming and so acquired five mortgage lenders, including subprime lender BNC Mortgage and Aurora Loan Services, all of which specialized in risky mortgage loans with high levels of defaults.

While the going was good between 2004 and 2006, Lehman's capital markets unit grew 56% thanks to the real estate businesses. But then, around March 2006, Lehman got greedy. They realized that, where before they were simply acquiring assets to move them to third parties through securitization, they could actually increase their market share and profits if they stored the assets as their own investments rather than passing them on. In this way, they retained the returns generated by those assets—and it seemed to be working. In 2007, they reported a staggering $19.3 billion in revenues and a record $4.2 billion net income.

But what they also retained, by holding these assets, were the risks and the illiquidity, a huge gamble that perhaps they were not fully aware they were taking. From 2006 to 2007, the firm aggressively increased its slice of the real estate market until it had $111 billion in assets and securities, double the amount it had held at the end of the previous year. The illiquidity of these assets made it very difficult to raise cash, hedge risks, and sell assets to reduce leverage on its balance sheet. But so long as the market held, Lehman remained afloat.

Then the cracks began to appear. The default rate on subprime mortgages began to climb, and voices began to emerge from credit ratings agencies and investors expressing concerns.

On March 13, 2007, the Lehman stock price dropped 5.5%—the largest single-day drop in five years. But just one day later, the firm posted record quarterly revenues and profits, ostensibly signalling that the company was in good health. "We see the subprime situation as being relatively contained," said Chris O'Meara, Lehman's chief financial officer, on a conference call to his investors.[138] Throughout that year, Lehman ramped up their practices even further, underwriting more mortgage-backed securities than any other firm and racking up a portfolio worth $85 billion. That was four times its shareholders' equity, and it would prove to be the last opportunity they had to shed some of their riskiest holdings.

Yet they did not see the need—or perhaps they were blind to it even then.

To pursue the most aggressive growth possible during this time, Lehman, like many of its peers, including Bear Steams, Merrill Lynch, Goldman Sachs, and Morgan Stanley, had adopted a high-risk business model built around massive amounts of leverage. This meant borrowing capital (i.e., taking on debt) to use as a funding source when investing to expand their asset base and generate higher returns. Lehman's ratio of debt to equity was a staggering 30.7x—up from 23.9x in 2004.[139]

Lehman's huge mortgage securities portfolio left it very susceptible to the crumbling housing market. When ratings agencies and analysts began pointing this out and suggesting they reduce

---

[138] Wilchins, D. "Lehman Profit Rises, Subprime Impact Offset," *Reuters* (March 14, 2007). Accessible at: https://www.reuters.com/article/us-lehman-results/lehman-profit-rises-subprime-impact-offset-idUSWEN539120070314.

[139] Lehman Brothers Holdings Inc. Form 10-K for fiscal year ended November 30, 2007.

their leverage, Lehman found themselves stuck. They could increase equity or sell some of their assets. They did the former and raised $6 billion in additional capital in early 2008, but to deleverage more, they needed to sell some of their real estate assets. This was tricky in a deteriorating market, and they failed to secure good prices for them. They were reluctant to let the assets go cheaply because they would take a loss—*and* it would cast doubt on the value of their remaining assets.

As the pot began to boil, Lehman began to panic. Every day, just to operate, they were borrowing billions of dollars in the overnight wholesale funding markets, offering up their securities as collateral. But soon people came to realise their assets were not worth as much, so they asked for more in collateral on the loans. Or they asked for different types of assets, not those connected to real estate. And then they stopped taking them altogether and demanded cash instead. Lehman found themselves frozen, unable to liquidate assets and lacking cash holdings.

Struggling to keep its head above water, the firm tried to spin off some of its most toxic assets—worth about $50 billion and shrinking fast—into a publicly traded corporation so that its own reputation would remain untainted. But credit rating agencies saw this for the misdirect it was, and the stock plummeted 77% in the first week of September 2008. Then Lehman tried to find a partner, unsuccessfully. The stock dropped another 45% on September 9. And the US Treasury refused to bail them out.

Like rats fleeing a sinking ship, hedge-fund clients and short-term creditors abandoned the tilting colossus. By the September 11, the stock dropped again by 42%. Then on Monday, September 15, with nothing left for it to do, Lehman declared bankruptcy; the stock fell 93% from its previous close.

The end had come.

The name Lehman is now synonymous with the infamous images of investment bankers streaming from their offices with cardboard boxes in their hands, ties loose, and faces grim. Although there are some valid questions around the Federal Reserve's decision not to bail the firm out like it did Bear Stearns and AIG, the mistakes that Lehman made—their gross miscalculations and poor risk management—were mistakes nonetheless, and a stark reminder of how mighty Goliaths can fall when they do not know their bets.

Looking back on 2008, Ed Clark, the former CEO of TD Bank Group—a Canadian multinational bank that came through the crisis comparatively unscathed—pointed out that people at firms like Lehman and others fundamentally misunderstood the importance of liquidity, and they were unaware of the bets they were taking.

The crisis revealed, he said, just how untransparent the banking system was. "There were things obviously going on underneath the surface that people either did not know about or did not really understand the implications of."

One of the key strategies we need to implement is to move away from the notion of the hero CEO, who makes dramatic decisions at the helm of the company and move back towards the more operational CEO whose primary concern is understanding what is going on in the core operations of the business. At a meeting of the seven big central banks in 2005, Clark recalls how people were discussing derivative products and hedge funds, and the CEO of one of the largest banks in the world at the time said, "Come on, let's admit it. We haven't a clue what's going on inside our firms. We're just hoping the guys below us do."[140]

To Clark, that was the wake-up call he needed, and he removed TD Bank Group from the structured credit derivative products from which everyone else was making so much money at the time. This led to universal criticism, but ultimately it was a

---

[140] "Former TD CEO Ed Clark on the lessons learned from the financial crisis," *BNN Bloomberg* (2018). Accessible at:
https://www.bnnbloomberg.ca/economics/video/former-td-ceo-ed-clark-on-the-lessons-learned-from-the-financial-crisis~1489309.

hedge based on the realization that the banking system was being run by people who did not understand the risks they were taking. And it saved his company.

The Lehman employees I have interviewed were a tight bunch who loved working for the firm, and to this day, they speak highly of the culture. They all seemed to feel that they were the fall guy for a disease that infected all of Wall Street. If there is one lesson to be learned from this and the other stories we have told here, it is that illiquidity kills—and cash can dry up in no time.

The Precautionary Principle

One reason why businesses ignore risk is because of denial—the risk may be too great or the problem too big, so it might be easier to ignore it until it becomes someone else's problem.

One expensive example is asbestos. The issue had been brewing for many years. On May 20, 2000, Middlesex Hospital in London was forced to cough up £1.15 million in compensation for the death of one of their senior hospital surgeons. The cause? Only 47 at the time, the surgeon had died of the asbestos cancer, mesothelioma, which he contracted through exposure to the blue asbestos dust that filled the communication tunnels in the hospital where the surgeon worked between 1966 and 1973. It is now estimated that about 5,000 people die every year in the UK from cancers brought about by asbestos, and approximately 125 million people worldwide are still at risk due to occupational exposure to the material.[141]

---

[141] Perraudin, F. "Britain's death toll from asbestos at crisis level, figures reveal," *The Guardian* (July 7, 2019). Accessible at: https://www.theguardian.com/society/2019/jul/07/britains-death-toll-from-asbestos-at-crisis-level-figures-reveal; Whitmer, M. "Asbestos Facts & Statistics," *Asbestos.com* (August 21, 2020). Accessible at: https://www.asbestos.com/asbestos/statistics-facts/.

The substance, a naturally occurring fibrous mineral, was widely employed in the latter half of the twentieth century as insulation and a fire retardant in industrial, commercial, and domestic settings. Initially, mining for asbestos began in Thetford, Canada, in 1879, but its popularity soon meant that it was mined in different forms in Australia, Russia, South Africa, and elsewhere, to the extent that worldwide production was 2 million tonnes in 1998.

In the first 20 years after mining began, more than 100 different products were created from the mineral, but early warning signs about its dangers also started to emerge.

Lucy Deane Streatfeild, one of the UK's first female Inspectors of Factories, categorized asbestos work as one of four dusty occupations that required observation because of their "easily demonstrated danger to the health of workers and because of ascertained cases of injury to bronchial tubes and lungs medically attributed to the employment of the sufferer."[142] Deane was followed by two other women Observers who, while not scientists, would today have been designated "competent observers." Both pointed to the dangers of asbestos as well, and yet, while their warnings were widely circulated to policy-makers and politicians, all three women were ignored.

A year after Deane's report of 1898, Dr. Montague Murray of Charing Cross Hospital witnessed the first case of lung disease attributed to the inhalation of asbestos dust in a 33-year-old man. According to the man, who had been working in a factory

---

[142] Gee, D. & Greenberg, M. "Asbestos: from 'magic' to malevolent mineral," in *European Environment Agency, Late lessons from early warnings: the precautionary principle 1896–2000*, Environmental issue report No 22/2001, 52–63, at 53. Accessible at: https://www.eea.europa.eu/publications/environmental_issue_report_2001_22/issue-22-part-05.pdf/at_download/file.

"carding room" for ten years, he was the only one left alive of an original group of ten.[143]

Murray's report came to the attention of the UK government inquiry into compensation for industrial diseases in 1906, but they decided that it did not warrant inclusion in the list of causes of industrial diseases. This was, perhaps, due to their (possibly willful) ignorance of the Observers' report and Murray's own statement that "one hears, generally speaking, that considerable trouble is now taken to prevent the inhalation of the dust so that the disease is not so likely to occur as heretofore."[144] Did the government realise the bet they were taking when they chose this course of inaction?

Further evidence cropped up in 1910 and 1911 thanks to dust experiments with rats, and this eventually led to the Factory Department pressing for the installation of exhaust ventilation in dusty processes. But further inquiries in 1912 and 1917 found no cause for further action. Meanwhile, insurance companies—always the canary in the coal mine—in the US and Canada were beginning to decline cover for asbestos workers due to assumed injurious conditions in the industry. But precautionary action went no further than this even as other warning signs cropped up and were ignored.

It was not until 1931 that something was done. After several scientific papers had been published on cases of asbestosis and the Medical Inspector of Factories had conducted a health study that concluded that 66% of asbestos workers employed for 20 years or

---

[143] According to Wilson College of Textiles, carding is a mechanical process where fibers are passed between moving surfaces covered with card clothing. It disentangles, cleans, and intermixes fibers to produce a continuous web or sliver suitable for subsequent processing.

[144] Murray, H. M., in *Departmental Committee on Compensation for Industrial Diseases, 2007, Minutes of evidence*, 127, paragraphs 4076–4104, Cd 3496 (London: HMSO, 1907).

more suffered from the disease, dust-control regulations, medical surveillance, and compensation arrangements finally came into force.

Unfortunately, the regulations neither banned asbestos nor were even enforced for the most part for almost 40 years, until 1969 when new asbestos regulations were put in place. During that time, a rising body of literature appeared linking asbestos exposure to lung cancer and mesothelioma cancer. Of particular influence were the studies of Dr. Irving Selikoff in the 1960s and 1970s, who, due to being banned from using company records, used trade union records to show that workers who installed asbestos insulation were in grave danger: of the 392 workers he examined with 20 years of asbestos exposure, 339 had asbestosis.[145]

By the Asbestos Textile Industry, Selikoff was described as a "disturbing sore thumb," a sentiment echoing the much earlier musings of the ex-Chief Medical Inspector of Factories, Dr. Legge, in 1932 on whether these sorts of figures might be swept under the rug with some sort of payment.[146] Each time evidence was brought up, parties with a vested interest in the production and installation of asbestos worked to hush up the evidence, and, tragically, regulatory authorities around the world let the matter lay dormant, refusing to act.

Meanwhile, the first instances of claimants winning court battles against asbestos factories began to crop up.

It was not until 1989, however, after the issue had been politicized, turned into a two-hour TV documentary for Yorkshire TV, come under bans around the world, and been buried under a mountain of scientific studies and compensation claims, that the UK government adopted a ban on all forms of asbestos.

---

[145] Selikoff, I. J. et al. "Asbestos Exposure and Neoplasia," *Journal of American Medical Association*, 188 (1964), 22–26.

[146] Tweedale, G. *Magic Mineral to Killer Dust: Turner and Newall and the Asbestos Hazard* (Oxford: OUP, 2000), 183.

By then, it was too late. One asbestos factory, Turner Brothers, was forced to make arrangements to pay up to £1 billion in claims. Lloyd's of London, the insurance underwriters, almost went under in the early 1990s from US pollution claims, many of which were asbestos-related.

Other asbestos companies, 12 in total, simply collapsed. Bill Sells, a former director of the world's biggest asbestos company, Johns-Manville, which had to file for bankruptcy in 1982 due to claims against it, wrote that medical research, assiduous communication, insistent warnings, and a rigorous dust-reduction programme "could have saved lives and would probably have saved the stockholders, the industry and, for that matter, the product."[147] It did not, primarily because denial had set in within management. Everywhere Sells looked, people were ignoring the warning signs and fudging safety precautions and measurements to ensure that the company looked good on paper. This happened across the industry and across multiple governments.

As he writes, "Manville and the rest of the asbestos industry did almost nothing of significance—some medical studies but no follow-through, safety bulletins and dust-abatement policies but no enforcement, acknowledgment of hazards but no direct warnings to downstream customers—and their collective inaction was ruinous."[148]

It cost hundreds of thousands of lives and billions of dollars, and nobody realized the extent of the bets they were taking.

So, what could they have done? The asbestos story teaches us a lesson in how something called the "precautionary principle" could have been, but was not, implemented as a form of risk thinking. The precautionary principle, in short form, is "safety first"—or

---

[147] Sells, B. "What asbestos taught me about managing risk," *Harvard Business Review* (March 1994). Accessible at: https://hbr.org/1994/03/what-asbestos-taught-me-about-managing-risk.
[148] Ibid.

"better safe than sorry." It states that when you have insufficient information about the risks of a product—be it asbestos, a new medicine, or the impact of a new technology—you should adopt a risk-management outlook that prioritizes precaution over profit.

The principle is based on the assumption that there is a social responsibility to protect the public from the potentially harmful effects of the progress of science and technology, and it is especially relevant in a corporate risk-management setting. Rather than wait until a causal relationship of harm can be proven beyond doubt, the precautionary principle would have you act in advance to establish preventative measures. Its most important rule is that lack of evidence of harm does not equal evidence of lack of harm. And we must act accordingly, putting safety measures in place even when we may not know exactly what they could be saving people from.

The trouble is figuring out how stringently to apply the principle. Too much caution, and you stymie any progress, but too little, and the consequences can be devastating. Economics is often the overriding factor here. Employers want profits, and employees want jobs. This combination can often put the long-term interests of a company at risk as short-term gains are prioritized. Again, this is where risk thinking steps in. It helps you identify the appropriate balance between precaution and progress.

In the case of the asbestos industry, the precautionary principle could have prompted several significant decisions. For example, it would have ensured that competent observers such as the early factory inspectors were listened to because they were able to anticipate the findings of later scientists—to the risk thinker, these are the type of non-traditional experts who you would want to include in your survey of expert judgment. Then, the early warning signs should have been followed up by extensive, long-term surveys of workers to accurately measure the risk, and companies should have put in place much more heavy risk-mitigation measures. This might have saved them from the billions of dollars in claims they later faced. And finally, the government could have implemented much tighter regulations that would have stimulated research into alternatives to asbestos (of which there were plenty).

Whether it is not knowing the type of people you have in your employment, refusing to experiment and explore new opportunities, creating globe-spanning lean supply chains in pursuit of pure efficiency, or operating at the limits of illiquidity, companies that fail to pay attention to their organizations and their changing ecosystems blind themselves to the risks they face. And they end up taking bets that are unnecessary or unknown.

In a world of radical uncertainty, there will always be the need to bet on particular outcomes not happening; it is impossible to hedge every downside and still achieve productivity. But risk thinking, through its scenario-generation process, provides a codified method for us to map the different futures in front of us so that, when we have to decide whether to bet or hedge, we do so equipped with the best knowledge available at the time. And importantly, risk thinking teaches us to appreciate when we have insufficient knowledge and yet still find a strategy for proceeding that utilizes imperfect action to improve our situation in the future. Thus, when new knowledge becomes available, we are in a position to act on it.

Regret: Know Yourself, Know Your Bets

If you go to Google and type in "worst business decisions ever made," you will find that the same seven or eight stories crop up in a different order across hundreds of outlets.

There is Excite, one of the original internet portals, which skipped on the opportunity to purchase Google in 1999 for a measly $750,000—today the latter's market value is more than $1 trillion and ever growing, while Excite slumped and was eventually picked up by Ask Jeeves in 2004 for a pittance.

Then there is Blockbuster, which in the 1990s had more than nine thousand video stores and an annual revenue of $6 billion, but which turned down the opportunity to purchase a new start-up company called Netflix for $50 million. Netflix is now worth $194 billion, although facing stiff competition from Amazon and Disney in the internet video marketplace.

Or have you heard the one about the American IT company Electronic Data Systems? In 1979, it was worth about $1 billion and wanted to invest in a small computer company to supply software. After searching around, they discovered the young Bellevue software company Microsoft, but when Bill Gates asked for $40–60 million, they flat-out rejected him. In 2020, Microsoft's net income was $44.28 billion, and Gates was the second richest man in the world (behind Amazon's Jeff Bezos).

These stories spread around the internet like wildfire, their details constantly warping as they are retold, and occasionally one or two will find their way onto the campuses of business schools as case studies. Digging into the details, we find they all vary quite a bit, and each case of business blunder serves up a unique lesson. But for the individuals involved in the decision-making, these colossal, missed opportunities demonstrate an important psychological component of risk thinking that economists are starting to turn their heads towards: regret.

Take Ross Perot, for example. In 1979, Perot was the head of the Dallas-based Electronic Data Systems and was responsible for passing up the opportunity to buy Microsoft. "I consider it one of the biggest business mistakes I've ever made," he said, looking back on his decision. "I should have just said, 'Now Bill, you set the price, and I'll take it.'"[149]

But why did Perot think it was the biggest mistake of his life?

---

[149] Andrew, P. & Manes, S. "I Blew It, Perot Says—He Didn't Buy Up Microsoft When He Had A Chance In '79," *The Seattle Times* (June 14, 1992). Accessible at: https://archive.seattletimes.com/archive/?date=19920614&slug=1497096.

To us, it seems obvious—each of us can instinctively understand that fear of missing out (commonly abbreviated as FOMO), the missed opportunity that we wish we had taken and the anguish it later causes us. But for a while, it was hard for economists to wrap their heads around—to quantify it and understand—the impact it had on investment decisions. After all, from a basic risk perspective, it was not so bad: Perot did not lose any money from the decision or end up in poverty (he was estimated to be worth a cool $4.1 billion at his death in 2019).

Think about the difference between risk and regret this way, as Harvard professor David Bell does: imagine that you have been playing the lottery every week for several years, and you always pick the same combination of numbers. But then one week, just to mix things up, you decide to change the combination you pick. You are still exposed to the same risk; your action has not changed the odds you face. But you would experience enormous regret if your old numbers were to come up the very week you switched.

The fear of missing out, FOMO, has also driven many investors to invest, sometimes under the craziest of valuations. Why? Because of the regret they would experience if they did not invest and the investment did well.

This psychological trick that our minds play on us is central to the way we learn from experience. It became interesting to economists once they realized that regret is not just something we can feel after the outcome of a decision is revealed to us, such as seeing our old lottery numbers come up on screen. It can actually influence the way we make decisions in advance. We frequently anticipate the regret we might feel if we make the wrong choice, and we consider this anticipation when we come to make a decision.

This theory of "anticipated regret" can make us act irrationally or in a biased fashion. It can both dissuade us from making a decision that, from a probabilistic perspective, might be in our favour, and it can motivate us to take a decision that rationally might be a bad one.

A classic example of this is a bubble in the stock market. In an extended bull market, when financial asset prices are on the rise and many people anticipate that they will continue to rise, the fear of missing out can drive prospective investors to ignore warning signs about an impending crash and dive into the market. This enthusiasm can push asset prices much higher than their true value as indicated by their underlying fundamentals. When the bubbles ultimately burst, the reverse happens and people begin panic selling for fear of being left in the market when it bottoms out.

There are plenty of ways for investors to eliminate (or at least reduce the influence of) regret by automating the investment process. For example, formula investing follows strict rules for investment decisions, and algorithms can be used to automate the execution of trades and their management.

But should we eliminate regret from the investment process? After all, it is a combination of the outcome of a decision *and* how we personally relate to that outcome that in many instances really defines whether an investment decision can be considered a "good" one or a "bad" one. To recognize regret is to acknowledge that we care about the consequences of our decisions; to admit it into our risk-thinking process is to be able to mitigate the worst of its influence. The fear of losing more money than we can afford, for example, may guide us towards more conservative positions than a traditional risk management technique such as *mean variance* (weighing risk, expressed as variance, against expected return) and *value at risk* (a statistic that measures how much a set of investments might lose during a given period under normal market conditions). Vice versa, taking regret into account, or the fear of missing out, when choosing an investment option might be a useful prompt to take the leap of faith required to capture a large upside.[150]

If we think back to our scenario tree, a sensible way of applying regret to the risk-thinking process would be to prune those branches of the tree where our anticipated regret would be higher than we can tolerate. We do this by insuring (or hedging) ourselves against those outcomes that cause the maximum regret. Often, they are the extremes—the double-digit standard deviation events that might be almost impossibly improbable but which, if they occurred, would cause not just loss, but immense regret as well.

We may never rid ourselves of regret completely. In many situations, the potential for regret may exist no matter which scenario happens to occur. But by applying this psychological component of risk thinking to our more structured probabilistic generation of scenario trees, it is possible to truly know the bets we are taking. For our emotional response to a bet that is won, lost, or simply missed out upon should be as much of a guide in the formal process of risk thinking as calculating the likelihood of each scenario and eliminating the ones with the highest negative numerical impact. Sometimes hedging against the biggest regrets is cheap, and other times, it is not. But sometimes it is worth paying whatever it takes to ensure peace of mind—even if it means walking away from a deal completely.

---

[150] Integrating regret into the decision-making process can be done quantitatively, as is outlined in Dembo, R. and Freeman, A. *Seeing Tomorrow: Rewriting the Rules of Risk* (New York: Wiley, 2001), 72–108. Put briefly, compute the difference in the horizon values between the portfolio and the benchmark under each scenario; the downside is zero whenever this number is positive, in which case we should feel happy about our portfolio; regret is the absolute value of the difference when this value is negative plus the psychological effect of the loss; average regret is the probability-weighted sum of the regrets under each scenario.

CONCLUSION: RISK THINKING AT ITS BEST

Apollo 13 was 55 hours, 3 minutes, and 18 seconds into its mission to the moon when Jack Swigert flipped a fan switch and there was a big bang.[151] Famously, commander Jim Lovell said in a calm voice over the radio to mission control: "Houston, we have a problem." And what had been a planned lunar landing mission would turn in minutes into a rescue mission.

Lovell and his crew, Jack Swigert and Fred Haise, were risk thinkers. Like Hadfield, they had spent years training for all eventualities. Yet in that moment of radical uncertainty, they had no idea what had happened.

Immediately, the astronauts began considering scenarios. One benign possibility was an instrumentation problem—a faulty reading. But the ominous sound of the explosion ruled that one out quickly.

What about a micro-meteor collision? Despite the very small chance of such an event, the downside impact would be huge:

---

[151] Details for this section are taken from the following: Dunbar, B., "Apollo 13," *NASA* (2009). Accessible at:
https://www.nasa.gov/mission_pages/apollo/missions/apollo13.html; Lovell, J. and Kluger, J. *Lost Moon: The Perilous Voyage of Apollo 13* (Boston: Houghton Mifflin Company, 1994); Cass, S. "Apollo 13, We Have a Solution," *IEEE Spectrum* (April 1, 2005). Accessible at: https://spectrum.ieee.org/tech-history/space-age/apollo-13-we-have-a-solution.

the invisible punch would rip a gaping hole in the spacecraft and the life-preserving pressure pocket inside would be whisked out into the vacuum. Immediately they hedged against this possibility. They moved to seal the hatch between the command module and the lunar module, which, had it been hit, would now be rapidly depressurizing.

But it was not a meteor.

The next candidate was a problem in the oxygen tank. Yet those were built with as few parts as possible, and the chances of a fault were extremely slight. Also, even if one failed, the other should have been more than capable of keeping the other components running. Except several other components were not functioning. They had failures in one tank, two fuel cells, and one bus—a statistical absurdity. To make matters more perplexing, the antennas on the ship had suddenly begun switching stations, and the ship itself started wobbling off its proper attitude as it hurtled towards the moon at 2,000 miles per hour.

Thoroughly perturbed, Lovell decided to perform one of the oldest pieces of analysis in the aeronautical books. He looked out the window.

What he saw was the beautiful and the damned. His spaceship was venting a ghostly gas that crystalized as it bled from the ship, stringing itself around them and out into space like a halo that went on for miles. It clearly had been an explosion in the oxygen tank, then, and the second was emitting its liquid lifeblood rapidly.

Lovell, Swigert, and Haise kept their cool. Already several hedges had come into play that had saved them, for it was just this type of scenario that had led NASA to install two oxygen tanks and multiple fuel cells in the first place. They had oxygen, though dwindling, and they had identified the cause of the spinning as the venting.

Back at Houston, it was less calm. The flight director, Gene Kranz, smoking heavily and pacing back and forth behind his console at mission control, executed some critical upside analysis, known, inversely in NASA-speak, as "down-moding." What rewards, at what risk, were still available to them? If a moon landing was off the cards, perhaps an orbit was possible. If not an orbit, perhaps a loop around for some hasty sightings.

Each of these was exhausted as the situation worsened until Kranz was left with only one upside: return the crew alive.

The first thing the mission control head asked for was to bring all people familiar with the capsule back into mission control from wherever they were. He wanted people in the room who knew everything about each and every component in the module's design. These were his experts.

There was an exact replica at mission control that they could work with to try to manage the situation. A wise move. This was their scenario generator, a physical tool to figure out different possibilities, and it proved to be essential. Little did they know, but they were setting the bar for excellent risk thinking with the way they separated the deterministic from the stochastic, their improvised methods for generating scenarios, and the way they implemented hedges for the most awful potential outcomes.

With the oxygen dwindling rapidly, the ground team decided to move the astronauts to the lunar command module. This was an oxygen- and power-starved tin can made for two, and the three crew members now had to use it to get back to Earth.

A significant challenge was adapting the command module's navigational platform alignment for use in the lunar module whose only requirement until then had been to jump down to the surface of the moon and hop back up again. Now the crew had to undertake midflight navigational adjustments that returned them to Earth safely.

At this point a decision had to be made. The craft was accelerating up to 5,000 miles per hour and closing in on the moon. The closer it got, the harder it would be to perform any midflight adjustments before entering the moon's field of gravity and losing radio contact on the backside.

Rapidly, the team on the ground generated two scenarios. Both were stochastic—involving significant uncertainty—and they each had their upside and their risks. The discussion back in Houston was fierce.

One option was a direct abort. This would use the service module's main engine to return before ever getting to the moon. The upside was a speedy return; the downside was a catastrophic failure of the propulsion system, which the initial explosion could have damaged, and the death of the wavering fuel cells. This could leave them stranded or cause another explosion that obliterated the craft. It was also a maneuver that had to be calculated fast, and which used up every last drop of fuel, so no adjustments could be made if they got it wrong.

Instead, they decided to use the lunar module's smaller engines, which had been designed primarily for descending to the moon's surface, to adjust course for a free-return trajectory—the famous slingshot around the moon. This hedge cost them some upside; the return journey would now take four days, but crucially it was safer and left fuel for another burn on the other side to correct their flight path and, importantly, speed up the craft.

But now, the challenge was how to eke out the oxygen to be able to have enough to get them home. They also had to arrive back with enough energy to deploy all the mechanisms for a safe entry and landing. Again, with their slide rules, the engineers figured out that all energy, except actual essential power needed to be turned off, to bring the level of power used to 12 amps—an amount insufficient to make coffee in a regular coffee pot!

The chief engineer who headed the design of the lunar module set about figuring out all possible ways this could be achieved, generating many re-entry scenarios simulated in the command module replica in Houston, under the same conditions as the Apollo module speeding home. Working day and night, he was about to give up when a junior engineer had the bright idea to bring the tiny bit of power back from the now shut-down command module into the batteries of the lunar module. With this tiny addition and a particular energy-efficient scenario plan to power up various functions for re-entry, they calculated that, by a hair's width, they probably had just enough to make it. The risk remained. Some other black swan could fly in, and there would be a shortage of power for a safe entry.

As luck would have it, another black swan did appear, one that had not at all been contemplated by the design engineers when building the module. A serious carbon dioxide buildup in the module could have had potentially fatal consequences. How to deal with this?

A group of engineers took an exact replica of all the materials available to the astronauts in the module, including their user manuals, plastic bags, duct tape, and other odds and ends, and they put them out on a table with a challenge to build a carbon monoxide remover!

Amazingly, they figured out how to do it, built it in Houston, and proceeded to guide the astronauts to build it in space. And it worked!

What next?

On Day 6, approaching Earth, they tried to power up the computer to guide them on a trajectory to a landing. They had to approach Earth at exactly the correct angle—or the module could bounce off the atmosphere, sending them to a slow death. To add insult to injury, the computers would not fire up. Another huge risk in a long line of risks they had faced in their six days of travel in space.

Once again, the engineers and Commander Lovell figured out an ingenious way to guide the module manually by keeping the Earth in the same position relative to the module in one of its windows.

So, crippled with almost no energy, with a jury-rigged carbon monoxide appliance and manual guidance, they entered the Earth's atmosphere for 4 harrowing minutes, hoping the heat shield on the monitor would be sufficient to protect them, facing yet another radically uncertain event. They knew this was their final bet; they just had to take it.

The heat shield held up, and they landed safely on Day 7.

As details of the incident had been communicated back to Earth, news reporters and analysts had put the crew's odds of survival at a meagre 10%. But astronauts do not think like that. They do not make single-figure forecasts. Each of their steps—the water conservation, the carbon dioxide syphoning, the navigational decisions, the multi-stage burns—played a part in the risk thinking methodology. This rolling reassessment of policy accounts for evolving scenarios and enables the charting of the best course of action for the immediate future. The risk thinking that got them home under the most dangerous circumstances had started four years before with scenario planning, training for the radical events that might befall them, hedging the systems with redundancy, and the amazing team of thousands that used structured expert judgment to bring them back to Earth.

As Lovell said in interviews after the fact, "When you're in a situation like this, you don't think of the odds, you think of only how to improve the odds … as we got over one crisis after another … our percentage went up."[152]

---

[152] "A conversation with Capt. James Lovell 50 years after Apollo 13," *USA Today* (April 13, 2020). Accessible at: https://youtu.be/tCgfawFAGW4; https://www.kennedyspacecenter.com/blog/featured-flashback-jim-lovell-recounts-apollo-13s-chance-of-survival

Risk Thinking in Today's World

As Canadian astronaut Chris Hadfield writes, NASA teaches astronauts to look on the "dark side," imagine the very worst that could happen and ask, "OK, what's the next thing that will kill me?"[153] They rocket up to space and face the totally unforeseeable, and, in some extreme cases such as the *Challenger* disaster in 1986 or *Columbia* in 2003, they do not survive. And yet, more often than not, they can navigate their way through each problem that comes at them.

Never has that been truer than in the case of *Apollo 13*. So, how can we learn from this? After all, we, as individuals, do not have NASA's budget or wealth of great engineers. How shall we as individuals deal with radical uncertainty?

Let us put ourselves in situations that we have witnessed recently and map that to how we should think better about our radically uncertain future.

The outbreak of icy weather that rushed through the heartland of America in early 2021 overwhelmed the Texas power grid, plunging millions into darkness, bursting water pipes, and corrupting drinking water. As the humanitarian crisis unfolded, two things became increasingly evident: the glaring faults in the country's aging infrastructure and our outdated methods for planning in an evolving, radical uncertain world.

Using statistical modelling to forecast future events works well over short time periods. The science of meteorology, for example, has advanced significantly in the twenty-first century—to the point where we were able to predict the arrival of this arctic blast several weeks in advance. Better still, we can say that the likelihood of the weather patterns that would cause this can be known a year in advance.

---

[153] Hadfield, *Astronaut's Guide*, 36.

What is broken is that we seek to plan by using a definitive forecast. This is true not only for our grid planners but everything from our central banks to our governments to our journalists who write primarily in the language of forecasting.

Texas exemplifies this failure. Its grid operators forecast how much energy residents would need over this winter. Using those parameters, they allowed several power plants to shut down for maintenance while other equipment was left overdue for upgrades. As the cold front hit, household power usage jumped dramatically as residents struggled to keep warm—it jumped outside the range that the operators had forecast, triggering rolling blackouts. Then conditions worsened further, disabling power plants and exacerbating the disaster.

Not only was the forecast wrong, but the operators had failed to prepare for the possibility that they could make a mistake.

The problem is radical uncertainty. That climate change is happening is a verifiable fact—it is deterministic—but its exact manifestations are often unknowable.

The Texas snowstorm was the result of a polar vortex—a massive expanse of swirling cold air in the polar regions—breaking much farther south than normal. There is solid science suggesting that global warming causes these arctic outbursts. Rising temperatures in the Northern Hemisphere appear to be weakening the circulating jet stream that holds the vortex in place. When heat in the stratosphere punctures that stream, arctic air spills south.

But it is almost impossible to predict exactly when this puncture will occur, how severe it will be, and how exactly it will interact with other macroclimate and microclimate factors across the United States. There is no way to predict that an event similar to the one in Texas will occur next January. You might as well be throwing a dart at a rock on Mars.

What is possible is to say that, most likely, given global

warming scenarios for the future, there will be more events like this. We can say that, most likely, Sacramento will experience many more hot days (temperatures above 100 degrees Fahrenheit) in the coming years. We can say that the west coast of Canada is more likely to get drier and the east coast wetter as the century progresses. We know that bigger and more frequent hurricanes are creating more destructive flood events and storm surges.

We can also say, with significant certainty, that if the concentration of carbon dioxide in the atmosphere keeps on increasing as it has over the past fifty years, there will be much more volatility in the weather. However, we cannot tell for certain whether southern England will be a tropical paradise or more like Scandinavia by the end of the century.

If one thing is clear, it is that the past is no longer a guide to this uncertain future. We must alter our current mode of risk management, which depends on forecasting to predict a singular state of the world, and move to a method that can comprehend a spectrum of possible scenarios about the future. And we must strategize accordingly.

We need to change our language about the future. We need to think like risk thinkers when describing a future—using the language of scenarios and planning for mitigation and adaptation (hedging).

Scientists and activists frequently demonstrate that we have the capacity for this. For example, many have long advocated for decentralizing the power system.[154] Microgrids would enable communities to generate and store their own green energy using rooftop solar panels and nearby wind turbines. A lot has been written and discussed about how our power grids will have to

---

[154] Singh, M. "'California and Texas Are Warnings': Blackouts Show US Deeply Unprepared for the Climate Crisis," *The Guardian* (February 19, 2021). Accessible at: https://www.theguardian.com/environment/2021/feb/19/power-outages-texas-california-climate-crisis.

be re-engineered to cope with the new world of renewables. Yet relatively little has been done to date. With the correct infrastructure, this would allow communities to operate locally and not be subject to some monolithic grid, with centralized generation, to bring us down.

Texas was and is particularly vulnerable. And it is not alone. Texas is not connected to other grids to avoid restrictions imposed by the federal government. So, it misses one of the biggest hedges available to utilities—the ability to share power from others when needed. If Texas politicians were to risk think rather than plan as they do, they would give very serious consideration to a change in policy. The correct form of an approach to having a robust strategy for the state's energy supply is to develop a broad range of scenarios and start thinking about the hedges they could implement to mitigate the radically uncertain risks they will face, particularly as climate change starts to rear its ugly head.[155]

Ultimately, we need to accept that our view of the future is like the view through our windshield of our car on a dark night. We only see what the headlights show us. And, as we get closer to objects, we see them better and can revise our driving strategy. The radical uncertainty is whether a moose is about to run out of the darkness into our path. How do we hedge against this? We slow down so that in the event the poor animal runs across the road, we and the animal will not be gravely hurt. This metaphor highlights the difference between drivers who speed through the night, even with poor visibility, and those who risk think. We do not want to land up in a pile-up like the collision of more than 100 vehicles, which happened in Texas during the storm.

---

[155] Dembo, R, http://www.caiso.com/Documents/Session1-RonDembo-MarkRothleder.pdf, Plenary presentation given to CAISO, October 2018, https://www.youtube.com/watch?v=qVUo0PSW3-E&feature=youtu.be.

Looking to the Future

The world today, according to University of Oxford moral philosopher Toby Ord, stands on a precipice.[156] As never before, we have obtained the power to destroy ourselves and now stand on the very brink of doing so. In fact, by his somewhat bold forecast, we face in this century a one in six chance of total human extinction; this, where just a century ago, the probability was more like one in six hundred.

Arriving at a single probability like this, as we have seen throughout this book, is a futile attempt to quantify the radical uncertainty of our environment. Nevertheless, Ord's more qualitative arguments ring true: along with our advances in technology, our increasingly reckless use of the power we have obtained are putting us in graver danger than our species has ever faced. Climate change, pandemics, and out-of-control AI are just a few of the most pressing dangers—and they will affect every one of us in the decades to come.

Supply chains wrap around the globe in complicated webs, interlinked with single, vulnerable strands that are highly susceptible to disruption. Meanwhile, manufacturing systems rely on complicated processes often with multiple thousands of moving parts, meaning contingencies have proliferated, and outputs are shot from glass cannons.

On top of this, our financial systems communicate instantly and are interdependent, making them volatile and inherently nonstationary, yet our portfolio managers measure them with standard deviations and normal distributions—instruments blind to black swans.

We have set AI loose on our systems, where it analyzes vast amounts of big but incomplete data, ignorant to the biases of the

---

[156] Ord, T. *The Precipice: Existential Risk and the Future of Humanity* (Bloomsbury, 2020).

sample while distorting its results with the biases of its creators. Meanwhile our environment becomes increasingly recursive: the more people and their machines communicate, the more feedback loops arise and create unpredictable impacts—people like and share videos, purchase books, clothes, and tech, buy and sell stocks simply because information enters their news feeds, their "suggested for you's," or because a president tweets doctored propaganda at three o'clock in the morning.

The result of these developments is that our societies and the economies that drive them exist in a frequently random world. It is one in which there is no "typical member" of a group, hardly any "normal distributions," a world that is nonlinear and fluid, massively scalable, where numbers are boundless, and the exponential commonplace. It is one where the past has little predictive power over the future, where measurements are commonly biased and typically sparse because events (pandemics, melting permafrost, terrorist attacks) are few and far between yet have the potential to be devastating. It is a world where the difference between the middle of the road and disaster can be a minuscule disruption that occurs halfway around the globe. Here, the winners take all, and the losers—be they companies, species, societies, or individuals—can be quashed in an instant, victims of complex, highly structured but nonlinear functions of hazard magnitude.

To navigate this increasingly uncertain environment, entities of all sizes, from the individual to the multinational, and of all types, from the financial to the governmental, must learn to think better about risk. This book has illustrated the risk-thinking process through a series of entertaining but didactic stories and examples. Through each one, we have sought to highlight a particular aspect: the pitfalls of forecasting, the use of structured expert judgment, the scenario-generation process, knowing your bets and mitigating the risks, and ultimately strategizing effectively in the face of radical uncertainty.

But each of these stories form part of a whole, and that whole is the codified transition from uncertainty into risk, and from risk into strategy. We see that process, whether in a highly structured, technology-driven, large-scale form for multinational corporations, or in the informal, critical thinking-driven, small-scale form for individuals as, essentially, a coherent and uniform practice.

A crucial factor that distinguishes this book from the others is that it provides a codified structure to that process of risk thinking.

For individuals and organisations who want to implement risk thinking, that first step is essential to the process. We have seen that traditional forecasting relies, incorrectly, on assumptions of tame randomness in a world that is inherently radical and that can readily produce unprecedented events seemingly out of the blue. The result, as Nicolas Taleb has neatly summed up, is that "we produce thirty-year projections of social security deficits and oil prices without realizing that we cannot even predict these for the next summer ... The inability to predict outliers implies the inability to predict the course of history."[157]

Every time we pin our hopes on a single number based on past data, we not only falsely represent the multiple possibilities of the future, but we create a dangerously false sense of security about the road ahead that allows policy-makers to shift the onus for their decision onto a statistic.

Traditional forecasting ignores the distribution of estimated potential outcomes surrounding the central forecast when establishing an action plan. And, since the models currently underlying forecasts are based on history, no thought is given to possible future outcomes that lie outside the bounds of historical experience.

Risk thinking stresses an action plan focused not on the central forecast but on the whole distribution, and it is a process that

---

[157] Taleb, Nassim Nicholas, *The Black Swan*, Random House, 2010, prologue.

accounts for possibilities that lie outside the bounds of experience, i.e., black swans. If we cannot remove our dependency on forecasting, we will continue to pin our hopes on a fixed narrative that undermines the creation and communication of an adaptable strategy that is cognizant of its own limitations and can therefore work to overcome them.

Our greatest resource for risk thinking is ourselves. As we move forward in a world ridden with radical uncertainty, we must learn to adopt the mentality of our risk-thinking heroes. We must learn to integrate what we all do intuitively in a structured, systematic fashion throughout our industries and governments. We must recognise appropriate strategy in the face of radical uncertainty. If we fail in this, if we fail to proactively risk think when we have the opportunity, we will go down to the most insidious killer of them all: complacency.

AUTHOR'S NOTE

From Risk Thinking to Riskthinking.AI

What happens when you want to apply what we have learned here to some big, hairy, real-world problem involving radical risk?

As is evidenced in this book, I have been driven to make a difference in our fight for a low-carbon, sustainable, equitable world. I would say, a bigger, hairier problem is hard to find. So, how does risk thinking help us have an impact on reversing climate change? One clear way is to attack the problem of measuring and managing the financial risk of climate change. For one thing, if all the world's companies, investment funds, and banks were regulated to price climate change risk into their operations, we would move to a much more sustainable world with the speed we need. If the markets priced carbon risk as we do credit or market risk, we would definitely see massive change.

Luckily, there are many other people who feel the same way. The Task Force on Financial Disclosures (TCFD)[158] initiative started in 2015 by Mayor Michael Bloomberg and the then governor of the Bank of England, Mark Carney; the Central Bank initiative (NGFS);[159] the Climate 100+[160] initiative started by the largest fund managers in the world, and many more have mobi-

---

[158] www.fsb-tcfd.org
[159] www.ngfs.net
[160] www.climateaction100.org

lized hundreds of trillions of dollars of commerce and finance to move in this direction. The momentum is already here. Their challenge has been the new technology and data sources that are needed to make it happen. I believe that risk thinking can play a big role in helping us get there. Whereas standard finance tools for measuring risk rely on historical data, correlations, probability theory, and mathematical models that often assume normality, perfectly efficient markets, and so on, measuring climate risk, or any other radically uncertain problem, cannot be solved in this way.

These problems have plagued the TCFD, the NGFS, and other initiatives since their inception. As I write this, there is a conference organized by the *Economist,* and just about every speaker, including regulators, professors, and bank CEOs worldwide, are asking the same questions.

For this reason, I founded Riskthinking.AI, a company focused on applying risk thinking to provide the data and tools for measuring and managing climate risk.

What data is needed? What analytics may be applied? Where do we get such data from? How can it be delivered? Where does one start?

At Riskthinking.AI, we started out in 2020 to answer these questions, just as the Covid-19 pandemic hit the world. The company comprised a ragged bunch—Andrew Wiebe, Brendan Reilly, and me—with combined deep knowledge and experience in climate science, data science, software engineering, and financial risk management. We had one advantage; we knew what the end result would look like. We took a risk-thinking approach as follows:

1. We identified climate and other risk factors that would affect the profitability of a corporation, government, multinational bank, and investment manager anywhere in the world.
2. With this information we generated forward-looking, multifactor scenarios (chapter 8—climate risk is a

combination of factors coming together to generate a climate event—fire, flood etc.).
3. Since correlations and probabilities were meaningless when looking forward 50 years or more, we looked for causation, driven by climate science.
4. We also looked for standards to help with organizing data. When we could not find any, we developed one, the Climate Risk Classification Standard (CRCS).[161] This standard codifies the way climate science today understands weather patterns and what causes them worldwide.
5. We then had to think about consistency across the various risks, *transition risk*[162], *physical risk, investment risk, liability risk*, and *reputation risk*, that a corporation, bank, or government might experience.
6. We found a way by conditioning on a transition and developing forward-looking multifactor scenarios that could ˊ mix risk factors from various domains—political, environmental, social, and financial (chapter 8 and appendix 1).
7. Since the world's climate knows no borders, is indifferent to politics, and experiences the same level of carbon concentration in the atmosphere everywhere, it became clear that we would need to cover every corner of the world, uniformly, at any level of resolution possible with the same data that applied to that geography—a daunting task.
8. It was clear from the start, because of our risk-thinking mindset, that we would have to know how each geographical area of the world was related to any other geographical area. The world's climate in one area is not

---

[161] https://riskthinking.ai/videos/crcs-climate-risk-classification-standard-overview/.

[162] *Transition risks* can occur when moving towards a less-polluting, greener economy. Such *transitions* could mean that some sectors of the economy face big shifts in asset values or higher costs of doing business.

independent of the climate in other areas. So, for example, if a company has physical resources in many parts of the world, it needs to know how the climate might affect each one of them simultaneously, and in what ways. Drought in Australia is intimately related to rain in East Africa, as an example.

With all of this in hand, we set out to gather all the open-source data from climate science and economics, all the climate models and their results that described possible futures, plus all of climate science knowledge of climate drivers and causality and policy sentiment about the future. We then derived the uncertainty distributions for all of the relevant factors. The end result was our data-exchange product that was the first truly comprehensive, science-based data source available anywhere (see figure below).

Figure E1
Riskthinking.AI's World Climate Data Exchange
To tackle the problem of measuring and managing the financial risk of climate change, we compiled the first truly comprehensive, science-based data source available.

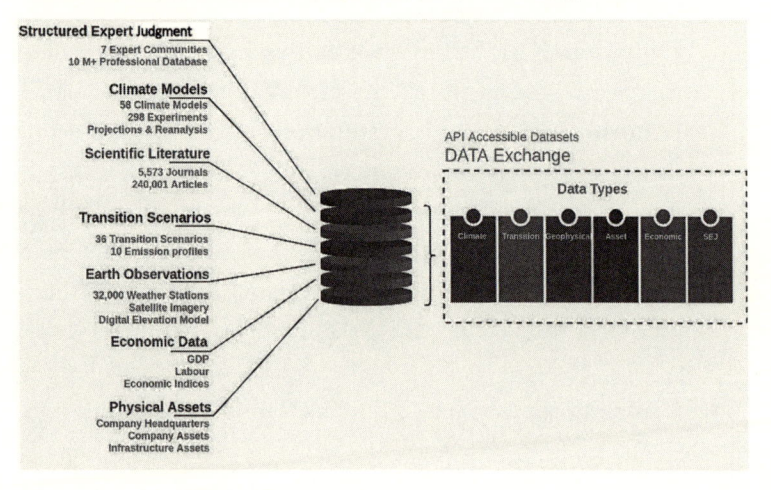

Source: Andrew Wiebe, Riskthinking.AI

To build our data exchange product, we had to develop standards that didn't exist.

The finance world has developed many standards to create regulations that enforce more and more sophisticated levels of risk management. This has enabled digital trading and risk management to be regulated and enforced. One example is the GICS.[163] In my former company, Algorithmics Inc., we worked closely with regulators, banks, and insurance companies that were grappling with how to deal with the growing risk derivatives impose on the financial system. The 1980s and 1990s saw a huge increase in the use of derivatives that brought new systemic risks to the markets. We were leaders in data, models, and standards for enterprise financial risk and in facilitating the regulations that helped control these emerging risks. Eventually, 70% of the world's top banks and 4 of 5 of the top insurers adopted our software to guide their risk-management functions.

A similar situation exists now. There are growing risks that climate change has imposed on the financial markets, and there are no standards to guide the systemic and other financial risks that result. That is why we developed the Climate Risk Classification Standard (CRCS).[164] CRCS provides a standard (i.e. unique metric) to compare the level of exposure to climate risk across enterprises or portfolios of assets just like S&P provides a unique standard for comparing default risk. We are able to do this because of our ability to use the entirety of available global scientific assessment data to create scenarios that appropriately span all possible outcomes and aggregate the resulting impacts into single rating, the CaR value (chapter 8).

---

[163] In 1999, MSCI and S&P Dow Jones Indices developed the Global Industry Classification Standard (GICS), seeking to offer an efficient investment tool to capture the breadth, depth, and evolution of industry sectors. GICS is a four-tiered, hierarchical industry-classification system.
[164] CRCS, the Climate Risk Classification Standard, https://riskthinking.ai/videos/crcs-climate-risk-classification-standard-overview/.

Let's take a look at why there is a need for such a standard.

Australia is a great example of the complexity of climate change risk and the need to understand and incorporate the causality of climate science in climate risk data. A 2020 report by the Australian Commission inquiry into Australia's extensive summer bushfires[165] includes detailed proposals to improve their national response efforts, tools, and climate data. Australian weather is heavily influenced by various climate drivers, such as the Indian Ocean Dipole (see chapter 8), the "El Nino, La Nina" systems in the Pacific Ocean, and more. Climate change has made these drivers more volatile, and this is why the commission concluded that the droughts in Australia were becoming more severe and were followed by floods that are becoming more and more severe.

Figure E2
El Niño, the Warm Phase of the El Niño – Southern Oscillation (ENSO)
El Niño is one of several climate drivers influencing global weather conditions, and climate change is making these drivers more volatile.

Source: NASA

---

[165] https://naturaldisaster.royalcommission.gov.au/publications/html-report; Also, two recent articles by BBC summarise these issues well: https://www.bbc.co.uk/news/world-australia-54742909
https://www.bbc.co.uk/news/science-environment-54725970.

So now, armed with codification of climate causality, we were able to create a product that covers every point on the Earth's surface with the climate risk data relevant to that geographic location as well as the other points/regions on Earth that are affected by the same climate drivers. This captures the essence of climate science as it relates to risk. We live in a big bathtub, and what we experience in Toronto, Sydney, London, and Singapore is influenced by the same climate driver, albeit in different ways.

The real value of risk thinking comes with what we can do with this data. Now that we have climate causation captured and aligned to every point on the Earth's surface, we can add historical data and future data as simulated by climate models. The historical data gives us a baseline. This we have from 1850 to 2010. Going forward, from now to 2100, we can use one or all of the 58 accepted climate models designed by the best institutions in the world. The power of risk thinking is to capture the uncertainty of every risk factor at each geographical location worldwide and to derive from this information forward scenarios algorithmically consistent on the multiple factors that cause climate disasters. For example, the heat, drought, and high winds that cause fires or the precipitation and storm surges that cause flooding or beach erosion as is happening in Australia today.

And, with these standards, the radical uncertainty quantified, the forward-looking scenarios generated algorithmically, we have all the ingredients to stress test future climate risk on our infrastructure, our portfolios, and our ability to grow food.

Ron Dembo
Toronto
March 2, 2021

ACKNOWLEDGMENTS

This book is the product of many years of thinking about how to model uncertain futures. It began with my research at Yale and then put into practice with my then fledgeling start-up, Algorithmics, in 1989. We developed an entire enterprise software system to measure the financial risk of banks, based on scenarios. This eventually was implemented worldwide and became a mainstay for risk management in 70% of the world's top 100 banks.

There were many colleagues, too many to mention all individually, who helped me formulate my ideas and turn them into successful software. I will mention only a few, with whom I have had the pleasure of many hours debating the pros and cons of various risk theories: Yaacov Mutnikas, Dan Rosen, Michael Zerbs, and Andy Aziz.

After selling Algorithmics and embarking on a quest to be useful in combatting climate change, I thought that I had left this behind until, one day in 2010, I was asked to give a 6-minute TED talk on how to think about risk at TEDGlobal in Oxford.[166] I worked hard on this talk, and it ultimately led to some of the ideas expressed in this book. The title of my talk was "Risk Thinking!"

Later, while on retainer to Goldman Sachs with Darren

---

[166] https://riskthinking.ai/videos/ron-dembo-tedglobal-discussing-risk-under-extreme-uncertainty/.

Cohen in 2017 and 2018, this popped up again, and these ideas were refined once more into a practical application. For this, I have to thank him as well as Atul Pawar, who became a big believer and implementer of risk thinking.

More recently, in my new start-up Riskthinking.AI, I have been working with Brendan Reilly and Andrew Wiebe, to make risk thinking a mainstay in banks, corporations, and governments with software and data for measuring the financial risk of climate change—one of the most pressing problems of our times. Their ideas and energy, and the teams they manage, have helped turn this dream of implementing the ideas on radical uncertainty into practice.

Finally, this book would not have happened without the excellent research and writing suggestions of Matthew Tibble and many hours of editing by Jeremy Clift. They improved the exposition tremendously. My daughter, Justine, with whom I have shared a love for writing, was also instrumental in improving the book with her constructive insights and excellent writing skills.

My wife, Ilana, with her incredible ability to synthesize information, played a big role in helping edit the final draft and eliminate unnecessary text. Her help made this book much more cohesive and accessible. I am grateful for this and very fortunate to have had her input.

APPENDIX 1

ALGORITHMIC-SCENARIO GENERATION

Imagine if we could automate scenario generation, span the range of possible future events, find the "black swans," understand the risk of "white elephants," and account for a full range of market sentiment. In this paper, we describe such a method. The only input required is the initial macro event or shock, financial or otherwise, that provokes a need for spanning future possible states of the world. Armed with that information, we can use machine-learning techniques and artificial intelligence (AI) to gather information about the macro-financial factors that could change significantly as a result of the event in question. We get these from history and the current market sentiment, and using the model we proposed below, we develop a *spanning set of scenarios* for possible future states of the world. With the knowledge we have gained, we can also automatically estimate the probabilities of these scenarios occurring, as influenced by the market view today and also with history that is relevant.

What do we mean by a "spanning set" of scenarios?

Definition of a Spanning Set of Scenarios

Let $f = \{f_1, f_2, f_3, \ldots, f_n\}$ be a finite set of random variables and $V(f)$ be a real valued function. An instance of f, $f^i = \{f^i_1, f^i_2, f^i_3, \ldots, f^i_n\}$ is defined as a scenario. A set of scenarios is defined to be a spanning set if it contains the maximum and minimum values of V for any valid choice of f^i.

We show later how, under certain circumstances, the scenario algorithm we will propose generates a spanning set.

Automating Scenario Generation

The factors $f_1, f_2, f_3, \ldots, f_n$ may or may not be independent. One convenient way to represent the state of the world at some future point (the horizon) would be to use a scenario tree. A simple version is the binary tree shown in figure A1.1. In this example, there are 3 factors, each of which only exhibits two states, up (U) with likelihood L(U) or down (D) with likelihood L(D).

Figure A1.1
A Binary Scenario Tree
To generate a spanning set of scenarios, it is necessary to combine multiple factors into a scenario tree. The dark line indicates a single scenario, Factor 1 down, Factor 2 up and Factor 3 down.

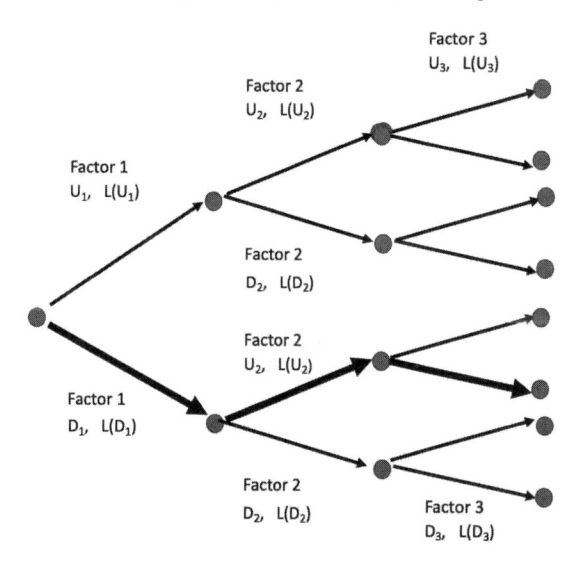

Source: Author

Naturally, there are more complex trees and possibly networks that could be used when analyzing a given situation. We use a binary tree to explain the algorithm for simplicity of presentation. The discussions below would apply to more complex trees as well.

So where could we get the values for U_i; D_i and their associated likelihoods $L(U_i)$; $L(D_i)$?

Imagine we could estimate the likelihood distribution of each factor at the horizon. Then one possible choice for U_i would be the upper extreme of the distribution, and D_i would be the lower extreme. The extremes may be chosen in a number of ways; for example, U_i could be set to the 99th percentile of the distribution.

Why would we want U_i and D_i to be the extremes?

First, the dimensionality of the problem could grow very large if we were to choose more than two points on the distribution. Second, the extremes hopefully allow us to generate extreme scenarios, both good and bad. We show later that this is true under certain assumptions.

Steps for Algorithmic-Scenario Generation

1. Identify macro factors affecting the issue being analyzed.
2. Generate a scenario tree for these factors.[167]
3. Generate the forward distributions for each factor at the horizon.
4. Identify the extreme values and the corresponding likelihoods for each factor.
5. The scenarios are the paths in the tree, their likelihoods are the product of the likelihoods along the path, and the value associated with each scenario is the sum of the values along the path.

There is clearly a lot of detail and many options behind each one of these steps. We discuss these below.

1. Identify macro factors affecting the issue being analyzed.

This is usually the domain of experts. It can, however, also be done automatically using machine learning. The question that it answers is: "What is the combination of material macro factors that affect the value being measured." For example, if we were analyzing a possible future strategy for a Californian electricity

---

[167] The ordering will be important if there are dependencies between factors.

distributor, macro factors might be the world temperature rise, electrical load in the future, precipitation, and so on. If we were looking at Brexit and its effect on a fund, the factors might be the value of the pound, various financial indices, or the deal reached with the EU. The factors are often a mixture of financial and non-financial ones. The algorithm handles arbitrary combinations of both.

2. Generate a scenario tree for these factors.

For this paper, we will restrict the analysis to trees, which does put some constraints on the types of dependence among factors that we can handle. Within this restriction, we can handle situations where the dependence between factors follows some order. In this case, the likelihoods on the arcs will be conditioned on the factors that came before them in the tree. Clearly, if the factors are independent, the tree represents all possible permutations and combinations of the factors. The tree is no longer a necessary representation; it is simply useful as a visual representation.

3. Generate forward distributions at the horizon.

This is the essential ingredient of the method, its source of it power, and the aspect to which it is most sensitive. As can be seen from the algorithm, we do not truly need the entire distribution. We only use extreme values and the likelihoods of upward and downward movements. The four numbers extracted from the distributions are enough to populate the tree for evaluation purposes. Still, when we have the entire distribution, it could be useful for deciding if an extreme value might be an outlier that should be excluded.

In many situations facing us, the history is scant, not very informative, or nonexistent, making the estimation of the future distributions of factors a difficult task. Good examples might be the analysis of the risk climate change will have on corporations, governments, and institutions; the risks inherent in reusable launch vehicles for space applications; the risks of the outcome of a referendum (e.g. Brexit); cyber risk; etc. It is in these situations that the usually accepted measures do not work well.

A source that could overcome these difficulties is the sentiment of the large numbers of people who influence the outcome of such future events or whose intuition could help where data is missing. The most important aspect of the forward estimation of factor values is that it spans the range of possible outcomes and that it contains values that might go against the general consensus. A single forecast is dangerous in such situations, but the range of expectations that is observable could be very useful. Think of Brexit where the vast majority of people predicted a no vote, but the yes vote prevailed. There were a small minority of people predicting no, and their view should always be taken into account in a risk assessment. So, how do we obtain this data?

One possibility is to poll a large number of people who are knowledgeable or otherwise engaged in the future values of the factor in question. Another is to use machine learning and AI to extract these sentiments from a broad base of information on the subject. Yet a third is to use historical proxies wherever appropriate. We suggest that an optimal situation would be to use combinations of all of the above.

4. Identify the extreme values and corresponding probabilities for each factor.

A key challenge is to eliminate spurious numbers (noise) from this estimation. These might occur when nonsensical answers are obtained from a poll or other means. There is a fine line, however, between crazy values and those that estimate true extreme situations from trusted sources. Certainly, "events that have never happened before in recorded history" will be a poor criterion for elimination. Possibly this could be achieved by a signal processing algorithm.

Theorem: Algorithmic-Scenario Generation

Assume $f = \{f_1, f_2, f_3, \ldots, f_n\}$ is a set of independent factors whose distributions are known at some horizon. Also, let each factor f_j be a random variable whose distribution at the horizon is F_j.

Let f^i_j, $f^i_j \in F_j$, be the ith realization of f_j at the horizon and $f^i = \{f^i_1, f^i_2, f^i_3, \ldots, f^i_n\}$. We refer to f^i as the ith multifactor scenario. Now define $V^i = V(f^i)$ the value associated with some institution, under the ith scenario, at the horizon. Let, S be the set of all feasible scenarios. Furthermore, assume that V is a monotone function of each of $f_1, f_2, f_3, \ldots, f_n$. Then the set of scenarios, S, is a spanning set.

Proof

In our algorithm, the scenarios are chosen to be all the permutations of $f^i_1, f^i_2, f^i_3, \ldots, f^i_n$ with f^i_j given by the maximum and minimum values of the estimated factor distribution for the up and down move at the node. Given the monotonicity and independence assumptions, at each node, we could choose the value that maximizes the gain in V(f), which could be either the lower or higher end of the factor distribution, and hence, by following the path of maximum gain, we will arrive at the path (scenario) that yields the overall maximum gain. In a similar fashion, we can generate the maximum loss. Hence, the paths in the scenario tree are a spanning set of scenarios.

Q.E.D.

Discussion Regarding the Assumptions of the Theorem

Many financial portfolios, in fact the vast majority of investment portfolios, are constructed with products that are linear and exhibit the monotone property required by the theorem. Many climate risk factors, such as temperature, also exhibit this monotone property over the long run—higher temperatures imply more drought, stronger storms, etc., which ultimately translate into higher costs. The assumption of independence might also be acceptable if the horizon is far away. In the immediate term, the factors are likely to be correlated but far less so as time passes. Still, this assumption is the more difficult one to live with. The theorem still holds if the dependence amongst the risk factors is ordered as it is represented in the tree, that is, each factor is conditioned only on a factor or factors appearing before it in the tree.

It might also be possible to use this result when monotonicity cannot be assumed by restricting its use to a local approximation to V where the assumptions hold.

The Initial Event and the Resulting Financial Shocks

To illustrate the methodology, we describe a complete end-to-end automatic scenario-generation process that is based on "the wisdom of the trusted experts," using a simple polling mechanism to obtain the information we need.

It starts with an event (for example, the French election, Brexit, a transition to a low-carbon future, a 2-degree warming by 2050, etc.), financial or non-financial, that could have an effect on the financial markets. Alternatively, it is conditioned on some scenario or transition such as is the case in climate change. In this case, the scenarios we generate for measuring risk are often conditioned on an assumed *transition scenario*.

There may be possible sub-events of interest (for example, a list of possible candidates who are eligible to win, a number of different possible transition scenarios, and so on. We can use experts studying the event to decide on the macro factors that could be affected by each possible sub-event (for example, various indices, spreads, GDP, etc.). In practice, we propose that trusted experts in the field, coupled with machine learning and artificial intelligence engines, be used to ascertain what macro-financial factors are important to consider. We believe that this is a function that could be executed well by machines guided by human experts. Once we have these factors, we can poll a large independent sample of actors in the financial markets for their opinions on the possible effect of the event on these factor movements over the time horizon in question. The result is a likelihood distribution for each macro factor. This gives us $L^u(F_i)$, the likelihood of an upward movement in factor i over the time horizon that has been chosen. Similarly, we can obtain, $L^d(F_i)$, the probability of a downward movement in the ith factor. In addition, we get the range the ith factor might move in, $R(F_i)$. This is all we need to generate a spanning set of scenarios.

In lieu of this poll, depending on the data available, we could also run artificial intelligence engines or models, such as the climate models used by the UN's International Panel on Climate Change, to derive these likelihood distributions or do a combination of trusted experts and polls.

As an example, let us consider the French election that was held in April and May of 2017.[168] There were three possible outcomes (transition scenarios). Let us imagine you owned a hedge

---

[168] The discussion and figures relating to this example are the patented result of work joint with Goldman Sachs. Dembo, R.S., Pawar, A., Nahum, E., and Phillips, A. Systems and Methods for Scenario Simulation, US Patent 20190197206, 2020. Applicant: Goldman Sachs & Co. LLC. Patent also issued in Japan (6805369-December 2020), Republic of South Korea (2218549), pending in Australia, Canada, China, Europe, Hong Kong, Singapore, PCT member states (51 countries).

fund, and it was late April, and you wished to understand the risk to major financial macro factors that affected your portfolio in the event of any one of the transitions.

To do so, you conducted a poll (shown in figure A2) to determine the uncertainty in each of the individual macro factors under each transition outcome at the horizon (a month after the election). In addition, you used machine learning algorithms to understand the uncertainty in the sentiment of the people most involved with the election or affected by it.

Figure A1.2
A Poll on the Outcome of the French Election in 2017
An example of the questions that would be sent out in a poll. Responders to this poll move the sliders to where they think the shocks could go.

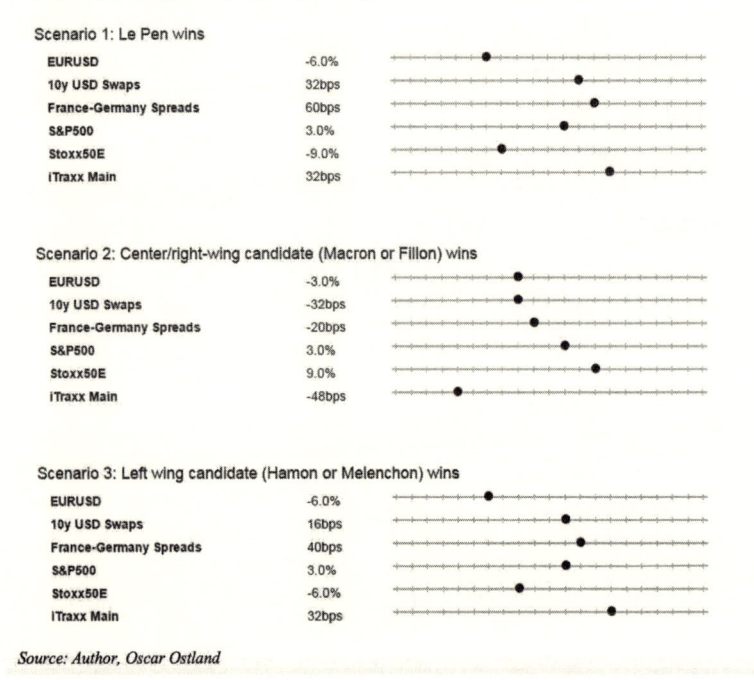

Scenario 1: Le Pen wins

EURUSD	-6.0%
10y USD Swaps	32bps
France-Germany Spreads	60bps
S&P500	3.0%
Stoxx50E	-9.0%
iTraxx Main	32bps

Scenario 2: Center/right-wing candidate (Macron or Fillon) wins

EURUSD	-3.0%
10y USD Swaps	-32bps
France-Germany Spreads	-20bps
S&P500	3.0%
Stoxx50E	9.0%
iTraxx Main	-48bps

Scenario 3: Left wing candidate (Hamon or Melenchon) wins

EURUSD	-6.0%
10y USD Swaps	16bps
France-Germany Spreads	40bps
S&P500	3.0%
Stoxx50E	-6.0%
iTraxx Main	32bps

Source: Author, Oscar Ostland

Figure A1.3
Estimated Likelihood Distribution
This example of an uncertainty distribution shows how we might extract upward and downward extremes for the scenario tree and the likelihood of an upward movement and a downward movement from the distribution of a macro-financial factor, e.g., the Euro.

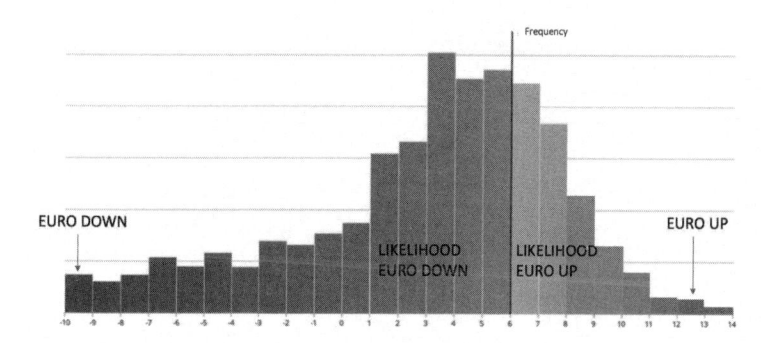

Source: Author

Figure A1.4
Macro-Factor Poll Distributions
This is an example of likelihood distributions of macro-financial factors obtained from a poll.

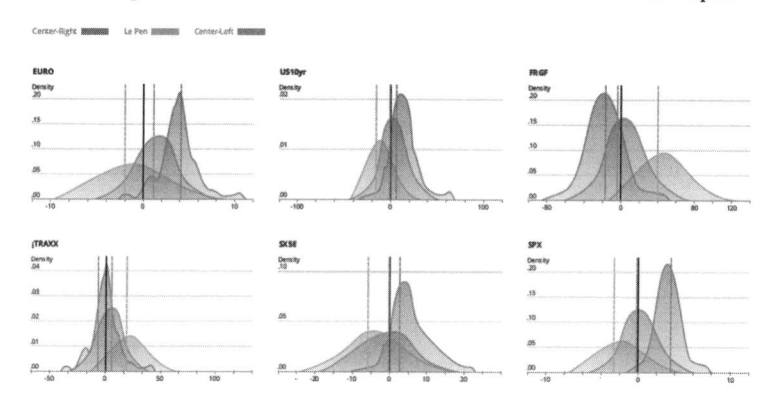

Source: Author, Oscar Ostland and Carmen Serravale

From these distributions one can extract possible ranges for the macro-financial factors as well as the likelihoods of upward and downward movements in these factors over the time period in question. (We use the term "likelihood" and not "probability" to reflect the fact that we are dealing with radical uncertainty.)

Table A1.1

An Example of Macro-Factor Shocks and
Their Likelihood Generated by a Poll

These are the four core values taken from the uncertainty distributions for each question.

Le Pen Wins						
	EUR	US10y	FRGE	SPX	SX5E	iTraxx
Likelihood Up	12%	20%	88%	20%	13%	79%
Likelihood Down	88%	80%	12%	80%	87%	21%
Shock Up	7.38	64.8	47.39	15.68	18.29	28
Shock Down	(7.06)	(37.00)	(47.50)	(10.56)	(16.27)	(34.00)
Center-Right Wins						
	EUR	US10y	FRGE	SPX	SX5E	iTraxx
Likelihood Up	77%	46%	13%	47%	75%	18%
Likelihood Down	23%	54%	87%	53%	25%	82%
Shock Up	4.79	47.3	46.15	7.44	10.36	29.94
Shock Down	(3.98)	(29.33)	(26.09)	(7.22)	(8.00)	(21.00)
Left Wins						
	EUR	US10y	FRGE	SPX	SX5E	iTraxx
Likelihood Up	13%	25%	71%	21%	17%	70%
Likelihood Down	87%	75%	29%	79%	83%	30%
Shock Up	7.27	54.4	25.92	11.94	13.65	24.6
Shock Down	(4.78)	(33.92)	(22.76)	(7.89)	(10.94)	(10.50)

Source: Author, Atul Pawar

Generating the Scenarios on the Financial Factors Affected by the Event

The next step is generating a possible set of scenarios that is derived only from this information and potentially information on the correlations between the macro-financial factors.

For this, we use financial networks. The simplest form of this is a decision tree. This can be used to demonstrate the method, and despite its simplicity, it will be very useful to illustrate how we generate a spanning set of scenarios.

Consider the binomial tree shown (partially) in figure 3 below, derived for the French election in 2017. Because there are 6 macro-financial factors that are affected whenever one of the candidates win. There are 2^6 possible paths for each possible win, making 3×2^6 possible paths in total, that is 192 possible paths = 192 possible scenarios.

By weighting the possible transition outcomes (for example with polling results) all three transition scenarios (regimes) may be combined for an overall result to get a distribution based on the 192 outcomes.

This is how, in the case of many transition scenarios for climate change, we can combine the likelihood of these transition scenarios to get an overall view of possible outcomes and their likelihoods to get a single picture of the risks we might face.

Figure A1.5
Scenarios for the French Election (Partial Tree)
Here we see how the multiple factors combine into a single scenario tree for the French election showing all possible transitions for the French Election.

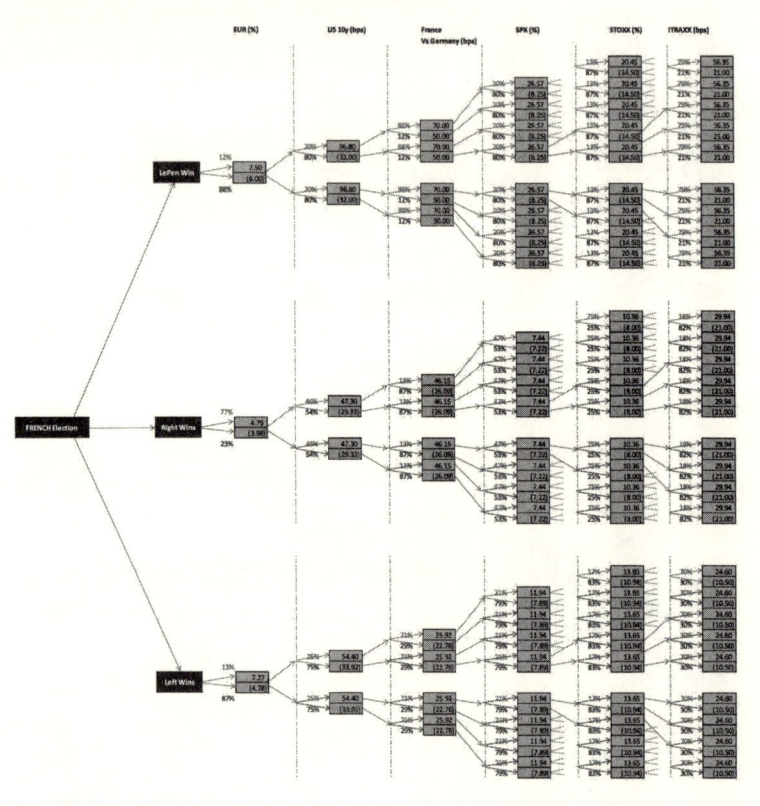

Source: Author, Atul Pawar

Here, we see how the multiple factors combine into a single scenario tree for the French election, showing all possible transitions for the French election.

There are 3 subtrees, one for each possibility—Le Pen, Center Left, Right winning. Each subtree has 2^n paths, where n = 6 is the number of macro-financial factors affected by the election results.

Each path through the tree corresponds to a scenario. For

example, in figure A1.7, Euro down, USD10y up, Fe/Ge up, SPX down, STOXX down, ITRAXX up.

For ease of exposition, not all paths are shown. When independence of the financial factor moves may be assumed the likelihood of a scenario is the product of the likelihoods along the path. The likelihoods of up and down moves and the size of the moves will be different in each subtree because they are conditioned on different events. This tree is for illustrative purposes only. The numbers shown are not indicative of the actual numbers that would be generated in a real application of this methodology. Thanks to Atul Pawar for generating the original diagram from which this was built.

Figure A1.6
A Multi-Factor Scenario on a Scenario Tree
An example of a multifactor scenario (path through a subtree) conditioned on a Le Pen transition.

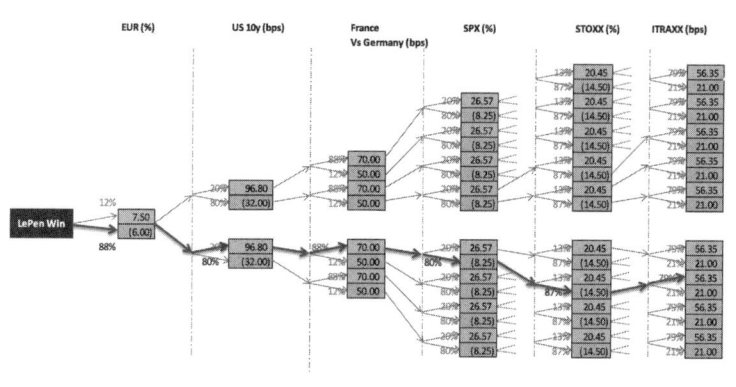

Source: Author, Riskthinking.AI

An example of a multifactor scenario (path through a subtree (conditioned on the sub-event—Le Pen wins)) is the scenario:

EUR down 6%; US10y up 96.8 bps; French/German Spreads up 70%; SPX down 8%; STOXX down 14.5%; ITRAXX up bps.

The example tree in Figure A5 is just one possible tree or network that we could use to automatically generate scenarios based on the information obtained on the market's views of possible moves that the macro-risk factors might experience, conditioned on this event. A macro scenario is a single path through the tree (see figure A5). The tree or network could be more complicated than the simple example depicted above; for example, a Bayesian network that is continually updated with new information as perceptions of those polled change with changing news. The likelihood of a macro scenario occurring is simply the product of the likelihoods of each event or conditional event along the path. In more complicated networks (trees), the order of the risk factors as they appear in the tree is important, and we need to consider correlations and ordering and dependencies between factors. Also, the correlations themselves could be changing from day to day.

To simplify the exposition here, we can assume independence or linear dependence in the order the factors appear in the tree. An actual example, consistent with the polling shown in figure A1.7, is shown below.

Figure A1.7
The Scenario Tree Conditioned on a Center-Right Win
For our purposes here we can assume independence or linear dependence in the order the factors appear in the tree.

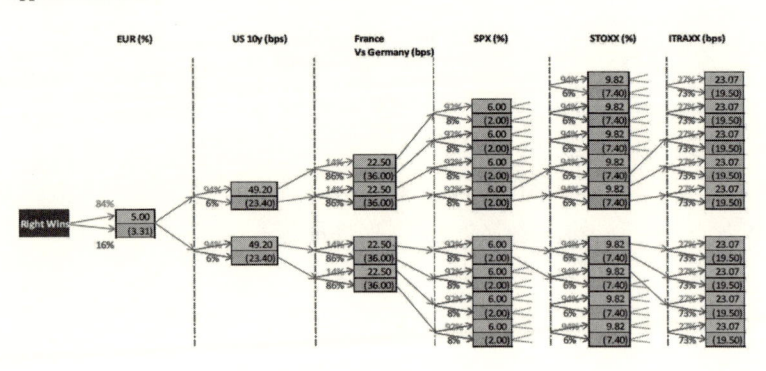

Source: Author, Atul Pawar

Figure A1.8
The Scenario Tree Conditioned on a Center-Left Win
The likelihood of a macro scenario occurring is simply the product of the likelihoods of each event or conditional event along the path.

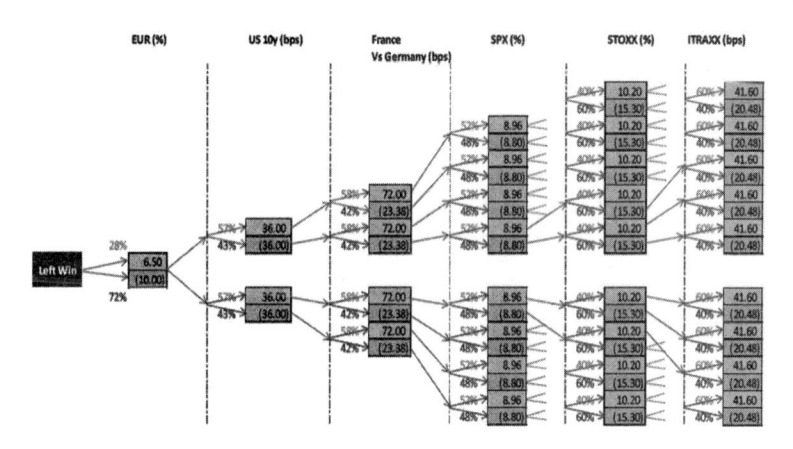

Source: Author, Atul Pawar

Figure A1.9
The Scenario Tree Conditioned on Le Pen Winning
Each of the end leaves in the tree corresponds to a particular macro-financial scenario, which is a combination of all the macro factors that appear along the path.

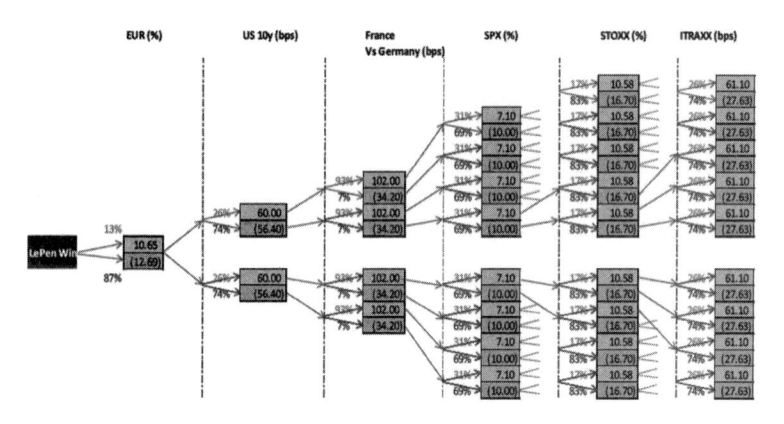

Source: Author, Atul Pawar

Generating Micro-Factor Shocks from the Macro-Factor Scenarios

Each of the end leaves in the tree corresponds to a particular macro-financial scenario, which is a combination of all the macro factors that appear along the path.

The next step is to convert these macro-factor scenarios into micro-factor shocks that can be used to value their effect on portfolios. This may be achieved automatically by using a number of existing methods that are not the subject of this paper. This is well studied and common practice. Typically, this is done using some form of a regression analysis, using conditional expectations.

In summary, once the principal event or transition regime has been defined, the macro-risk factors can be generated using a machine learning algorithm or using experts. The individual macro scenarios at the horizon are then generated by combining a machine learning algorithm or an automated poll of a large number of independent experts. The multifactor scenarios are then formed using a financial network (tree) that results in a spanning set of multifactor scenarios under the assumptions of linear dependence and monotonicity.

The contribution of this method is the marrying of expert judgment with machine learning and AI to develop a financial network that estimates a spanning set of multifactor macro-financial scenarios. Coupled with macro-to-micro factor conversion, this creates a fully automated scenario-generation system to measure the financial impact of a particular transition regime.

Why Does This Scenario-Generating System Generate a Spanning Set?

By construction, in the example tree in figure A1, for every move in a factor we consider a counter move. The paths are simply all possible combinations of these macro-financial shocks. There are 2^n paths, where n is the number of macro variables that we will shock for any sub-event. Assuming that we have not omitted a factor that is important (a risk of such a process), we will span the range of possible macro shocks that need to be considered.

So, without knowing the contents of the portfolio, we are likely to catch both upside and downside moves in any portfolio. It is true, however, that for highly nonlinear portfolios, one would have to have a very fine-grained set of possible shocks and factors to catch all possibilities (think of a portfolio of binary options and the difficulty of catching the precise points/combinations that result in the binary options being exercised). For the 95% of portfolios being managed around the world, however, this simple process is likely to work well.

APPENDIX 2

STRATEGY FOR AN ELECTRICITY DISTRIBUTOR

In Texas, in February 2021, we saw what havoc a climate event could inflict on the electricity supply of a US state. How should Texas manage its electricity distribution strategy going forward? Can risk thinking help them? If so, how? An interesting parallel, explored here in appendix 2, might offer some clues.

This risk-thinking example concerns the California Independent System Operator (CAISO), which is in charge of bulk distribution of electricity and transmission lines in California. The example shows how risk thinking could be applied to guide long-term strategy where the radical risk stems from a combination of financial, climate, and social risk factors.

CAISO was concerned about the unknown effects that climate change (such as its impact on temperature and the frequency and intensity of wildfires and droughts) could have on their planning and ability to deliver electricity efficiently and securely. In addition, they wanted to consider possible transitions occurring in transportation and the generation of electricity. In October 2018, they were considering joining their grid with other Western utilities to construct a resilient grid, make more effective use of renewables, and handle the possible growth of electric vehicles

(EVs). They wanted to understand how to address a combination of risk factors, most of which were very hard to quantify over a long horizon. I was hired to prepare a talk and a paper to show how this might be done.[169]

Some key factors that might influence their strategy were identified as:

- the average temperature in California in 2050 (to account for all the unknowns that might result from climate change such as higher temperatures, increased frequency and higher severity of droughts, wildfires, etc.)
- the progress toward renewable targets (California has a goal of 100% renewables by 2045)
- the ability to form a regional grid with other Western states to be able to mitigate extreme events by sharing electricity between states (can this kind of political cooperation be achieved?)
- the anticipated load growth resulting from the possible future growth in electric vehicles (California had managed to keep load growth constant over the past 30 years while growing the economy by increasing efficiency—historical performance was no measure of what could happen in the future).

Of course, there were possibly more factors, but the purpose was to demonstrate a methodology and not to prepare a strategic plan.

We started by defining a scenario tree that showed the different possible paths these factors might take between then and 2050, their planning horizon (figure A 2.1).

---

[169] R. Dembo and Mark Rothleder, "Session 1: Opening Keynote— Explore various grid scenarios for GHG and cost model outcomes," *2018 Stakeholder Symposium* (October 17, 2018), accessible at:
http://www.caiso.com/informed/Pages/MeetingsEvents/Stakeholder Symposium/SymposiumLiveStreaming.aspx.

Note that their decision involved a mixture of climate change factors as well as political, social, and financial factors that influenced their business—but which were not caused by climate change. This is one of the scenario tree's primary benefits: its ability to combine multiple risk factors from disciplines and areas of interest that rarely communicate or overlap.

Figure A2.1
CAISO's Scenario Tree for Delivering Energy in 2050
CAISO identified multiple factors that could affect their ability to deliver energy safely and securely in 2050, including average temperature, renewables progress, regional grid, and load growth.

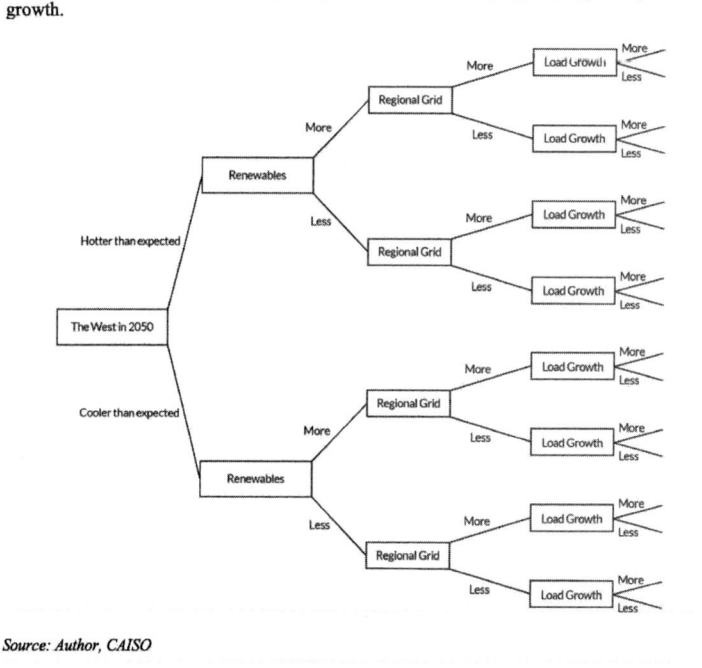

Source: Author, CAISO

The paths in this tree are the scenarios of the combined factors that need to be accounted for in CAISO's strategic planning.

Figure A2.2
A Single Scenario in CAISO's Scenario Tree
The path equates to a single scenario that can be expressed in simple terms.

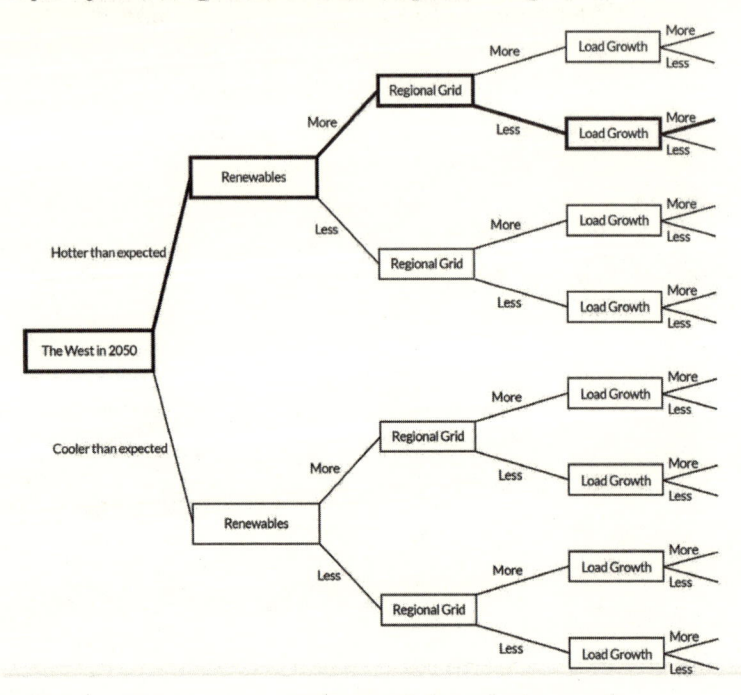

Source: Author, CAISO. Key: 'more' = 'more than expected', 'less' = 'less than expected'.

By selecting a single path through the scenario tree, CAISO can produce a scenario that is easily expressible in layman's terms:

According to this scenario, by 2050, California's average temperature will have risen more than expected. The growth of renewable energy generation will be more than was expected, and the regional grid will not have materialized as much as was expected. Load growth, by contrast, will be more than was expected.

In order to evaluate this tree, we need four values for each factor, the possible upside and downside values for each factor, and their probabilities. We get these from the forward-looking data contained in the uncertainty distributions, in particular by looking at the extremes and the possible likelihoods of the upside and downside (as in chapter 6).

To generate these uncertainty distributions for each of these factors in 2050, CAISO took a poll of its members (Figures A2.5–7, presented at the end of this appendix). In this example, the CAISO members represent the experts and thus are the source of the forward-looking data (as we explained in detail in chapter 2). With these distributions, the tree can be evaluated, and CAISO can then determine the possible scenarios requiring examination.

CAISO maps the scenario data that it has generated on combinations of temperatures, fires, drought, etc. onto infrastructure data to get estimates of the costs or benefits that would result for each and every scenario. Fires will threaten transmission lines; sea level rise will compromise coastal grid infrastructure; higher temperatures will increase demand and decrease supply; droughts will decrease hydro availability, and so on.

Measuring the impacts to CAISO's abilities to meet demand would require identifying all of CAISO's generating sources (or the utilities that run them such as PG&E), transmission lines, and other infrastructure necessary to supply California with electricity, excluding the electricity generated by individuals or companies not under CAISO's jurisdiction. This turned out to be a nontrivial exercise. The valuation of one such scenario (the worst case) is shown in figure A2.8. This was estimated at a massive $53 billion shortfall should this scenario or something like it occur.

Having run these evaluations, CAISO's next task would be to strategize. They would have to decide which of the scenarios they would ignore—perhaps due to minimal impact or low likelihood of occurrence—versus those that they wished to hedge against. This would ultimately be their business decision.

Figure A2.3
The Possibility of Future Wildfires in California
The geographical component of the scenario generation is key to assessing the risk to different assets.

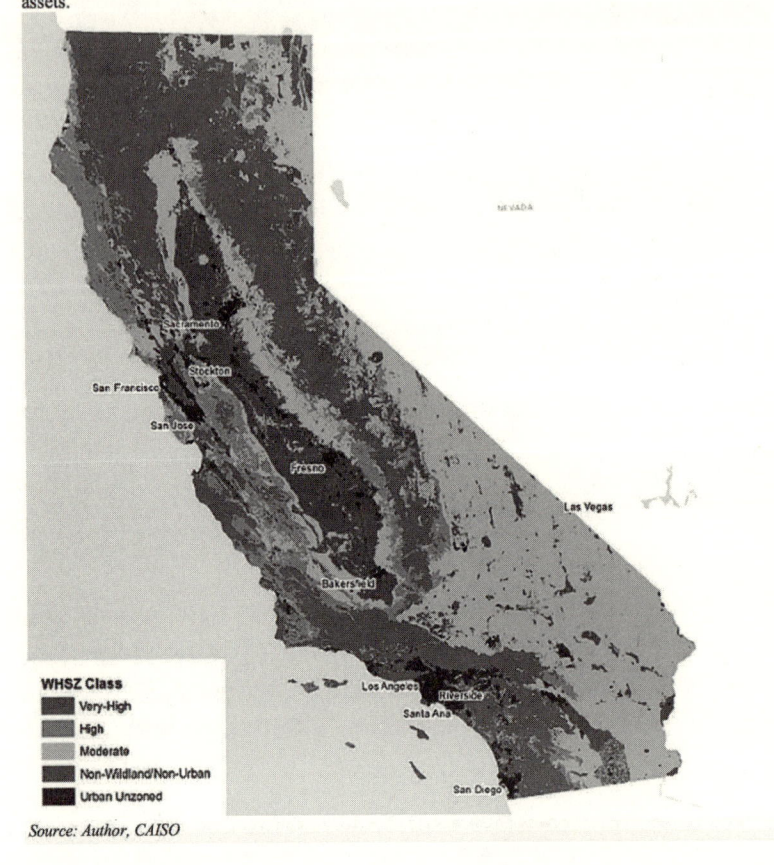

Source: Author, CAISO

Figure A2.4
CAISO's Infrastructure in California
By comparison with Figure A2.3, it is possible to see considerable overlap of high-risk zones and existing CAISO infrastructure.

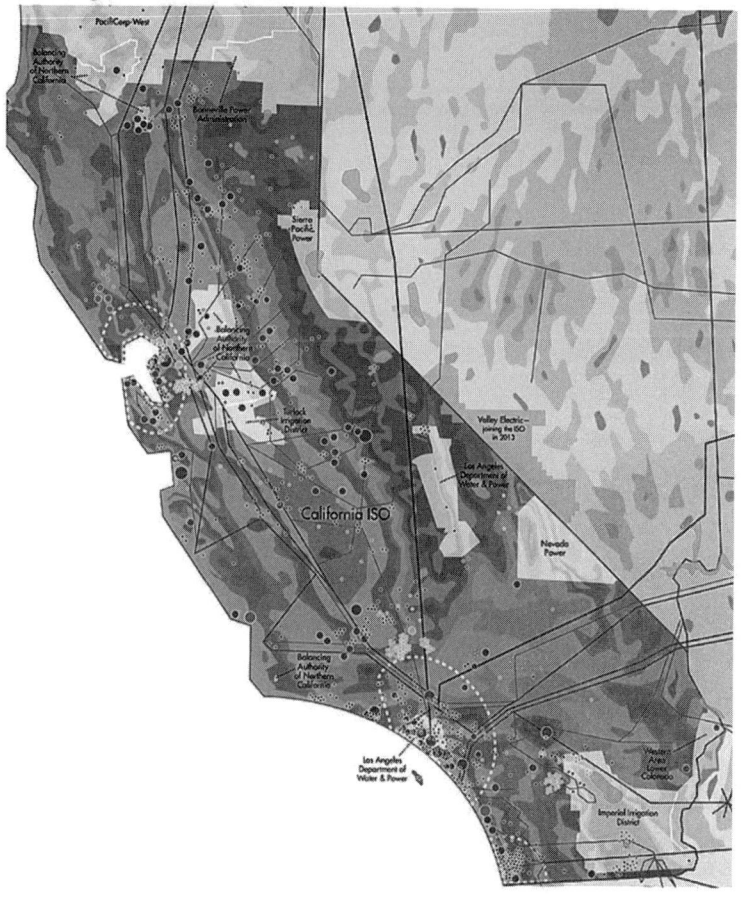

Source: Author, CAISO

CAISO would have to repeat this analysis periodically or when new events and information arose that would require a reassessment of the scenarios and the risk factors. As time passes and the data gets better and better, scenarios will improve, and the strategy chosen will evolve. That strategic evolution is a core thesis of risk thinking.

As fate would have it, only a few weeks after my talk, California experienced one of the worst fires in its history, most likely exacerbated by climate change. The fire brought the state's largest utility provider, PG&E, down from a $23-billion, must-have utility investment to a bankrupt company in the space of a month or so. It turned out that their transformers, located (unprotected, i.e., unhedged) in a clearly identified high-risk zone, set off the fire, which killed 22 civilians and caused millions of dollars' worth of damage. They went down to a fury of lawsuits. A single spark brought one of the world's largest utilities to its knees—talk about radical risks!

We conclude with a final word on implementation. One drawback of moving from a forecasting world to a world of risk thinking is the need to upgrade the abilities of organizations to measure the effects of arbitrary forward-looking scenarios on their costs·or benefits. Most organizations would require a significant effort to do so today, but ultimately, this would lead to better planning. The experience that banks had when forced to run a single stress test for the Federal Reserve System, CCAR,[170] was that it was difficult and costly but has ultimately organized banks' data and improved their management of capital and liquidity. We see a similar opportunity here with risk thinking as applied to corporates.

Below, we illustrate the various risk-thinking tools used in this example: the survey, the uncertainty distribution, and the scenario tree.

---

[170] https://en.wikipedia.org/wiki/Comprehensive_Capital_Analysis_and_Review.

Figure A2.5
Example of CAISO's Poll
From the responses to this poll, it is possible to form uncertainty distributions for each risk factor.

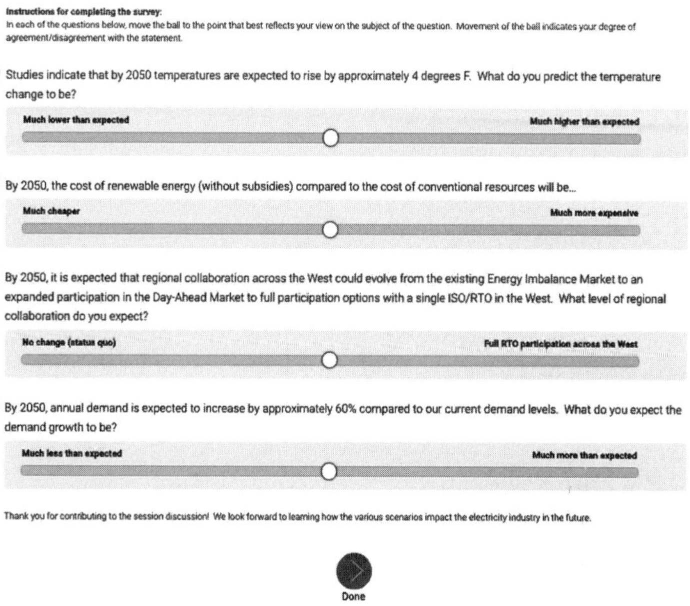

Instructions for completing the survey:
In each of the questions below, move the ball to the point that best reflects your view on the subject of the question. Movement of the ball indicates your degree of agreement/disagreement with the statement.

(1) Studies indicate that by 2050 temperatures are expected to rise by approximately 4 degrees F. What do you predict the temperature change to be?

| Much lower than expected | | Much higher than expected |

(2) By 2050, the cost of renewable energy (without subsidies) compared to the cost of conventional resources will be...

| Much cheaper | | Much more expensive |

(3) By 2050, it is expected that regional collaboration across the West could evolve from the existing Energy Imbalance Market to an expanded participation in the Day-Ahead Market to full participation options with a single ISO/RTO in the West. What level of regional collaboration do you expect?

| No change (status quo) | | Full RTO participation across the West |

(4) By 2050, annual demand is expected to increase by approximately 60% compared to our current demand levels. What do you expect the demand growth to be?

| Much less than expected | | Much more than expected |

Thank you for contributing to the session discussion! We look forward to learning how the various scenarios impact the electricity industry in the future.

Done

Source: Author, CAISO

This survey is not meant to be a definitive analysis of CAISO's future risk. Its purpose is to demonstrate the method on a simplified problem. In particular, since the results from this survey implicitly assume the higher-temperature branch in the scenario tree, we would also need to do a similar poll for the lower-temperature branch. The conditional probability distributions for the factors, renewables, regionalization, and load growth will almost certainly be different for each major branch of the tree.

Figure A2.6
Results of the CAISO Poll for Temperature and Renewable Energy
Temperature rise was predicted to be close to the consensus expectation, whereas the cost of renewable energy was predicted to be lower.

Studies indicate that by 2050 temperatures are expected to rise by approximately 4 degrees F. What do you predict the temperature change to be?

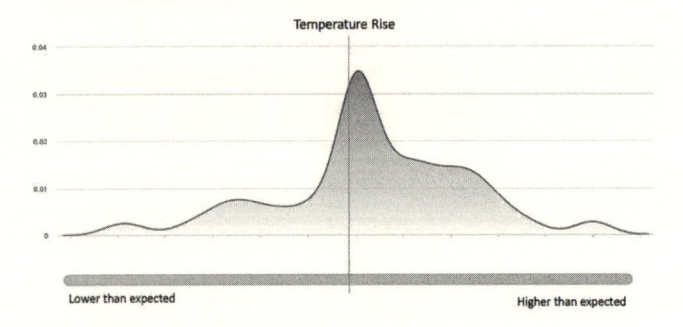

Temperature Rise

Lower than expected — Higher than expected

By 2050, the cost of renewable energy (without subsidies) compared to the cost of conventional resources will be...

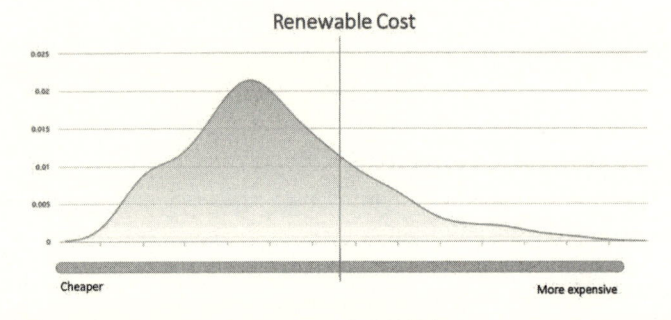

Renewable Cost

Cheaper — More expensive

Source: Author, CAISO; thanks to Joanne Serina and Mark Rothleder

Figure A2.7
Results of the CAISO Poll for Regionalization and Load Growth
Regionalization was predicted to be higher than the consensus expectation, whereas load growth was predicted to be nearer the consensus.

By 2050, it is expected that regional collaboration across the West could evolve from the existing Energy Imbalance Market to an expanded participation in the Day-Ahead Market to full participation options with a single ISO/RTO in the West.
What level of regional collaboration **do you expect?**

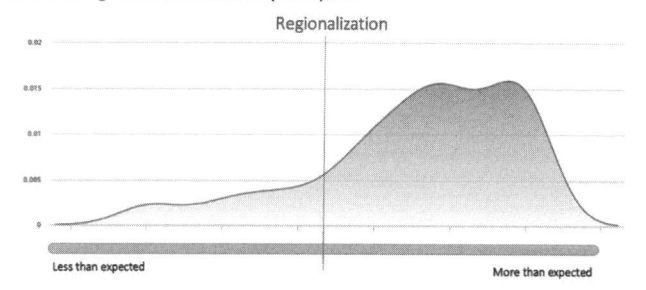

Regionalization

By 2050, annual demand is expected to increase by approximately 60% compared to our current demand levels.
What do you expect the load growth **to be?**

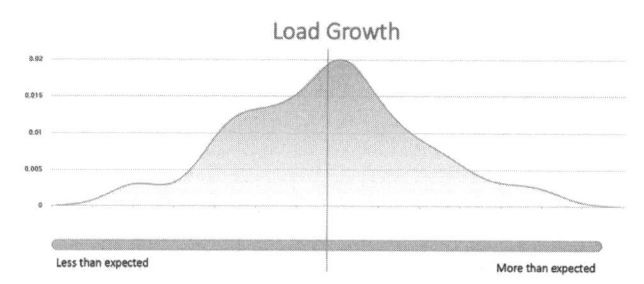

Load Growth

Source: Author, CAISO

These results are not meant to be a definitive analysis of CAISO's future risk. They are meant to demonstrate the method on a simplified problem.

Figure A2.8
The CAISO Representative Worst-Case Scenario
By selecting a path through the scenario tree, it is possible to identify a single scenario that can be expressed in simple terms.

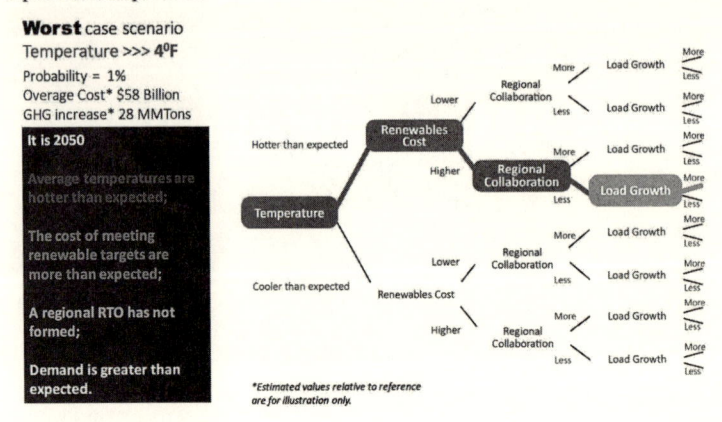

Worst case scenario
Temperature >>> 4⁰F
Probability = 1%
Overage Cost* $58 Billion
GHG increase* 28 MMTons

It is 2050

Average temperatures are hotter than expected;

The cost of meeting renewable targets are more than expected;

A regional RTO has not formed;

Demand is greater than expected.

*Estimated values relative to reference are for illustration only.

Source: Author, CAISO

These results were not meant to be a definitive analysis of CAISO's future risk. They were meant to demonstrate the algorithm in the context of a simplified problem.

FURTHER READING

Those who want to follow up on ideas in this book can read and add comments on our blog: https://riskthinking.ai/category/blogs/.

ABOUT THE AUTHOR

Ron S. Dembo has been an associate professor at Yale, an entrepreneur, consultant, CEO, and author. He founded Algorithmics, which he grew to become the largest supplier of enterprise risk systems to banks before it was sold to Fitch. He was made a lifetime fellow of The Fields Institute of Mathematics in 2007 and has received many awards for his work in optimization, risk management, and climate change. He is Founder and CEO of Riskthinking.AI, which produces data, software, and algorithms for measuring and managing climate related financial risk.